W9-DAQ-025

Copy, Combine, & Compose

COPY, COMBINE, & COMPOSE

Controlling Composition

Roseann Dueñas Gonzalez
MaryCarmen E. Cruz
Ann Barger Thomson

University of Arizona

Wadsworth Publishing Company/Belmont, California/A Division of Wadsworth, Inc.

English Editor: Kevin Howat
Production Editor: Gary Mcdonald
Cover Designer: Adriane Bosworth
Copy Editor: Jonas Weisel
Signing Representative: Nancy Tandberg

© 1983 by Wadsworth, Inc. All rights reserved. No part of this book may be reproduced, stored in a retrieval system, or transcribed, in any form or by any means, electronic, mechanical, photocopying, recording, or otherwise, without the prior written permission of the publisher, Wadsworth Publishing Company, Belmont, California 94002, a division of Wadsworth, Inc.

Printed in the United States of America
2 3 4 5 6 7 8 9 10 — 87 86 85 84 83

ISBN 0-534-01341-4

Library of Congress Cataloging in Publication Data

Gonzalez, Roseann Dueñas.
  Copy, combine, and compose.

  Includes index.
  1. English language — Rhetoric.   2. English language — Grammar — 1950-   I. Cruz, MaryCarmen E.
II. Thomson, Ann (Ann Barger)   III. Title.
PE1408.G5736   1983   808'.042   82-20196
ISBN 0-534-01341-4

CONTENTS

PREFACE

Copy, Combine, and Compose: Controlling Composition uses a successful, time-tested approach for improving student writing: controlled composition. In this approach, students practice basic syntactic, grammatical, and usage skills, not in meaningless, isolated sentences, but in a meaningful complete composition.

The unique feature of this controlled composition text is its emphasis on the three C's: copy, combine, and compose.

COPY   This feature of the text follows the traditional controlled composition idea of copying and manipulating grammatical and syntactic items within the meaningful framework of a paragraph. In addition, this text offers strategies for the teaching of rhetorical concerns; in particular it introduces the innovative concept of teaching documentation skills through controlled composition exercises. The numerous paragraphs for practice are examples of acceptable college writing, usually written in a "middle" tone on stimulating and informative topics such as religion, medicine, marriage, sports, politics, art, archeology, psychology, astrology, history, and music.

COMBINE   This aspect of the text represents a new dimension of controlled composition, one that focuses on combining sentences for rhetorical purposes. In the unit devoted to this practice, students are shown *when* — under what circumstances — and *how* to combine sentences to communicate their ideas effectively.

COMPOSE   This component of the text leads students from manipulating to creating paragraphs of their own. Every set of paragraph practices is followed by the "On Your Own" section, which contains guided writing suggestions complete with prewriting questions and topic sentences for developing paragraphs. These highly structured, well-developed topics for writing are followed by open-writing suggestions, which are less structured yet comprehensive.

This text can be used effectively as a core text or as a supplementary exercise book for college students who are working at the paragraph or essay level. The text provides students with opportunities for improving basic and complex skills in syntax, tense, usage, style, sentence combining, and documentation. At the same time, this text provides model paragraphs as well as detailed paragraph topics to stimulate discussion and writing. Also, the teaching at the beginning of each chapter carefully explains the items the students will practice, and the grammatical and usage skills that the students may need reinforced are briefly reviewed in the Handbook at the end of the text. This text will be equally beneficial to students in the traditional classroom as well as for students in writing laboratories and other individualized learning programs.

What *Copy, Combine, and Compose* has most to offer is flexibility in teaching. It is divided into five units: Practicing Basic Skills; Focusing on Time; Writing for a Specific Audience; Incorporating the Ideas of Others; and Combining Sentences for a Purpose.

Each of the five units in the text concentrates on a specific area of writing improvement. Any one or all of the units can be used, according to the needs of individual students or class.

Unit A: Practicing Basic Skills

This unit focuses on learning to use articles, pronouns, plurals, and possessives correctly and teaches how to avoid problems with subject-verb agreement, fragments, run-ons, comma splices, nonparallel constructions, and misplaced dangling modifiers. This unit points out the miscommunication that can result from problems with these basic skills, and students learn to clarify meaning by eliminating these weaknesses. After students have had repeated opportunities to correct problems involving these basic skills, they will develop the ability to recognize and correct these problems in their own writing.

Unit B: Focusing on Time

This section concentrates on the tenses of English verbs. It explains the formation and use of the present, past progressive, perfect, and future tenses to help students write precisely. Once students have mastered verb tenses, their compositions should reflect accurate relationships between ideas and events.

Unit C: Writing for a Specific Audience

Unit C is concerned with the considerations writers make when they write for a specific audience. What tone to assume, as well as what point of view to maintain, are dictated by the intended audience. In addition, students practice choosing the most appropriate words as well as recognizing and avoiding trite language and wordiness.

Unit D: Incorporating the Ideas of Others

This unit stresses supporting ideas in composition through the incorporation of direct quotations, reported speech, or paraphrases. The unit also gives students the opportunity to manipulate techniques that they often have trouble mastering: using passive-active voice, direct quotation, and reported speech. Such skills add clarity and color to their writing. In this section students recognize the reasons for and the mechanics of supporting ideas with the ideas of others. They recognize when the passive voice weakens their writing and, equally important, when it is effective. Students also gain practice in distinguishing between active and passive voice, learning to recognize the impact that accuracy in using these voices has in developing ideas.

Unit E: Combining Sentences for a Purpose

This unit focuses on combining sentences to help students develop a mature writing style. However, because random sentence combining as an end in itself is not meaningful, this section helps students to learn to combine sentences for definite purposes within the context of a paragraph. This section emphasizes combining to avoid choppy, awkward sentences and to create sophisticated, well-written sentences. Students learn not only how they can combine sentences but also why certain sentences should be combined. As a result, students are able to evaluate the relationship between sentences in order to combine appropriately and to construct more effective sentences.

Advantages for Students

PRACTICING IN A MEANINGFUL CONTEXT   Students copy paragraphs while transforming, substituting, or manipulating language in the meaningful context of the paragraph. Based on topics that complement the reading and writing students are asked to do in their college writing, the paragraphs should interest the students and generate ideas for their writing.

USING MODEL PARAGRAPHS   Students are exposed to model paragraphs as they practice the grammatical, syntactic, or rhetorical principles of each chapter. Thus, through repeated practice in reading and copying, students become more aware of the organizational and developmental patterns of mature, well-developed paragraphs.

BUILDING CONFIDENCE IN WRITING   Because the focus is on only one grammatical, syntactic, or rhetorical item at a time, students' errors will probably be limited to that one item. As the students reduce their number of errors, they will become more confident in their writing skills.

WRITING WITH SUCCESS   After working on at least two controlled practices, progressing to a guided writing exercise, and finishing with the open writing exercise, students experience the success necessary to begin creating their own mature compositions.

LEARNING TO DOCUMENT   The creative exercises on how to incorporate the information of others to support one's own ideas provide a nonthreatening context for students to practice this typically difficult concept, which in turn they will transfer to their own writing.

Advantages for Teachers

RECOGNIZING PROBLEM AREAS EASILY   Controlled composition allows teachers to focus on one particular grammatical or syntactic feature in a controlled setting. Thus, they can help students with a specific problem area.

ORGANIZING TIME   Because students apply the concepts as they learn them, teachers do not have to spend a great amount of time on isolated problems. Instead, they can devote time to working with the students on more demanding areas of their writing.

INDIVIDUAL INSTRUCTION   Since this book does not have to be followed sequentially, teachers can select those chapters that will be most beneficial to their students. They can simultaneously assign specific chapters to different students, depending on the individual weaknesses of each student.

PROMPT REINFORCEMENT   The practices facilitate grading. Because extended comments on students' practices are not necessary, teachers can grade the practices and return them to the students almost immediately. In addition, the exercises also lend themselves very well to peer correction or small group work. Therefore, teachers are able to give their students immediate feedback.

Acknowl-edgments

The authors wish to thank the following reviewers: Peter E. Sotiriou, Los Angeles City College; Larry McDoniel, St. Louis Community College at Meramec; William Condon, Arkansas Technical University; Susanne Stevens, Skyline College; Mark Reynolds, Jefferson Davis Junior College; Eric P. Hibbison, J. Sargeant Reynolds Community College; and Cathie Platt, Piedmont Virginia Community College.

Our gratitude goes out to our colleagues at the University of Arizona who have encouraged and helped us: Charles Davis, Director of Composition; Frank Pialorsi, Director, Center for English as a Second Language; Ed Dryden, Head, English Department; Jean Zukowski/Faust, English Department; and John Hollowell, Director of Composition at the University of California at Irvine.

To our dear Wadsworth editor, Kevin Howat, who smiled his way through three preliminary editions, and to Gary Mcdonald, our production editor, we give our sincere thanks. To Janey Ninde, Judy Gonzales, Sonya Nuñez, Merle Turchik, Toni Pennington, Jill Weber, and Becky Galas we give special thanks for ribbons-worth of typing well done! We send a heartfelt thank you to Victoria Vasquez for her perseverance, encouragement, and magnificent deciphering and typing of our manuscript; and thanks also goes to Ellen Cohen for her assistance.

Deepest appreciation and thanks go to our families and friends whose support was constant: Roberto Gonzalez, Marisa Gonzalez, Mrs. Maria Luisa Dueñas, Mrs. Carmen C. Cruz, Casey Christensen, Stanley E. Tims II, David Thomson, Mr. and Mrs. David Barger, Ariel Ballesteros, and a very special thanks for many late nights to Bob Gonzalez without whose pagination, food runs, and counsel we couldn't have survived.

To the Student

Why do people have such a hard time putting their thoughts on paper? Have you often felt frustrated because you spend a great deal of time wondering where a punctuation mark goes, how to spell a word, or whether your sentence sounds "good?" You're not alone. In fact, few writers find writing a quick, easy process. However, mastering basic skills does help the experienced writer. Correcting run-ons, poor punctuation, or awkwardly worded sentences are skills that can become automatic habits if the writer practices. The paragraphs in this book try to give you the practice you need to feel confident about these writing skills.

This book may be different from any writing textbook you've used before. You won't be correcting a list of sentences that are not related to each other. You will also not have to correct the separate sentences and then become frustrated because you can't find those errors in your own writing. You will be reading and practicing with well-written paragraphs. Each lesson talks about only one writing skill that you may not have developed yet. For example, in one chapter you may look only at capitalization; in another you'll look at writing complete sentences. Then you will copy the model paragraph, changing it according to what you have learned. You must pay attention only to copying correctly and using what you learned in the chapter.

You don't have to worry about organization or developing ideas in the practice. The paragraphs are already well developed and well written. The more you copy, the better you should become at imitating and creating the mature structures in the model paragraph. The better you imitate a particular point of writing and think about it, the more it will become a habit in your own writing. Once you have practiced the structure, you will get a chance to write ideas of your own in the guided and open writing exercises. The suggestions should help you to organize and develop your ideas in those paragraphs. Because the best way to improve writing is to practice, and because the best way to practice is to imitate examples of good writing, working in this book should help you to get off to a good start.

If you follow this outline, you will notice your writing skills improve. We hope that you find practicing with this book both enjoyable and beneficial. Follow this outline for each chapter your teacher assigns:

1. Read the explanations in the chapter.

2. Read the practice. Copy the paragraph, following the directions before each practice.

3. Have your instructor check your paragraphs. Review any errors you have made.

4. Try every guided writing exercise and at least one open writing exercise.

5. Apply what you learn in the chapters to your own writing.

As you proofread the paragraphs that you write, ask yourself the following questions:

1. Who is your audience?

2. Is your language appropriate for that audience?

3. Are your sentences clear, complete, and effective?

4. Have you accurately included the ideas of others to support your own?

5. Are your paragraphs free of run-ons, comma splices, dangling modifiers, subject-verb agreement errors?

6. Are the verb tenses correct?

On the basis of your answers to these questions, rewrite your paragraphs.

UNIT A

Practicing Basic Skills

CHAPTER 1

Using A and An

Although *a* and *an* may sometimes cause problems for writers, the rules for using these are easily learned.

1. Use *a* before all words beginning with consonant sounds.

a *c*ity	a *k*ennel
a *j*udge	a *h*ouse
a *l*ater hour	a *t*ender moment
a *w*ise owl	a *b*lack eel

2. Use *a* with words that begin with *u* when it sounds like *you*. The *u* in this case has a consonant sound.

a *u*nique experience
a *u*seful item
a *U*tah resident

3. Use *an* before all words beginning with vowel sounds, including silent *h*.

an *u*mbrella	an *h*our
an *i*rresponsible person	an *e*xcellent meal
an *e*xample	an *h*erb
an *o*celot	an *a*lmond

4. Don't be confused by *h*. Sometimes an initial *h* is silent and sometimes it is not.

an *h*onorable man	but	a *h*umorous article
an *h*omage	but	a *h*ome
an *h*eir	but	a *h*earty meal

5. Another vowel that sometimes sounds like a consonant is *o*. Use *a* with words beginning with *o* when the *o* sounds like a *w*.

     a *o*ne-track mind   a *o*ne-sided argument

     a *o*ne-way street   a *o*ne-time winner

6. When the *o* does not sound like a *w*, use *an*.

     an *o*rphan   an *o*minous note

     an *o*nion field   an *o*ptometrist

P R A C T I C E   1 A

Working with A and An

DIRECTIONS: Read the following paragraph. Then copy the paragraph, making the changes or adding the insertions listed here. With each change or insertion you may have to change *a* to *an*, or *an* to *a*. Check your work carefully.

In sentence	2	change <u>extraordinary</u> to <u>unique</u>, and change <u>fantasy-like</u> to <u>exotic</u>.
In sentence	3	change <u>energetic</u> to <u>dedicated</u>, and change <u>enormous</u> to <u>one-hundred-word</u>.
In sentence	5	insert <u>amusing</u> before <u>stream</u>.
In sentence	7	insert <u>attentive</u> before <u>housesitter</u>.
In sentence	8	insert <u>over-protective</u> before <u>parrot owner</u>.
In sentence	9	change <u>assortment</u> to <u>variety</u>, and insert <u>occasional</u> before <u>apple</u>.
In sentence	10	insert <u>unusual</u> before <u>combination</u>.
In sentence	11	change <u>fine</u> to <u>excellent</u>.
In sentence	12	change <u>delightful</u> to <u>entertaining</u>.
In sentence	13	insert <u>unmistakable</u> before <u>air</u>.
In sentence	14	change <u>highly valued</u> to <u>honored</u>, and change <u>growing</u> to <u>increasing</u>.

Bird Talk

(1) Parrots are becoming one of the most popular pets in America—and for good reason. (2) The parrot is an extraordinary bird that can be taught to talk, can be easily cared for, and can create a fantasy-like atmosphere anywhere. (3) With the help of an energetic parrot owner, a parrot can develop an enormous vocabulary. (4) In addition, a parrot can be trained to say "pretty boy" or "Polly wants a cracker," and it also can learn to whistle or even to imitate human singing. (5) No matter what an owner decides to teach a bird, training a parrot takes much patience, but the reward is a stream of chatter. (6) Another reason for the parrot's popularity is that this pet does not require much care. (7) For example, even a spoiled parrot does not need a housesitter for the purpose of daily walks and daily feeding. (8) In fact, a parrot owner may leave his or her pet with enough food for five days and have no fear that the parrot will overeat. (9) Still another advantage of owning a parrot is its inexpensive diet, which consists of an assortment of seeds, nuts, corn, and grain—along with an apple, banana, or carrot. (10) Perhaps the most likely reason the parrot is becoming such a well-liked pet is that it is a combination of tameness and wildness. (11) Because the parrot can live in almost any environment, it makes a fine, tame companion for many people. (12) In addition, because it can be easily trained, it is a delightful performer. (13) At the same time, its colorful feathers give it an air of the mystery of the parrot's native home, the jungle. (14) Thus, the parrot, once a highly valued gift presented to kings and noble families, is now appreciated by a growing number of people.

P R A C T I C E   1 B

Working with A and An

DIRECTIONS: Read the following paragraph. Then copy the paragraph, making the changes or adding the insertions listed here. With each change or insertion you may have to change *a* to *an*, or *an* to *a*. Check your work carefully.

In sentence   1   change <u>ridiculous</u> to <u>absurd</u>.
In sentence   2   change <u>subterranean</u> to <u>underground</u>.
In sentence   3   insert <u>1000 percent</u> before <u>increase</u>.

In sentence 4 change new to innovative.

In sentence 5 insert historic before revival.

In sentence 7 change evident to clear.

In sentence 8 change great to impressive.

In sentence 9 insert well-constructed before underground.

In sentence 11 insert artistic before one.

In sentence 14 insert uninformed before impression.

In sentence 15 insert effective before plastic.

In sentence 16 change conventional to usual.

In sentence 18 insert seemingly before impractical, and change responsible to effective, and change continuing to eternal.

Dwellings of the Future

(1) In the 1930s, when renowned architect Frank Lloyd Wright dreamed of living in a house built underground, many Americans considered the idea a ridiculous one. (2) When he designed and built a subterranean arena in 1950—the "Cabaret Theater" at Taliesin West in Arizona— most other architects rejected the concept. (3) Recently, however, there has been an increase in the number of underground houses built in the United States. (4) Building into the earth is a new approach to the problem of modern living. (5) Moreover, it is a revival of the ancient cave-dwelling tradition. (6) Why the sudden interest in earth shelters? (7) The most important reason for building earth shelters is an evident one: people want to reduce their heating and cooling bills. (8) The design of these underground houses makes it possible to save a great amount in energy bills. (9) Sitting ten to twenty feet below the earth, an underground home is cooled in the summer by the slowly penetrating cold from the last winter. (10) Also it is evenly warmed in the winter by the past summer's heat. (11) Another reason for going underground is one encouraged by environmentalists. (12) They believe that a building should blend into its environment. (13) Some people, however, do not trust this style of architecture. (14) They usually have an impression of underground housing as damp, dark, moldy, and spidery. (15) On the contrary, underground homes are well insulated with a plastic foam, which blocks out excess heat and moisture. (16) Furthermore, an underground home often has more light than a conventional American home because of the location of the windows and skylights. (17) Man's future, then, may be directed away from the traditional form of housing toward an economical and comfortable form: subterranean housing. (18) Thus, an impractical dream has evolved into a responsible solution to a continuing need for shelter.

O N   Y O U R   O W N

Ideas for Guided and Open Writing

GUIDED WRITING EXERCISE: In a paragraph of approximately 100–150 words, discuss a few prominent characteristics that people reveal about themselves by the jewelry they wear. Be sure to give reasons for your conclusions. For example, "Punk rockers who wear nails and safety pins as jewelry may be revealing their rejection of the traditional beliefs of society." Consider some of the following people for your paragraph: an elderly man wearing an elaborate bracelet, a young sportscaster wearing a diamond pin, a middle-aged woman wearing a thin necklace dotted with a delicate ruby, a grocery checker wearing a heavy necklace made of animal teeth, a businessperson wearing a Mickey Mouse watch, an energetic carpenter wearing an earring made with a penny. Try incorporating four of the following words into your statements in order to practice the use of *a* and *an*.

exotic	dainty	egotistical	ambitious
humorous	sophisticated	extravagant	old-fashioned
adventurous	obnoxious	healthy	shy

Use other descriptive words or other types of people and jewelry as you see fit. If you wish, you may begin your paragraph with the following: "Jewelry sometimes reveals important personality characteristics of the people who wear it."

OPEN WRITING IDEAS: The following topics are suggestions for open writing exercises to help you practice the structures presented in this chapter. Develop these ideas into paragraphs of 100–150 words. Focus your attention on the appropriate use of *a* and *an*.

1. Observe people in a public place such as an airport, bus station, or cafeteria, and describe one person you observed. Tell how he or she looked and behaved. Be specific in your description; for example, you might talk about an angry customer, a crying child lost in a crowd, or a frustrated mother trying to balance luggage in one arm and her infant in the other.

2. Describe one typical kind of character portrayed in one of the following kinds of television programs: daytime soap operas, situation comedies, westerns, talk shows, game shows, or nighttime dramas. Discuss his or her physical appearance, behavior, and appeal to the audience.

CHAPTER 2

Using Capitalization

Learning capitalization rules will help you in checking your work. Study the following rules carefully.

1. Capitalize the first word of every sentence.

Chili is spicy.

Cotton clothing is cooler than polyester clothing.

2. Capitalize the first word of a quoted sentence.

Quotation at the beginning of a sentence: "That's all I can do," she exclaimed.

Quotation in the middle of a sentence: The statement "All's well that ends well" is very often true.

Quotation at the end of a sentence: Porky Pig is known for saying, "That's all, folks."

Whenever the quotation is interrupted, do not capitalize the word of the second set of quotation marks.

Quoted sentence interrupted by unquoted words: "In my opinion," the adjustor said, "your fender was already bent before this accident occurred."

3. Capitalize names of people and animals.

Mary Ann Pacheco	King Kong
Jim O'Brien	Rin Tin Tin

4. Capitalize titles of persons when the titles come before their names. When the title is used alone, do not capitalize it.

I saw Professor Garcia during his office hours.
He is a professor of literature.

> The Reverend Polanski performed the wedding ceremony.
> The reverend of the new church visits the sick every day.

Always capitalize the titles of the current President and Vice President of the United States, whether they are used alone or with names.

> Barbara Walters interviewed President Reagan last night.
> The President will discuss his economic policy on television tonight.

Unless they are accompanied by a name, do not capitalize these titles when they refer to the presidents or vice presidents of other countries.

> Many people were saddened by the death of President Anwar Sadat of Egypt.
> Leaders from around the world attended the president's funeral.

5. Capitalize names of family titles when the titles are used as a name. Do not capitalize after possessive pronouns such as *my, his, her, our,* or *their.*

> Although Grandfather is seventy, he can jog three miles a day.
> My grandmother, who is fifty, ran in the Boston Marathon last year.
> Would you carry these books for me, Dad?
> My father never minded washing dishes.

6. Capitalize the names of specific groups or organizations.

PEOPLE OF GEOGRAPHIC REGIONS	Texans, Israelis, Mideasterners, Southerners
TRIBAL GROUPS	the Navajos, the Bantu, the Zulus, the Apaches
LANGUAGE AND ETHNIC GROUPS	English, Spanish, Russian (*Black* is usually capitalized, although *white* is not.)
SPORTS TEAMS	the Phoenix Suns, the University of Arizona Wildcats, the Los Angeles Dodgers
POLITICAL AND PUBLIC SERVICE ORGANIZATIONS	the Democratic Party, a Republican, the American Civil Liberties Union, the United Nations, the Girl Scouts of America, the New Mexico Opera Company

7. Capitalize names of religions, references to gods, and most words of religious significance.

Catholic	Koran	Ten Commandments
Jewish	Bible	Baptists

Judaism	God	St. Paul
Zeus	Venus	Buddha

8. Capitalize the names of places and things.

GEOGRAPHICAL AREAS	China, the North Pole, Mars, Sells Papago Reservation, the Middle East, Earth. (The *earth* is not capitalized when used with *the* or *our*; the *moon* and the *sun* are never capitalized.)
STREETS AND STRUCTURES	Words such as *avenue, highway, post office, bridge,* and *airport* are generally capitalized when they are part of a title.

Highway 10	Statue of Liberty
Pan-American Highway	Dodger Stadium
Speedway Boulevard	London Bridge

INSTITUTIONS, GOVERNMENT AND INTERNATIONAL BODIES, AND BUSINESS FIRMS

Institutions: North High School, Johns Hopkins University

Government bodies: Social Security Administration, World Court

Business firms: International Telephone and Telegraph, Exxon Corporation

VEHICLES

Ships: the *Queen Mary,* the *U.S.S. Hope,* the *Titanic*

Airships: *Air Force One,* the *Concord*

Spacecraft: *Voyager 2, Apollo 11*

Cars: the Fox, the Citation, the Phoenix, the Mustang

Trains: the Orient Express, the Cannonball Express

CALENDAR AND HISTORICAL EVENTS, PERIODS, AND DOCUMENTS

Calendar Events: New Year's Day, Hanukkah, April, Halloween

Special Events: the Olympics, the Kentucky Derby, the New York State Lottery

Historical Events: the Industrial Revolution, the Spanish-American War, World War II

Periods: the Space Age, the Age of Enlightenment, the Great Depression

Documents: the Bill of Rights, the Treaty of Guadalupe-Hildalgo, the Constitution

9. Capitalize direction words that refer to regions of the country. Do not capitalize direction words when they refer to points of the compass.

> People who move to the Southwest often miss the dramatic changing of seasons of the East.

> First, you drive three miles east and then turn south on Skullbone Drive.

10. Capitalize the names of academic subjects if they are followed by a course number.

> Jeanne took a few courses in chemistry and biology in high school.

> She had to register for Chemistry 200 and Biology 101 this semester.

11. Capitalize all the words in titles of songs, television programs, books, magazines, short stories, plays, essays, and poems — except for articles (*a, an, the*), short prepositions, and conjunctions. Capitalize an article only when it begins a title.

SONG	"Yesterday"
TELEVISION PROGRAM	Saturday Night Live
BOOK	*A Portrait of the Artist as a Young Man*
MAGAZINE	*Time*
SHORT STORY	"The Week of the Life of Manuel Hernandez"
POEM	"My Grandmother Would Rock Quietly and Hum"

12. Capitalize the names of the seasons only when they are personified.

> Then Spring awakened the forest with her cool rain.

> Last winter was the coldest I have ever experienced.

13. Capitalize the words *freshman, sophomore, junior,* and *senior* only if the words are part of an event.

> The Freshman Orientation this year was successful.

> The Senior Spring Fling made a profit this year.

> The Junior Rodeo Dance was boring.

> Joann's freshman year was a disaster.

> Bobby's girlfriend was a senior.

14. Capitalize the openings and closings of letters.

Dear Joe, Yours sincerely,

Hi, Mary, Very truly yours,

Notice that only the first words of the closings are capitalized.

P R A C T I C E 2 A

Using Capitalization Rules

DIRECTIONS: Read the following paragraph. It is written without any capitalization. Copy the paragraph, capitalizing words where necessary. Check your work carefully.

A Time of Transition: Part I

(1) the latter part of the seventies and the first year of the eighties was a transitional period in recent american history. (2) to a great extent, the early and middle part of the decade had been a period of self-examination; people thought about themselves and their feelings more than they ever had before. (3) during the final years of the seventies, however, and in 1980, people started to turn their attention outward, away from their private interests. (4) they became interested in important national events that were filled with tragedy, excitement, frustration, and discovery. (5) for example, astronomers, as well as national aeronautics and space administration space scientists, waited anxiously for the information collected from the pioneer saturn mission and the voyager I. (6) sports fans were excited to see the u.s. olympic hockey team win a gold medal in the finals against the russians. (7) meanwhile, other fans won and lost bets as the philadelphia phillies gained their first world series victory. (8) citizens around the country watched in anticipation and fear as mt. st. helens erupted, sending blinding clouds of ashes down upon residents of washington state and nearby cities in oregon. (9) further south, in the summer of 1980, residents in the southwest experienced one of the most serious heat waves in the twentieth century. (10) moreover, blacks in miami, florida, began to protest and riot because of racial injustices. (11) the nation watched as investigations were conducted by the civil rights commission and by the national association for the advancement of colored people. (12) this period was an important time of change and a time of renewed social awareness.

PRACTICE 2B

Using Capitalization Rules

DIRECTIONS: Read the following paragraph. It is written without any capitalization. Copy the paragraph, capitalizing words where necessary. Check your work carefully.

A Time of Transition: Part II

(1) during the five years up to ronald reagan's election in 1980, people began to pay less attention to their own personal problems and became concerned with religious, social, and political issues affecting the nation. (2) whereas organized religion had been losing popularity for many years, suddenly the moral majority gained political power. (3) in addition, while the catholic church continued its stand against abortion, the national organization for women campaigned for personal choice. (4) people of all ages and backgrounds looked for the answer to the question "who killed j.r.?" as they watched the nighttime drama "dallas." (5) in addition, the world of fashion promoted calvin klein jeans, gloria vanderbilt blouses and jeans, pierre cardin shirts and jackets, and other designer clothing. (6) millions of people across the country—and across the world—played old beatles and john lennon albums in final tribute to john lennon, one of the most influential songwriters and musicians of the century. (7) partly as a result of his assassination, average citizens, as well as members of the house and senate, continued to argue over gun control. (8) moreover, the cubans' exodus to miami on the freedom flotilla made citizens throughout the country either sympathetic or very angry. (9) in order to help these refugees start new lives in the united states, white house administrators worked with city, county, state, and federal agencies. (10) in addition, throughout this time, the nation was united in its campaign to end the iranian hostage crisis. (11) as the 1980 election day approached, republicans, democrats, and independents united in their enthusiasm. (12) after ronald reagan became president, wall street reported a boost in the economy. (13) this period of transition closed with people feeling hopeful and optimistic about the future.

PRACTICE 2C

Using Capitalization Rules

DIRECTIONS: Read the following paragraph. It is a letter written without any capitalization. Copy the letter, capitalizing where necessary. Check your work carefully.

A Letter

(1) dear casey,
   (2) i just received your letter about your trip, and it sounds like it was fantastic. (3) i especially enjoyed your story about meeting the old u.s. park ranger patrolling the campgrounds at glacier national park. (4) his stories of grizzlies and wolverines must have been frightening to mother and dad, who've always worried about the dangers of camping. (5) i'm sure they enjoyed the rest very much, though, especially since dad's been so involved in trying to write an article on wildlife for the revised edition of the backpack guide. (6) i'm glad to hear you got to see old faithful and the grand tetons. (7) the rockies are so spectacular in the spring. (8) i'm sorry that you didn't get as far as lake louise and the salt lake near the columbian ice fields. (9) i hope you can travel along highway 1 next year; it's known as the scenic route, and it's one of the most beautiful in the west. (10) oh, by the way, i've also been trying to rent the house on union street for roger. (11) his firm, harned and associates, is gaining a very good reputation among city designers and architects, and i should have no trouble renting the house. (12) architectural remodeling digest just did a review of his work this fall, so he should get an automatic membership in the designers association of southern california. (13) the kids are fine. (14) pam just entered seventh grade at mt. st. james catholic school after being on the honor roll all last year. (15) the principal, father george, thinks she'll do very well. (16) paul received the best player medal in football at plumber high school and is hoping to get a scholarship to union state college next fall. (17) celina is excelling in physics and spanish. (18) intermediate physics was an easy class for her, but physics 208a is very difficult. (19) barbara is still head volunteer at the red cross and conducts blood mobiles twice a week. (20) janice came up with the question "can i wear make up now?" which makes me feel like i'm getting old quickly. (21) oh well, as they say, "i'm not getting older, i'm getting better." (22) i loved hearing from you.
   (23) much love,
   (24) carmela

O N   Y O U R   O W N

Ideas for Guided and Open Writing

GUIDED WRITING EXERCISE: The chamber of commerce for the town in which you now live or in which you grew up has asked you to write a promotional brochure for a group of visiting Russian tourists. The purpose of the brochure is to provide a brief picture of the city. Write a 100–150 word paragraph describing one area or one aspect of the city to these tourists. Take your readers on a brief tour, concentrating on the most striking and interesting area or aspect that you believe would interest these visitors. You may describe historical sites, landmarks, meeting halls, convention centers, shopping centers, churches, museums, restaurants, parks, or neighborhoods. In addition, consider mentioning major streets the visitor should know in relation to these specific sites. If you wish, you may begin your paragraph with "A visit to —— reveals . . ." or "—— is a city of many . . ." or "The character of —— is best described as. . . ." Pay attention to appropriate capitalization as you write.

OPEN WRITING IDEAS: The following topics are suggestions for open writing exercises to help you practice the structures presented in this chapter. Develop these ideas into paragraphs of 100–150 words. Focus your attention on proper capitalization.

1. Discuss one song, book, poem, or movie that has been influential or memorable in your life. Tell the time of your life that it was influential and why it is still meaningful. Identify the artist or author of the work.

2. Describe someone you know who reminds you of one of the following: preppie, used-car salesman, jock, absent-minded professor, cowboy, and so on. In your description, mention some of the following personal habits or preferences: what the person wears, eats, reads, or enjoys doing.

CHAPTER 3

Using Plural Nouns and Possessives

Some writers have trouble making nouns plural and making nouns show possession. Using the following rules may help students check their work.

Noun Plurals

1. For most nouns, add *s* to form the plural.

photographer	photographers
submarine	submarines

2. For singular nouns that end with *s*, *z*, *sh*, *ch*, or *x*, add *es* to form the plural.

kiss	kisses
Mr. Gomez	the Gomezes
circus	circuses
fox	foxes

3. For nouns that end in *y* preceded by a consonant, change *y* to *i* and add *es*.

spy	spies
worry	worries
dairy	dairies

4. For nouns that end in *o*, consult the dictionary when in doubt. Here are some general rules.

For some nouns that end in *o* preceded by a consonant (including all musical terms), add *s*.

silo	silos
soprano	sopranos

Other nouns ending in *o* preceded by a consonant add *es*.

echo	echoes
hero	heroes
potato	potatoes

Nouns that end in *o* preceded by a vowel add *s*.

portfolio	portfolios
radio	radios
igloo	igloos

5. Nouns that end in *f* and *fe* vary.

Some add *s*.

belief	beliefs
cuff	cuffs

In others, the *f* changes to *v*, and *es* is added.

half	halves
life	lives
loaf	loaves

Some *f* and *fe* words are formed in both ways.

hoof	hoofs or hooves
scarf	scarfs or scarves

6. Some nouns have irregular plural forms. These nouns form the plural through a spelling change.

tooth	teeth
ox	oxen
child	children
man	men
mouse	mice
foot	feet

7. Compound nouns written as one word add *s*. Hyphenated compound nouns, however, add the plural ending after the first word in the combination.

bystander	bystanders
landlady	landladies
cupful	cupfuls
mother-in-law	mothers-in-law
maid-of-honor	maids-of-honor
court-martial	courts-martial

8. Some nouns have identical singular and plural forms.

a tame *deer*	a herd of *deer* in the field
a woolly *sheep*	a flock of *sheep*
the dangerous *species* of bees	the many *species* of rodents
the *series* of questions	three new television *series*
a *fish* out of water	a lot of *fish* in the sea

9. Some English words borrowed from foreign languages retain their foreign plural forms.

the television *medium*	all of the public *media*
the most important *criterion*	all of the *criteria*
the first *crisis*	all of the *crises*
the best *analysis*	the three *analyses*
the single *basis*	the three *bases* of philosophy
a 1956 *alumnus* of East High	the three *alumni* of 1958
one butterfly *larva*	many butterfly *larvae*
a fine *thesis*	the four best *theses*
a Pythagorean *hypothesis*	several scientific *hypotheses*
an extraordinary *phenomenon*	the various *phenomena* of the universe

10. Some nouns have two plural forms: the original foreign or the regular English plural. The English plural, which is usually preferred in all writing, is the first choice in the following examples.

the *formula* for aspirin	secret *formulas* or *formulae*
a book *index*	lists of *indexes* or *indices*
outside *stimulus*	the variety of *stimuluses* or *stimuli*
the *radius* of the circle	along the equal *radiuses* or *radii*
a long *memorandum*	many *memorandums* or *memoranda*
an obligatory *curriculum*	three school *curriculums* or *curricula*
a course *syllabus*	two separate *syllabuses* or *syllabi*
an edible *fungus*	three kinds of *funguses* or *fungi*

P R A C T I C E   3 A

Using Plurals

DIRECTIONS: Read the following paragraph. Then copy the paragraph, changing the words in parentheses to their plural forms. Check your work carefully.

Circuses: The Greatest Shows on Earth

(1) (Circus) have been performing for (audience) since the beginning of recorded history. (2) Today these glittering (spectacle) still excite (thousand) of (community) throughout the world. (3) Such (motto) as "The show must go on" and "Always be prepared" seem to be the (criterion) for producing successful (show), which are colorful (phenomenon). (4) The (performance) illuminate the (arena), usually filled to their (capacity) with young and old (spectator). (5) Every possible detail creates brilliant (reflection)—from the (hoof) of the high-stepping (horse) to the gleaming, bared (tooth) of sleek (tiger, lion, and panther). (6) Dressed in yards of (bead, satin, rhinestone, and ruby), (lady) perform as (winged fairy and princess). (7) (Clown, trapeze artist, acrobat, and juggler) fascinate (bystander)—(man, woman, and child) alike. (8) Sometimes risking their (life) to perform a (series) of dramatic physical (feat), these (performer) swirl and turn in the middle of (cloud) of (scarf, ruffle, and heavy fold) of (fabric). (9) When the many (doorway and entrance) into the (arena) open, all (eye) are focused on the (performer). (10) (Monkey, chimpanzee, ostrich, and bear) strut, walk, and dance to the commanding (echo) of the (trainer). (11) In another part of the arena, entire performing (family) of (brother-in-law, sister-in-law, niece, and nephew) are encouraged by the (hurray and smile) of the audience. (12) Then, as the final act finishes, the glamour and excitement of circus (activity), which have sparked the (imagination) of (million) of people, are stilled until another performance. (13) The reality of the crumpled (box) of popcorn, spilled (drink), and half-eaten (sandwich) left behind in the empty (bleacher) are the only (reminder) that the circus was in town.

Possessives

To show ownership of something by one or more persons or things, use the possessive form.

Singular Possessives

To write the possessive forms of most singular nouns, add *'s*.

a camel	a camel's hump
the moon	the moon's shadow
the poem	the poem's rhythm
the tarantula	the tarantula's habits
Charles	Charles's idea

Usage is divided, however, about singular proper names ending in *s*. You may see only an apostrophe, as in *Charles'*. But most often an apostrophe and *s* (*'s*) are used. The only universal exceptions are the names *Jesus* and *Moses* and Greek names of more than one syllable ending in *es*.

SINGULAR	SINGULAR POSSESSIVE
sparrow	the sparrow's young
doctor	the doctor's office
Ms. Willis	Ms. Willis's apartment
Jesus	Jesus' teachings
Moses	Moses' law
Hercules	Hercules' feats

Plural Possessive Forms

To form the plural possessive of any noun, first write the plural form. If the plural ends in *s*, add an apostrophe after the *s* (*s'*). If the plural does not end in *s*, write the plural form and then add *'s*.

SINGULAR	PLURAL	PLURAL POSSESSIVE
sparrow	two sparrows	two sparrows' eggs
secretary	the four executive secretaries	the four executive secretaries' desks
Ms. Willis	the Willises	the Willises' house
child	children	the children's friends
deer	deer	the three deer's antlers
daughter-in-law	daughters-in-law	the daughters'-in-law gift

Shared and Separate Ownership

When ownership is shared with another person or thing, only one of the persons or things needs to show possession. For example, Marisa and Camille own some records together. The last name listed (in this case, the second name) shows possession.

Marisa and Camille's records were stolen.

The following are other examples of shared ownership:

Marg Carter and Dick Shelton's short story collection will soon be published.

The poem and story's inspiration came from visiting the Navajo reservation.

To show that two people own the same things separately, each noun should be in the possessive form. For example, if Marisa and Camille separately own records, then each name would have to show possession.

Marisa's and Camille's records were stolen.

Study the following situations. Are they examples of shared or separate ownership?

1. Our friends and relatives all parked cars outside our trailer.

Our _____ cars blocked the street.

This situation is an example of separate ownership. Because the friends and relatives own separate cars, then each word should show possession:

Our friends' and relatives' cars blocked the street.

2. Ernesto and Belen have two children.

_____ children attend preschool.

This situation is an example of shared ownership. Because Ernesto and Belen have shared ownership of their children, only the second name needs to show possession.

Ernesto and Belen's children attend preschool.

P R A C T I C E   3 B

Using Possessives

DIRECTIONS: Read the following paragraph. Then copy the paragraph, changing the words in parentheses to their possessive forms. Check your work carefully.

Macamaw City

(1) One-hundred-year-old Chester Beltimer, Macamaw County, (Washington) oldest resident, was honored last week by Macamaw (City) Chamber of Commerce for his outstanding career as postmaster, county supervisor, deputy sheriff, and church pastor. (2) Asked last week what he feels the major change has been in the character of the city over the years, he said that he feels it to be the (resident) attitudes toward living in a small town. (3) "Years ago," he said, "the (townspeople) emotions were tied directly to their (family) needs and to their (neighbor) needs. (4) The (church) influence was important back then, and the (community) responses to an (individual) problems were based on brotherly love." (5) He went on to tell about a time when (Frank) and (Mary Jane Homer) daughter had to undergo a serious operation. (6) "No sooner had the (town) two (doctor) reports been written," he said, "than the (mayor) and the three (county supervisor) wives collected donations for the (girl) medical expenses." (7) Even the (schoolchildren) (teacher) efforts to help brighten the suffering (parent) spirits revealed a sense of genuine love and concern.
(8) Today, however, most of these same (people) hopes have changed greatly. (9) These (adult) attitudes about the town have turned toward progress and achievement. (10) "(Evelyn) and (Jack) original general store, for example, has been replaced by one built by (Port Angeles) largest (law firm) partners. (11) Years ago each (resident) sense of community would have been threatened by these (city folks) actions. (12) Today, though, the (town member) attitudes as well as the individual (business) policies reflect the (politician) goals of expansion and success." (13) He continued, "One more thing has happened to weaken the (citizen) unity. (14) When the (Farris) and the (Kostolias) farms were bought up last year by the (state) major electronics firm, this small (community) morale dropped. (15) I'm afraid Macamaw City won't be able to survive as it has for all these years."

P R A C T I C E   3 C

Using Plurals and Possessives

DIRECTIONS:　Read the following paragraph. Then copy the paragraph, appropriately changing some words in parentheses to their plural forms and some of the words in parentheses to their plural possessive forms. Check your work carefully.

Swap Meet in Glendale

(1) The first swap meet held in Glendale, California, proved to be one of the greatest (success) of all the (town) community (activity). (2) Entire (family)—(husband, wife, baby, child, son-in-law, and daughter-in-law)—came in (automobile) and in (bus) to shop, exchange (story), and enjoy (themself). (3) All age (group), from (newborn to ten-year-old to senior citizen), came from nearby (town, county, and city) to attend the swap meet, which was located away from all (house) and near the (county) new airport. (4) Many people packed entire picnic (lunch); others snacked on (loaf) of freshly baked bread, homemade (pastry), and other (dish) being sold in (booth). (5) Up and down the aisles, (man, woman, and child) looked through (thousand) of (toy, watch, brush, and household item) for (bargain). (6) (Child) pulled at their (parent) (sleeve), (mother) quieted their (baby) (cry), and (father) carried their (family) (purchase). (7) (Child) stood in long (line) to ride (pony and merry-go-round). (8) Around the corner, book (lover) glanced through (box) and (shelf) lined with new and old book (edition). (9) At another booth, music (buff) examined (oboe, cello, piano, and banjo). (10) Elsewhere, people looking for fresh (vegetable) were delighted to find homegrown (tomato, potato, radish, and ear of corn), as well as many (variety of squash). (11) (Photographer) looking for old (photo) searched through (stack of album) of (photograph). (12) Others found extra (lens, filter, and carrying case) for their (camera). (13) As the (day) (activity) came to a close, price (quote) came down considerably. (14) By the end of the swap meet, many (people) (foot) ached as they walked among the various (row) of (item). (15) The success of this (community) first swap meet spurred many nearby (community) to establish their own (swap meet).

ON YOUR OWN

Ideas for Guided and Open Writing

GUIDED WRITING EXERCISE: A controversy has recently arisen in some states about the legal rights of sexually active minors who want to keep their discussions with their doctors confidential. Private doctors do not have to keep this information confidential. In fact, some doctors feel it is their duty to report the sexual activity of their teenage patients to the parents of those teenagers. These doctors give such information freely to parents; others, however, give the information only at the parents' request. Yet in still other cases, some doctors believe that if they were to reveal the sexual activities of their teenage patients, these teenagers would be afraid to seek necessary medical attention.

What do you believe? In a well-developed paragraph of 100–150 words, defend or attack the idea that parents have the right to find out from their youngsters' physicians or clinics whether or not their children are sexually active. If you wish, begin your paragraph with "Parents have (or do not have) the right to obtain the medical records of their teenagers." In your discussion consider only one of the following situations: a teenager asking for help obtaining an abortion, asking for help obtaining contraceptives, or asking for help curing venereal disease. Should the doctor volunteer information that was not requested, or should he or she provide information only upon request? Does the age of the patient make a difference? If so, how?

OPEN WRITING IDEAS: The following topics are suggestions for open writing exercises to help you practice the structures presented in this chapter. Develop these ideas into paragraphs of 100–150 words. Focus your attention on plural nouns and possessives.

1. With the recent increase in the number of immigrants and refugees into this country, bilingual-bicultural education has become an important issue among parents, educators, and legislators. Should classes be taught in two languages in schools where a certain percentage of the student population represents a particular language and cultural background? Or do you believe that instruction should be only in the dominant language, English? Which is most beneficial for the student and for society? Explain your beliefs.

2. Since full-length movies are now being shown on cable television, many people are staying home for entertainment. To counter this trend, movie theaters are turning to the concept of full-scale entertainment centers. Built into the design of the new movie theaters are bars, restaurants, and even game rooms. What is your opinion of building such recreation centers?

CHAPTER 4

Using Pronouns Correctly: Reference and Agreement

A *pronoun* is a word that substitutes for a noun or another pronoun. Pronouns refer to other nouns or pronouns mentioned earlier. Consider the following sentence:

Joseph had begun cooking Joseph's supper when Joseph's sister walked in.

The sentence sounds repetitious. Here is the same sentence with the appropriate pronouns included:

Joseph had begun cooking *his* supper when *his* sister walked in.

Notice that each of the pronouns agrees in number with *Joseph*, a singular noun. Pronouns have singular and plural forms:

	SINGULAR	PLURAL
FIRST PERSON	I, my, me	we, our, us
SECOND PERSON	you, your, you	you, your, you
THIRD PERSON	he, his, him she, her, her it, its, it	they, their, them

1. A pronoun must agree in number with the noun it refers to. A singular noun takes a singular pronoun, and a plural noun takes a plural pronoun.

Using straw, gum wrappers, and feathers, the birds quickly built *their* new nests. (*Their* refers to *birds*.)

The aardvark, a native of Africa, uses *its* sticky tongue to capture insects. (*Its* refers to *aardvark*.)

2. Use a singular masculine pronoun to refer to pronouns such as *any, anybody, anything, another, everyone, everybody, everything, each, either, the other, someone, somebody, something, nothing, no one, one,* and *nobody.*

Everybody should bring *his* own car.

Someone forgot *his* briefcase at the meeting.

This rule is very controversial. Many people argue that these pronouns can also be referred to by a singular feminine pronoun, such as:

Everyone should carry *her* own luggage.

Somebody forgot *her* umbrella at the meeting.

Another more acceptable alternative is to use *his or her* such as in the following example:

Anybody who wishes to carpool should register *his or her* car here.

Although using "his or her" is acceptable in formal writing, sometimes people overuse it. To avoid the "his or her" problem, many people rewrite their sentences to plural:

People who wish to carpool should register *their* cars here.

Another alternative is to omit the pronoun entirely, by rewriting the sentence as in the following example:

HIS OR HER	In the United States, almost no one drinks *his or her* beer hot.
PRONOUN OMITTED	In the United States, almost no one drinks beer hot.

In your own writing you can use either the masculine or the feminine to refer to these pronouns, or you can use "his or her" exclusively. You may want to try plural pronouns, or you may try to avoid pronouns as much as possible. Whatever you prefer, choose one alternative and use it consistently in your paragraphs.

3. Words connected by *and* take a plural pronoun.

Mary Louisa and *Paul* have completed *their* nursing degrees.

However, if words are connected by *nor* or *or,* the pronoun usually agrees with the word closest to the verb.

Neither the *two sisters* nor *Mike* is particularly satisfied with *his* work.

4. Remember a special rule for *collective nouns.* Collective nouns refer to a group of people or things as singular units, such as *jury, family, committee,* and *group.*

Collective nouns take a singular or plural pronoun, depending on whether the collective noun is used in a plural or singular sense. In the following examples, notice that *jury,* as well as *family, committee,* and *group,* can be considered a single body or a group of separate individuals.

The *jury* ended *their* day without a decision. (The sentence is referring to separate individuals within the group.)
The *jury* reached *its* verdict. (The sentence is referring to the jury as a single group.)

His *family* always exchanges *their* gifts on Christmas Eve.
His *family* spent *its* vacation at Pine Top.

The *committee* are voicing *their* opinions.
The *committee* is discussing *its* agenda.

The *group* are completing *their* college applications.
The *group* is submitting *its* yearly report.

5. Use the reflexive pronouns correctly. Reflexive pronouns are pronouns that "reflect" or rename the subject. For example, the following sentence is repetitious and incorrect:

John thought of *John* as a leader.

However, substituting a reflexive pronoun to refer to John corrects the sentence.

John thought of *himself* as a leader.

Study the following sentences to see examples of correct and incorrect ways of using reflexive pronouns:

INCORRECT	Direct the letter to John and *myself.*
CORRECT	Direct the letter to John and *me.*
INCORRECT	As for *myself,* I enjoy modern poetry.
CORRECT	As for *me,* I enjoy modern poetry.

	SINGULAR	**PLURAL**
FIRST PERSON	myself	ourselves
SECOND PERSON	yourself	yourselves
THIRD PERSON	himself, herself, itself	themselves

Use reflexive pronouns for special situations such as the following:

She hurt *herself* playing football.

He confused *himself* more and more.

6. *This* and *that* precede, or go before, singular nouns to point out a particular object. *These* and *those* precede plural nouns to point out particular objects.

SINGULAR	*This* note was found in the medicine cabinet.
PLURAL	*These* notes were found in the medicine cabinet.
SINGULAR	*That* young woman will be a fine musician some day.
PLURAL	*Those* young women will be fine musicians some day.

This and *that* also substitute for singular nouns; similarly, *these* and *those* substitute for plural nouns.

> *This* is the book I requested.

> *Those* are the famous catacombs in Rome.

P R A C T I C E   4 A

Changing Singular to Plural

DIRECTIONS: Read the following paragraph. Assume you are a psychologist in the year 2110 giving a lecture on psychological discoveries of the previous century. The paragraph is a part of your lecture. Copy the paragraph, changing:

> *anyone* to *people*
> *individual* to *individuals*
> *person* to *people* or *persons*

These changes will require you to change pronouns, articles, and other words referring to these pronouns. Check your work carefully.

Questions for Health

(1) In their book entitled *Type A Behavior and Your Heart,* San Francisco heart specialists Meyer Friedman and Ray H. Rosenman identified certain characteristics of Type A personalities. (2) They believed that the attitudes and behaviors seen in Type A personalities were the primary causes of heart disease. (3) These doctors hoped that a person would become familiar with the typical traits and behavioral patterns of the Type A personality. (4) As a result, this informed person would perhaps be alert to similar personal behavior in himself and could take steps to make changes in his or her life. (5) Friedman and Rosenman believed that a Type A individual could change his behavior; therefore, the doctors outlined the following specific questions such a person should ask in order to identify his own Type A characteristics. (6) The doctors recommended that the individual should consider his past year's behavior when answering these questions. (7) A person must consider whether those characteristics he found in himself are occasional or consistent patterns. (8) An individual should ask himself if he found himself hurrying through meals, work, and leisurely activities to make more time for his other work. (9) Also, this individual should ask himself whether he or she frequently found himself attempting two or more tasks at once in order to save his time. (10) In addition, the person must ask himself if he considered himself important based on the number of his accomplishments. (11) This individual must also determine if he or she has had difficulty recognizing and admitting his own personal faults. (12) These questions are a general guide for anyone wanting to examine his or her own behavior and attitudes. (13) According to Friedman and Rosenman, a person who answers yes to a majority of these questions should recognize himself or herself as a Type A personality. (14) Once recognizing his Type A personality, an individual can take steps to eliminate his negative behaviors and improve his overall health.

P R A C T I C E   4 B

Changing Singular to Plural

DIRECTIONS: Read the following paragraph. Then copy the paragraph, changing *bat* to *bats*. These changes will require you to change pronouns, articles, and other words referring to *bats*. Check your work carefully.

The Bat: A Mystery of the Night

(1) Perhaps because of its terrifying appearance and its habits of hiding by day and emerging at dusk to find food for itself, the bat long ago found itself associated with mysterious, dark, and sometimes frightening scenes. (2) Not surprisingly, as a result of its eerie features, it also found itself in the company of witches, demons, and other suspicious figures of the human imagination. (3) Even though false beliefs about the bat still exist, research conducted many years ago on the bat has revealed that it did not deserve such a terrifying reputation. (4) In fact, research revealed some interesting information about this winged mammal. (5) Research showed that the bat did not move much during the day. (6) It usually attached itself in an upside-down position to darkened areas in caves, barns, rocky cliffs, and even tree branches. (7) This creature became active at sundown, when it tried to nourish itself with insects, frogs, pollen, nectar, lizards, fish, and even other bats. (8) Thus, it looked for food when the skies were cleared of most birds that ate the same kinds of food that the bat did. (9) Researchers were most surprised by the ability of this remarkable animal to fly in the dark without hurting itself by running into trees, cliffs, and other obstacles. (10) Researchers have discovered that the bat echolocated; in other words, it sent high-frequency sound waves that echoed back to the bat from objects in its surroundings. (11) In this way, the bat directed itself toward its food and away from obstacles. (12) Because the bat developed at the same time as birds did many millions of years ago, this night creature most likely found itself competing fiercely with birds for the same food. (13) Because the bat could maneuver at night, it developed a nightly feeding cycle. (14) Probably the most frightening characteristic of the bat was thought to be its exaggerated facial features, such as large lips and nostrils. (15) These features, however, actually helped the bat in its echolocation. (16) Most people will continue to imagine the bat as a frightening yet fascinating mammal to study.

P R A C T I C E   4 C

Changing Plural to Singular

DIRECTIONS: Read the following paragraph. Then copy the paragraph, changing the underlined words to singular. These changes will require you to change pronouns, articles, and other words referring to the underlined words. Check your work carefully.

The Origins of Dating: Part I

(1) Dating, as it is known today, began in our society in the late nineteenth century because of new economic conditions and changing women's roles. (2) Before this time, young <u>people</u> rarely had casual meetings with <u>members</u> of the opposite sex since young <u>men</u> and <u>women</u> never found themselves unchaperoned. (3) This situation gradually changed, however, as methods of mass production developed and as new <u>laborers</u>—the working-class <u>women</u>—joined the American work force. (4) These newly employed women usually worked in factories or mills, but they slowly began to move into the business world in offices and stores as well. (5) This move created more jobs for young middle-class women, who before this time had satisfied themselves usually by becoming <u>teachers</u> and <u>governesses</u>. (6) In addition, these young women enrolled in colleges that previously had been all male. (7) Although these ambitious <u>women</u> never found themselves completely free from supervision, they could now associate with men more freely. (8) Furthermore, as World War I developed, they socialized more and more with their male peers. (9) As their <u>fathers</u>, <u>brothers</u>, and <u>boyfriends</u> went off to war, the <u>women</u>, now left at home, took over positions traditionally held by men, such as secretaries, clerks, and sales personnel. (10) While these skilled young <u>women</u> proved themselves in the business world, they also decided to continue their education by going to high school and college, where they had the chance to make friends with men and women their own age. (11) Another development that greatly increased the relationships between <u>men</u> and <u>women</u> was the invention of the automobile. (12) This new form of transportation made it easier than before for young men and women to go out on dates. (13) On these dates the young people of this time no longer felt as restricted as they once had. (14) Instead, they could enjoy themselves without the constant supervision of their parents.

P R A C T I C E   4 D

Changing Plural to Singular

DIRECTIONS: Read the following paragraph. Then copy the paragraph, changing the underlined words to singular. These changes will require you to change pronouns, articles, and other words referring to the underlined words. Check your work carefully.

The Origins of Dating: Part II

(1) As the telephone became a popular household item, young <u>men</u> in the early part of the century could communicate with their sweethearts privately for the first time. (2) Like the telephone, the moviehouses provided these young <u>adults</u> with a new kind of privacy. (3) These young <u>people</u> could now go to a somewhat secluded place to meet their friends and dates. (4) In addition, in the moviehouses they found themselves influenced by movie stars whose romantic behavior they could copy. (5) In fact, everywhere they turned, they found themselves surrounded by stories and pictures of these romantic idols in newspapers, magazines, and on the recently invented radio. (6) Influenced by the media, young <u>women</u>, in particular, began to change their behavior at this time. (7) The "old-fashioned <u>girls</u>" became the newly accepted <u>flappers</u>. (8) They wore their skirts, which for centuries had been ankle length, above their knees. (9) They shingled, bobbed, and marcelled their hair, which had once reached their waists, and they replaced their whalebone corsets with brief panties. (10) As a part of their new freedom, they dated young men they met at school, parties, or work. (11) Therefore, mainly because of the changes that the <u>women</u> of this time began to experience, dating became an acceptable part of American society.

PRACTICE 4E

Making Special Considerations

DIRECTIONS: Read the following paragraph. Assume you are an anthropologist in the year 2080, giving a lecture on human behavior in the previous century. The paragraph is a part of your lecture. Copy the paragraph, changing the underlined words to the singular forms in parentheses at the end of the sentence. These changes will require you to make changes in pronouns, articles, and other words referring to these words. Check your work carefully.

Clues to Meaning Through Kinesics

(1) Anthropologists agree that in the last century almost <u>all people</u> used kinesic signals when they spoke. (everyone) (2) They gestured with their head, hands, or other parts of the body to communicate a message. (3) Sometimes more powerful than words themselves, the gestures revealed the true feelings of the <u>speakers</u>. (speaker) (4) For example, <u>people</u> in love often showed their emotions through their eyes; their eyes appeared to sparkle because their pupils were dilated. (a person) (5) <u>People</u> also used other gestures to show their interest in a topic. (a person) (6) For example, <u>businessmen</u> sitting in a conference often demonstrated their involvement in the lecture by leaning forward in their chairs and resting their chins on their hands. (a businessman) (7) Although <u>some persons</u> may have used gestures to express interest, <u>others</u> may have frequently used gestures to show boredom or restlessness. (one person) (another) (8) For instance, <u>Americans</u> often revealed their boredom or dissatisfaction by crossing their legs while sitting and slightly kicking their feet. (an American) (9) One very interesting discovery is that gestures were found in every language, but the same gesture in one language could mean something different in another language. (10) For example, <u>Americans</u> wishing to show agreement nodded their heads up and down; to show disagreement, they shook their heads back and forth. (an American) (11) <u>East Indians</u>, on the other hand, nodded their heads to show disagreement, yet they shook their heads to signify yes. (an East Indian) (12) Similarly, often to express doubt about something, <u>speakers</u> of American English slightly touched their noses. (a speaker) (13) In contrast, <u>Europeans</u> expressed their doubt, not by touching their noses, but by resting one of their index fingers underneath one of their eyes and pulling slightly downward. (a European) (14) Thus, gestures were not meaningless; they actually contributed to <u>people's</u> expressing their attitudes, emotions, and opinions about something. (a person's)

O N   Y O U R   O W N

Ideas for Guided and Open Writing

GUIDED WRITING EXERCISE: "Look out for number one" became the motto during the seventies, which is called the "Me Generation." During this period, people joined therapy groups, religious cults, and other specialized clubs and organizations in order to "learn about themselves." In addition, people wanted to discover their true feelings in order to "find themselves." Is focusing on the individual good for society? Specifically, consider how this kind of thinking affects family life, community cooperation, or personal relationships with other people. In a well-developed paragraph of approximately 100–150 words, discuss how intense concentration on the individual affects society. You might begin your paragraph with "Focusing on the self helps (or hurts) . . ." Make sure your pronoun reference is clear and that your pronouns agree in number.

OPEN WRITING EXERCISE: The following topics are suggestions for open writing exercises to help you practice the structures presented in this chapter. Develop these ideas into paragraphs of 100–150 words. Focus your attention on the appropriate use of pronoun agreement and reference. Decide which topic you feel is better for a singular subject and which is better for a plural subject.

1. The United States is described as a wasteful country. Consider how people in your family, neighborhood, school, city, or state are wasteful. Using these people as examples, tell what such wastefulness reveals about the average American citizen.

2. Abigail Van Buren and her sister, Ann Landers, two widely read syndicated columnists, are household names across the United States. Why would thousands of people write every week for advice from persons they have never met?

CHAPTER 5

Understanding Pronoun Form

Using pronouns correctly requires an understanding of the forms of pronouns.

All pronouns have three forms: subject, object, and possessive.

PRONOUN FORMS

SUBJECT	OBJECT	POSSESSIVE
I	me	my (mine)
you	you	you (yours)
he	him	his (his)
she	her	her (hers)
it	it	its (its)
we	us	ours (ours)
you	you	your (yours)
they	them	their (theirs)
who	whom	whose
whoever	whomever	whoever's

The subject form of pronouns is used when pronouns function as subjects of sentences, as in the following examples:

He discussed the movie at length.
She and *I* are great friends.
They traveled to Hawaii last summer.

The object form of pronouns is used when pronouns function as objects. Objects are nouns or pronouns that receive the action of the verb or that follow prepositions. Prepositions are words such as *in, at, to, from,* or *during* that show location, space, and time.

> The reporter thanked *her* for the information.
> Amos baked *them* his favorite cookies.
> This secret is between only you and *me.*

The possessive form of pronouns is used to show possession. Possessive pronouns are used before nouns.

> Those are *her* books
> That car is *hers.*

Notice that an -*ing* verb can be used as a noun. It requires a possessive pronoun before it.

> *Hector's* getting an *A* in the course was a surprise. (*Getting* is an -*ing* verb used as a noun. Therefore, *Hector* must show possession: *Hector's.*)
> *His* getting an *A* in the course was a surprise. (The pronoun must show possession: *His.*)
> *Rachel's* deciding to become a lawyer made everyone happy. (*Deciding* is an -*ing* verb used as a noun. Therefore, *Rachel* must show possession: *Rachel's.*)
> *Her* deciding to become a lawyer made everyone happy. (The pronoun must show possession: *Her.*)

Note that the possessive pronouns do not have or require an apostrophe. Don't be confused by *it's* or *its* and *theirs* or *there's*:

> The cat meowed for *its* milk. (possessive pronoun)
> *It's* a good day for swimming. (contraction for *it is*)
> The attorneys opened up a new office; *theirs* is the one with the golden eagle on its shingle. (Theirs is a pronoun referring to *their office.*)
> *There's* a new play opening tonight. (*There's* is a contraction for *there is.*)

The use of *who* causes students problems unnecessarily. This pronoun, like almost all other pronouns, has three forms: subject, object, and possessive.

SUBJECT	**OBJECT**	**POSSESSIVE**
who	whom	whose
whoever	whomever	whoever's

The following examples show how these three forms are used.

SUBJECT	*Who* is the winner of the drawing? (*Who* is the subject.)
	Whoever wants the kittens can take them. (*Whoever* is the subject.)
OBJECT	To *whom* is the letter addressed? (object of *to*)
	They will vote for *whomever* they judge to be most competent. (*Whomever* is not the subject. To find the subject, find the verb first. Then ask, "Who judges?" The answer is *they*. *They* is the subject. *Whomever* is the object of *for*.)
POSSESSIVE	I don't know *whose* book this is.

Don't confuse *who's* and *whose*. *Who's* is a contraction for *who is*, and *whose* is possessive.

Who's the author of *The Old Man and the Sea*?

Whose glasses are these?

The following is a list of general rules to help you understand pronoun forms.

1. Pronouns after *than*, *as*, or *but* may be in the subject or object form. The form of the pronoun depends on whether the pronoun is the subject or the object of the following verb, which may be either stated or implied.

Rabbi Plotkin is somewhat older than *he* (is).

She loves him more than (she loves) *me*.

My friend is not as devious as *I* (am).

She teases my brother as much as (she teases) *me*.

2. Pronouns that follow *and* or *or* can be in the subject or object form, depending on whether they act as subjects or objects of the sentence.

Maria Luisa and I went to the opera together. (Not *Maria Luisa and me*)

Cambridge gave *Tommy and me* some licorice. (Not *Tommy and I*)

Nobody applauded except *Sigworth and her*. (Not *Sigworth and she*. *Her* is the object of *except*.)

In each sentence, cover the name. Without the names *Maria Luisa,* *Tommy,* and *Sigworth,* the correct pronouns are clear. For example:

I (not *me*) went to the opera.

3. In formal writing, use the subject form directly after the verb *to be*.

Subject — Verb *to be* — Pronoun in subject form

It was Marvin.

It was *he.* (not *him*)

When a pronoun follows the verb *to be,* it renames the subject and therefore is in the subject form.

Was it Becky?

Was it she? (not *her*)

P R A C T I C E   5 A

Using Pronouns Correctly

DIRECTIONS: Read the following paragraph. Then copy the paragraph, choosing the appropriate word in parentheses. Check your work carefully.

Arranged Marriages

(1) In most of the world's societies, marriage is a way of continuing the family and ensuring (its, it's) economic survival. (2) In these societies, marriage partners are chosen not by the young people (themselves, theirselves) but by (their, they're) parents. (3) The families of both the prospective bride and groom look for a mate (who, whom) is as wealthy or wealthier than (they, them). (4) According to Dr. Lloyd Saxton, a renowned authority on this subject, "In arranged marriages. (theirs, there's) little attention given to love. (5) While (its, it's) hoped that the couple will be compatible, (its, it's) not always possible for the prospective bride and groom because (theirs, there's) little, if any, direct contact between (she, her) and (he, him) before the marriage." (6) In some of these societies, parents often use the services of marriage brokers. (7) (Theirs, There's) is the responsibility to look for and contact parents of a marriageable son or daughter (who, whom)

might be acceptable to (their, they're) client. (8) The brokers swear to (their, they're) client's health, education, skills, training, social status, and appearance. (9) In some societies, the marriage brokers arrange for the dowry. (10) The dowry is money or property that the bride's parents give to the bridegroom. (11) It becomes solely his or is shared by both (he, him) and his bride. (12) In other societies, however, the groom pays a bride price to the family of the woman (who, whom) he is to marry. (13) (His, Him) paying the bride price finalizes the engagement. (14) When selecting an appropriate bride, the groom's family and (he, him) look for a woman (who, whom) is an acceptable member of the community and (whose, who's) social class is the same as (theirs, there's). (15) Only when the son or daughter totally rejects (whoever, whomever) the parents and the marriage arranger select as a mate will the arrangement not be finalized. (16) In general, however, the couples in these societies appreciate (their, they're) parents' help, and therefore the tradition of arranged marriages flourishes.

P R A C T I C E   5 B

Using Pronouns Correctly

DIRECTIONS: Read the following paragraph. Then copy the paragraph, choosing the appropriate word in parentheses. Check your work carefully.

Sex-Role Typing of Children

(1) During (their, they're) early years of schooling, children become increasingly aware of the culturally acceptable behavior for (their, they're) sex roles. (2) Learning behavior that is considered appropriate for (their, they're) sex is called sex-role typing. (3) Sex-role typing is promoted in many ways; of course, (its, it's) greatest promoters are parents, (who, whom) are most successful in teaching the sex-role patterns in children. (4) In fact, it is uncommon to find a child (whose, who's) parents have not influenced him or her with sex-role attitudes. (5) For example, parents often expect (their, they're) son to be aggressive, adventurous, and physically active. (6) However, the daughter is the one (who, whom) the parents expect to be emotional and tender. (7) As a result, parents often find (themselves, theirselves)

tolerant of certain behavior from a son that they would not accept from a daughter. (8) For example, parents might encourage a son to be independent but would expect a daughter to be more passive than (he, him). (9) As a result, a son is often given what are considered male-typed toys: trucks, airplanes, boats, soldiers, and guns. (10) A daughter, on the other hand, is not given the same toys as (he, him); instead, she is usually given female-typed toys: dolls, plastic dishes, cooking utensils, and doll houses. (11) Consequently, a child's sex-role behavior is often greatly influenced by the toys given to siblings and (he or she, him or her). (12) Parents, then, play an important part in (their, they're) children's learning culturally acceptable sex roles. (13) Not until parents' attitudes change will sex roles in society change.

ON YOUR OWN

Ideas for Guided and Open Writing

GUIDED WRITING EXERCISE: Many colleges and universities in the United States have established coeducational dormitories for their students. In some coeducational dormitories, male students live down the hall from female students. In other coeducational dormitories male and female students live next door to one another. Many administrators, parents, and students approve of coeducational living. Those who support these kinds of dormitories believe that coeducational dormitories give students a chance to interact with each other and to make good friends. However, many other parents and students argue that coeducational dormitories limit a person's privacy. In addition, these people say that coeducational dormitories encourage sexual relationships. In a well-developed paragraph of approximately 100–150 words, argue for or against living in coeducational dormitories. Discuss three advantages or disadvantages of living in coeducational dormitories. You might begin your paragraph with "Living in a coeducational dormitory makes a college student ——, ——, and ——." Concentrate on using the appropriate pronoun form.

OPEN WRITING EXERCISE: The following topics are suggestions for open writing exercises to help you practice the structures presented in this chapter. Develop these ideas into paragraphs of 100–150 words. Focus your attention on appropriate usage of pronouns.

1. Football is described as an aggressive sport. This sport seems violent, and its spectators seem fanatic, especially to Europeans. Think about the most exciting football game you have ever seen. Think about how strange it might seem to a visitor to the United States, and describe the game in a way that a foreigner will understand why you liked the game.

2. Listen to several different radio stations and pay special attention to what kinds of voices the disc jockeys have, how fast or slow they talk, and what kinds of things they talk about. Consider at least three types of disc jockeys. Discuss only one, and tell why the audience likes him or her.

CHAPTER 6

Checking for Subject-Verb Agreement

Subject-verb agreement is a problem for many writers. Because these writers are not familiar with the rules for subject-verb agreement, they usually guess at the correct form or make a decision based on what "sounds" better. However, the basic principle of subject-verb agreement is a simple one: **The verb always agrees in number and person with its subject.** Study the following examples and notice how a singular subject affects the verb and how a plural subject affects the verb.

SINGULAR	PLURAL
She *reads* slowly.	They *read* slowly.
My brother *drives* a truck.	My brothers *drive* trucks.
My mother *is* a good cook.	My parents *are* good cooks.
My friend *was* gone.	My friends *were* gone.
Bill *has* never *been* to court.	Bill and Tom *have* never *been* to court.

When the subject is singular (that is, only one person or one thing is talked about), the verb must also be singular. Notice that verbs and nouns differ in this aspect: Nouns add *s* to form their plurals, whereas verbs add *s* to show the singular form for third person singular. Making the verb agree with the subject seems simple in most cases, but some situations present problems. Become familiar with the following subject-verb agreement traps, and avoid some common errors.

1. Don't be confused by phrases or clauses interrupting the subject and verb.

45

This carton of eggs *takes* up too much room in my sack. (*Carton*, not *eggs*, is the subject.)

This pair of slacks *needs* mending. (*Pair*, not *slacks*, is the subject.)

2. When the subject is a *which*, *that*, or *who* pronoun, the verb must agree with the noun that the pronoun refers to.

The museum was filled with tapestries that *were* priceless. (Notice that the verb *were* agrees in number with the plural noun *tapestries*.)

He told a joke that *was* very funny. (Notice that the verb *was* agrees in number with the singular noun *joke*.)

She is one of those poets who *enjoy* reading before large audiences. (Notice that the verb *enjoy* refers back to *poets*, a plural noun. Therefore, *enjoy* must be plural in form.)

P R A C T I C E   6 A

Changing Singular to Plural

DIRECTIONS: Read the following paragraph. Then copy the paragraph, changing *cockroach* to *cockroaches* and *roach* to *roaches*. These changes will require you to change verbs, pronouns, articles, and other words referring to *cockroaches* and *roaches*. Check your work carefully.

The Enduring but not Endearing Cockroach

(1) The common cockroach dates back to the Paleozoic Age. (2) Because the cockroach was able to escape the evolutionary processes that completely changed or eliminated other insects of that time, it is the oldest of all existing winged insects. (3) The roach is considered by entomologists, scientists who study insects, to be the most adaptable of all living creatures. (4) In fact, it is able to adjust to any living conditions and any diet. (5) For example, the cockroach can live in the most remote land areas on earth; the roach is known to live even in barren polar wastelands as well as hundreds of feet below ground level in dark, lifeless mines. (6) In addition, the astounding ability of the cockroach to adapt to any diet is the major reason it

survives. (7) The cockroach is never discouraged, even when it cannot find the diet it prefers: human and animal wastes. (8) Indeed, the cockroach amazingly survives well on such varied diets as nylon, paper, and other man-made products, as well as all foods eaten by humans. (9) It sometimes breeds within empty grocery bags, existing on the glue used to manufacture these bags. (10) Surprisingly enough, the cockroach has occasionally even been known to eat a meal of the soft skin and fingernails of sleeping humans. (11) If, however, the roach is not able to find any food at all, it is capable of surviving solely on water for as long as two months. (12) Although society has been concerned about the extinction of many animal species, it has tried tirelessly to reduce the numbers of this persistent insect in the world. (13) The war waged against the oldest of all insects, the cockroach, has continued for centuries and is unlikely to end in the near future.

P R A C T I C E   6 B

Changing Singular to Plural

DIRECTIONS: Read the following paragraph. Then copy the paragraph, changing the underlined words to their plural forms. These changes will require you to change verbs, pronouns, articles, and other words referring to the underlined words. Check your work carefully.

**Type A
Personality**

(1) According to heart specialists, whether or not a person smokes, drinks alcohol, exercises sufficiently, or eats properly, he or she will most likely have a tendency toward heart disease if the individual has Type A personality characteristics. (2) A Type A personality has particular attitudes and responses not only to stressful situations, but also to everyday living situations. (3) For example, an individual with such a personality is ordinarily aggressive and ambitious, and he or she is unable to assign responsibility to others. (4) Such a person is usually overly concerned about work and deadlines and is generally unable to relax during free time without feeling guilty. (5) In addition, although the Type A personality is usually thought of as self-assured and self-confident, he or she often feels insecure about his or her

position in life. (6) Moreover, a <u>person</u> who has this type of personality often is obsessed with money or numbers. (7) Such an <u>individual</u> also exhibits an excessive competitive drive. (8) He or she tends to measure personal worth by his or her achievements. (9) The Type A <u>personality</u> is usually guided by very strong physical and emotional drives. (10) Such a <u>person</u>, then, would be likely to have strong, intense reactions to situations that may not be very important. (11) The Type A <u>personality</u> tends to overreact to many situations. (12) Heart specialists feel that these strong, exaggerated reactions are the major threat to the health of the Type A <u>personality</u>. (13) By describing and analyzing the major characteristics of such an <u>individual</u>, psychologists and psychiatrists hope to alert everyone to the dangers of such behavior.

P R A C T I C E   6 C

Changing Plural to Singular

DIRECTIONS: Read the following paragraph. Then copy the paragraph, changing *remoras* to *remora*. This change will require you to change verbs, pronouns, articles, and other words referring to *remoras*. Check your work carefully.

Hitchhikers of the Sea

(1) Examples of cooperative living are found throughout nature. (2) Remoras, members of the Echeneidae family of fishes, provide one such example. (3) Remoras are known for practicing commensalism, which means "being at table together." (4) Remoras are thin tropical fish, ranging in length from one to three feet. (5) They cling to larger marine animals and even to ships by means of powerful suction discs at the top of their heads. (6) Using this suction device, the remoras are able to hitch rides from one feeding area to another. (7) Although they occasionally hitch rides from a variety of marine animals, remoras most frequently look for a shark as a host. (8) As the shark or other traveling companions feed, the remoras either scoop up the remains or swim away looking for food. (9) After finishing a meal, the remoras search for another ride and stay firmly attached until another feeding time approaches. (10) Not only do the remoras benefit from this practice, but fishermen who use remoras to catch sea turtles also benefit.

(11) The remoras fasten themselves to turtles so tightly that the fishermen can use them to bring in the turtles. (12) Fishermen tie a line to the remoras and throw them into the sea. (13) Once the remoras attach themselves to turtles, the remoras along with the turtles are pulled ashore and separated from the companion. (14) The remoras, then, have provided humans with a clever and practical means of obtaining food. (15) In addition, they represent a unique cooperation that exists among living creatures.

P R A C T I C E   6 D

Changing Plural to Singular

DIRECTIONS: Read the following paragraph. Then copy the paragraph changing the underlined words from plural to singular. These changes will require you to change verbs, pronouns, articles, and other words referring to the underlined words. Check your work carefully.

Anorexia Nervosa

(1) Anorexia nervosa is an eating disorder that often appears in childhood or adolescence but can also appear later in life. (2) It is a perplexing condition, which literally means "loss of appetite as a function of nerves." (3) Over 90 percent of all cases occur in women. (4) People who have anorexia nervosa almost always have an excessive fear of gaining weight, frequently to the point of obsession. (5) In addition, women who suffer from this condition usually have a distorted image of their bodies. (6) They continue to feel that they are normal or overweight even after they have become extremely thin and weak from undernourishment. (7) In some extreme cases, women afflicted with anorexia nervosa continue to eat and then intentionally vomit what they have just eaten. (8) Another puzzling feature of this condition is that women who are known as anorexic commonly continue to do regular physical exercise long after they have begun to suffer physically. (9) Although causes of anorexia nervosa are unknown, doctors believe that some people with this disorder have an extreme fear of maturation and sexuality. (10) Afraid of accepting adult responsibilities, some women may stop eating altogether. (11) In fact,

as a result of both the physical changes and the emotional stress they suffer, some <u>women</u> may cease menstruation entirely. (12) In addition, studies reveal that as many as 60 percent of all anorexia nervosa patients eventually die as a result of self-starvation. (13) Consequently, anorexia nervosa <u>victims</u> seem to suffer from physiological and psychological problems. (14) Researchers, however, do not know how much of this destructive disease is physical or psychological in origin. (15) Nevertheless, <u>women</u> with this disorder no longer need to feel helpless since physicians and psychologists are gaining success in treating this disease.

More hints for checking for subject-verb agreement:

1. Expressions such as *in addition to, accompanied by, together with, as well as, along with, besides,* and *including* do not affect the verb. Because these expressions do not join two subjects, they do not make the subject plural.

> A good *attitude,* as well as good grades, *is* an important ingredient for successfully completing medical school. (The subject is *attitude;* therefore, the verb is singular.)

> The *President,* accompanied by the Vice President, *was walking* away from a group of reporters. (The subject is *President;* therefore, the verb is singular.)

> *High taxes,* together with inflation, *frighten* even the most economically secure in our society. (Notice that *high taxes* is plural; therefore, the verb is plural.)

2. Pronoun subjects such as *either, neither, each, one, everyone, everybody, no one, someone,* and *somebody* are singular. These pronouns are often confusing because most of them seem to be plural in meaning; however, they are still considered singular, and they take a singular verb.

> *Everybody* usually *eats* his or her lunch after the meeting. (*Everybody* is singular; therefore, the verb is singular.)

> *Each* of the women *is* equally qualified. (*Each,* not *women,* is the subject.)

> *Neither* of the computers *is* operating today. (*Neither,* not *computers,* is the subject.)

> *Is either* of the speakers available for discussion after the lecture? (*Either* is singular; thus the verb is singular.)

> *None* takes either a singular or plural verb, depending on what it refers to. If the noun after *none* can be counted as separate items

(such as *potatoes*, *albums*, or *rockets*), the verb is plural. If the noun after *none* cannot be counted (such as *pudding*, *money*, or *information*), the verb is singular.

None of the potatoes *are* left.

None of the pudding *is* left.

3. Subjects joined by *and* are usually plural.

The steam engine and the *cotton gin* were invented in the nineteenth century.

However, when two or more things joined are considered a unit, the verb is singular.

Gilbert's best friend and roommate at school *has been* accepted to West Point. (one person)

Vinegar and oil frequently *is used* as a marinade. (one thing)

Peanut butter and jelly frequently *is* the favorite lunch of many American children. (one thing)

4. Singular subjects joined by *or*, *nor*, *either . . . or*, or *neither . . . nor* usually take a singular verb.

Neither money nor success *substitutes* for good health.

Either rock or country music *is* featured at the annual concert.

When the subjects joined by *or* or *nor* differ in number, the verb should agree with the subject closest to it.

Neither the *briefcase* nor the *papers* were ever found.

Either the *students* or the *professor* has misunderstood.

5. Nouns that are plural in form but singular in meaning usually take singular verbs.

News often *travels* fast in a small town.

This *series* of incidents *leads* to that conclusion.

Measles, once a tragic disease, *is* no longer considered fatal in the United States.

Other words that appear to be plural but are actually singular are *aesthetics*, *astronautics*, *linguistics*, *genetics*, *mathematics*, *mumps*, *politics*, *physics*, *rickets*, and *semantics*. Nouns such as *athletics*, *acoustics*, and *statistics* are considered singular when referring to them as a field of knowledge. However, when they refer to activities, qualities, or individual facts, they are plural.

Acoustics is the study of sound production, control, transmission, and reception. (*Acoustics* refers to a field of knowledge.)

The *acoustics* in this room *are* poor. (*Acoustics* here refers to qualities.)

6. Nouns borrowed from other languages such as *data* and *media* often cause subject-verb agreement problems for students. Some borrowed nouns are the following:

SINGULAR	**PLURAL**
medium	media
datum	data

The *medium* of television *is* an effective way of advertising.

The *media* frequently *contribute* to the growth of the crime rate in this country.

(*Datum* is very rarely used.)

The *data* you requested *are* interesting.

7. Plural nouns that are used as singular units of measurement require a singular verb.

In some parts of the world, *five dollars* barely pays for one gallon of gas.

Seven years of bad luck *is* the result of breaking a mirror.

8. Collective nouns such as *jury, family, committee,* and *group* take singular verbs if these nouns are considered a single body. However, collective nouns can also take a plural verb if they refer to separate individuals in a group.

The *committee* always *meets* on Tuesday nights.

The *committee* finally *were* able to reach a decision.

P R A C T I C E   6 E

Making Special Considerations

DIRECTIONS: Read the following paragraph. Then copy the paragraph, choosing the appropriate verb form in parentheses. Check your work carefully.

Einstein: Man of the Future

(1) The name Albert Einstein has come to represent genius. (2) Even the least educated person, as well as the most educated scholars, (has, have) at least some knowledge of Einstein and his accomplishments. (3) Although theoretical physics (is, are) the area in which he is most famous, it (represents, represent) only one of the fields he worked in throughout his lifetime. (4) Not only was Einstein technically involved in mathematics, philosophy, and other fields, but he was also worried about how scientific research would affect society. (5) In fact, although politics (was, were) of little interest to him, one of his greatest concerns (was, were) the political issues affecting the well-being of humanity. (6) For example, even though his own research in nuclear physics (was, were) instrumental in the development of the atomic bomb, he, like many people today, actively sought to regulate nuclear activity worldwide. (7) The greatest worry and fear of this eminent scientist (was, were) that his accomplishments would be used against mankind; Einstein's greatest hope and dream, however, (was, were) to serve his fellow man. (8) Certainly Einstein's works and his life in general (shows, show) him to have influenced not only the physical sciences but the social sciences as well. (9) For example, Einstein, thoughtful and withdrawn as a child, did not speak fluently until he was over nine years old. (10) His late language development still (puzzles, puzzle) experts in the field of linguistics, which (has, have) traditionally held that learning to speak at an early age reflects superior intellect. (11) Neither linguistics nor psycholinguistics, which (deals, deal) with the relation between language and thinking, (has, have) been able to explain Einstein's genius in light of his late language learning. (12) Indeed, while the myths and mysteries surrounding this complex and gifted man (continues, continue), he remains one of the most significant figures in all of history.

P R A C T I C E   6 F

Making Special Considerations

DIRECTIONS: Read the following paragraph. Then copy the paragraph, choosing the appropriate verb form in parentheses. Check your work carefully.

Changing Attitudes About Age: Part I

(1) Caught in a youth-oriented society, Americans sixty-five years and older are often labeled as unproductive, chronically ill, or noncontributing members of our society. (2) Refusing to accept this stereotype, senior citizens, as well as the American population in general, (is, are) changing the image of older people in America. (3) Politics (has been, have been) the major means through which the aged are becoming an increasingly respected group. (4) The Senate Special Committee on Aging, along with the House Select Committee on Aging, for example, (serves, serve) the aged by encouraging recommendations from interested citizens concerning the problems of older people. (5) Each of these committees (holds, hold) hearings throughout the country and (strives, strive) to give older people a chance to voice their opinions on matters relating to senior citizens. (6) In addition, other old-age interest groups such as the National Council of Senior Citizens and the American Association of Retired Persons (has, have) lobbied reasonably effectively on behalf of the interests of older persons. (7) Each of these groups (pressures, pressure) lawmakers to pass laws in favor of older citizens. (8) Furthermore, the work of these groups (has been, have been) responsible for helping promote the status of senior citizens through community meetings on health care, employment, and housing for the aged. (9) Interestingly enough, none of these influential groups (is, are) run entirely by retired persons. (10) In fact, most of the support for these programs (comes, come) from young and middle-aged people. (11) For example, the National Council on the Aging (is, are) a group of over a thousand agencies that (represents, represent) the concerns of the aged. (12) This group of agencies (has, have) effectively organized people of all ages to publicize and encourage alternatives for older people. (13) the 150 billion dollars that (has been, have been) given to federal programs for the aged (is, are) proof that these political groups (is, are) succeeding. (14) The ultimate success or failure of the dedicated individuals within these groups still (remains, remain) to be seen, however. (15) Each citizen, young or old, (has, have) a responsibility to make certain none of these efforts (fails, fail).

P R A C T I C E   6 G

Making Special Considerations

DIRECTIONS: Read the following paragraph. Then copy the paragraph, choosing the appropriate verb form in parentheses. Check your work carefully.

Changing Attitudes About Age: Part II

(1) The work of many dedicated, concerned citizens (has been, have been) important in erasing or changing negative ideas about the elderly. (2) However, the media (has been, have been) the most effective in improving the image of the senior citizen. (3) Although many people believe that news usually (depicts, depict) the elderly in a negative way, in fact, data (shows, show) that the elderly themselves believe that television, newspapers, magazines, and books (promotes, promote) a fair picture of senior citizens. (4) In a current survey, two-thirds of the people polled (indicates, indicate) that they believe television treats older people with respect. (5) A majority also (indicates, indicate) that television shows older people as important, wise, and successful members of their families and communities. (6) Another series of studies (provides, provide) information showing that public affairs and talk shows usually (presents, present) aging favorably. (7) Like television and radio, popular magazines generally (portrays, portray) older characters as vivid, warm, and loving individuals to be respected. (8) The media, then, according to this poll, (continues, continue) to be aware of older Americans and their opinions. (9) However, neither the media nor politics (has been, have been) as successful as the active elderly themselves in creating a new concept of old age. (10) Seeing themselves as sources of wisdom, experience, and energy, today's senior Americans are demanding their rightful place in society.

ON YOUR OWN

Ideas for Guided and Open Writing

GUIDED WRITING EXERCISE: Choose a magazine and study its advertisements. Look specifically at the advertisements with people in them. In general, how do the advertisements portray men and women? What is the advertisement saying about the people? Choose one advertisement, and in a well-developed paragraph of 100–150 words, discuss the image(s) implied for either a man or woman in the advertisement. You might begin your paragraph with "The man (or woman) in a recent advertisement for —— portrays an image of ——." Notice the physical appearance of the person in the advertisement—that is, the person's posture, expression, clothing, surroundings, and so forth. In addition, think about the tone of the advertisement. Consider, for example, whether it is sensual, comic, serious, businesslike, casually sophisticated, and so forth. Finally, consider the audience of the advertisement. What kind of person is reading the magazine? How do all these factors affect the image(s) implied? Pay attention to proper agreement between subjects and verbs.

OPEN WRITING EXERCISES: The following topics are suggestions for open writing exercises to help you practice the structures presented in this chapter. Develop these ideas into paragraphs of 100–150 words. Focus your attention on subject-verb agreement. Use idea number 3 to practice agreement with special items.

1. Some of the most successful beauty and fashion models are paid up to $500 an hour. State why you feel or do not feel this is an appropriate salary for such a position.

2. Consider some of the most outstanding teachers you have had. Think of the characteristics they had in common. In general, what are three characteristics of the ideal teacher?

3. You are an influential member on the planning board for developing studies at a new high school. Name one nontraditional course such as economics, communications, the media, politics, or statistics that you would recommend most high school seniors take. Offer specific reasons for your opinions.

CHAPTER 7

Correcting Run-ons and Comma Splices

A *run-on* sentence is two or more sentences written together without any punctuation between them.

The President's Inaugural Ball was the gala event of the year it was attended by a number of celebrities.

Similar to the run-on is the *comma splice.* A comma splice is two sentences linked together with a comma, which is insufficient punctuation by itself to separate two sentences.

RUN-ON	A good stereo system needs an effective amplifier it also needs adequate speakers.
COMMA SPLICE	A good stereo system needs an effective amplifier, it also needs adequate speakers.

Run-ons and comma-splice errors occur most often when the two sentences are closely related in meaning.

RUN-ON	The bridge collapsed at three in the morning it could not withstand the sudden earthquake. (The second sentence gives a reason explaining the statement made in the first.)
COMMA SPLICE	Eugene reacted dramatically to his intense pain, he became irritable and aggressive.

Notice that the second sentence in each example begins with a pronoun (*it* in the first example and *he* in the second) that refers to a noun in the preceding sentence (the *bridge* in the first and *Eugene* in the second). The close relationship between the pronouns and the words they refer to may make a writer think that the second sentence is part of the first and does not need to be punctuated as a separate sentence.

Beware of words such as *then, now, consequently, therefore, however,* and *nevertheless.* These words show relationships between sentences; however, using them with just commas or with no punctuation between the sentences is incorrect.

RUN-ON	The owner of the car inspected his tires then he quickly got into his car.
COMMA SPLICE	That South American country has changed governments, now the country may be able to improve its economy.

There are various ways of correcting run-on and comma-splice sentences. One method may seem more appropriate than another, depending on the sentences. When deciding how to correct a run-on and a comma splice, consider the following questions:

Are the sentences related?

How important is the relationship between the sentences?

How much do you want to emphasize their relationship?

How can you make the meaning as clear as possible?

In order to learn how to correct run-ons and comma splices, you first should understand what makes up a sentence. A sentence is made up of one or more clauses. A *clause* is a group of words with a subject and a verb.

In 1903, the Wright brothers, two adventurous men, invented the "Kitty Hawk," the first airplane to fly. (*Wright brothers* is the subject; *invented* is the verb.)

Any clause that makes sense by itself is called an *independent clause.* Every independent clause can be a sentence.

Charles A. Lindbergh made air travel history in 1927.

A clause that does not make sense by itself is called a *dependent clause.* A dependent clause must join an independent clause in a sentence.

Charles A. Lindbergh made air travel history in 1927 when he flew by himself across the Atlantic Ocean. (*When he flew by himself across the Atlantic Ocean* is a dependent clause. It would not make sense if it were separated from the independent clause.)

Study the following methods for correcting run-ons and comma splices:

1. *Rewriting as two separate sentences.* The easiest way to correct a run-on or comma-splice sentence is to rewrite it as two separate sentences. This method works best when the two parts of the run-on or comma splice are not very closely related.

RUN-ON	Eduardo normally returns to Mexico every summer he never stays long.
CORRECTED	Eduardo normally returns to Mexico every <u>summer. He</u> never stays long.
COMMA SPLICE	The sun sank lower and lower, the sky grew dark and somber.
CORRECTED	The sun sank lower and <u>lower. The</u> sky grew dark and somber.

Pattern: | *Sentence 1. Sentence 2.* |

2. *Using a comma and a conjunction.* Since too many short sentences may make your writing seem choppy, consider joining some of your run-on or comma-splice sentences with a comma and a conjunction (*for, and, nor, but, or, yet, so*). A *conjunction* is a word that joins two words or two parts of a sentence. You can remember these conjunctions by remembering the first letter of each conjunction: They spell *fanboys.* Be sure to choose the conjunction that best shows the relationship between the parts of the sentence.

RUN-ON	Bob's commitment to his latest cause was great his tactics were very offensive.
CORRECTED	Bob's commitment to his latest cause was <u>great, but</u> his tactics were offensive.
COMMA SPLICE	The members of the rock band broke their guitars, they weren't able to break any attendance records.
CORRECTED	The members of the rock band broke their <u>guitars, yet</u> they weren't able to break any attendance records.

When rewriting a run-on or comma splice in this way, (1) use a comma and a conjunction to connect the two sentences or independent clauses, and (2) begin the part after the comma and conjunction with a small letter.

> **Pattern:** | **Independent clause, <u>conjunction</u> independent clause.**

3. *Using a semicolon.* You can also join two sentences with a semicolon. However, before using a semicolon, be sure that the two sentences are closely related in meaning.

RUN-ON	Playing tennis is a popular form of exercise in the United States it is not only fashionable but also healthful.
CORRECTED	Playing tennis is a popular form of exercise in the United <u>States; it</u> is not only fashionable but also healthful.
COMMA SPLICE	Angela's temperature is over 101 degrees, she must have the flu.
CORRECTED	Angela's temperature is over 101 <u>degrees; she</u> must have the flu.

For this type of correction, remember to (1) place the semicolon directly after the first sentence, and (2) begin the part after the semicolon with a small letter.

> **Pattern:** | **Independent clause<u>;</u> independent clause.**

4. *Using a semicolon and a connector.* Words such as *then, now, moreover, thus, however, nevertheless, therefore, consequently,* and *furthermore* are called *connectors* when they are used to join sentences. When the relationship between two sentences is not made clear with just a semicolon, join the sentences with a semicolon and one of these words. The connecting word should be followed by a comma.

RUN-ON	The three young women vowed never to marry they fell in love and married one by one.
CORRECTED	The three young women vowed never to <u>marry; however,</u> they fell in love and married one by one.
COMMA SPLICE	Many fairy tales contain frightening episodes, nevertheless, they perform an important function in the development of young children.

CORRECTED   Many fairy tales contain frightening episodes; nevertheless, they perform an important function in the development of young children.

Sometimes these words come in the middle of a sentence. Because they interrupt the sentence, they are also called *interrupters.* Put a comma before and after an interrupter in the middle of a sentence.

The audience screamed for an encore; the tired band, *however,* did not return to the stage.

The manager, *therefore,* sent the ushers home.

Pattern: | **Independent clause; connector, independent clause.** |

5. *Rewriting the sentence.* Sometimes the best way to correct a run-on or a comma-splice sentence is to rewrite the sentence by combining the sentences with subordinators, which are words such as *when, while, as, although, because, whenever,* and *even though.* The relationship between the sentences determines which word you need to use.

RUN-ON   Ed's argument was illogical it was impossible for him to win the case.

CORRECTED   Because Ed's argument was illogical, it was impossible for him to win the case.

When you rewrite the sentences in this way, the part beginning with a subordinator becomes a dependent clause. The other sentence is called an independent clause. If the dependent clause is first, you place a comma after it. If the dependent clause is last, no comma is necessary.

Pattern: | ***Dependent clause,* independent clause.**
 ***Independent clause* dependent clause.** |

P R A C T I C E   7 A

Eliminating Run-ons

DIRECTIONS: Read the following paragraph. Some of the numbered word groups are complete sentences; others are run-ons. Copy the paragraph, correcting the run-ons as you write. Use each of the five patterns outlined in this chapter to make your corrections. Check your work carefully.

The Common Cure

(1) Mild analgesics are drugs that relieve minor headache, muscle, and joint pain, usually without affecting mental alertness or without causing drowsiness. (2) Aspirin, the most widely used of all medicines, is a mild analgesic it is used to relieve tension headaches and the pain of arthritis. (3) It is also used to reduce fever and sunburn pain most people, of course, take it to feel better in spite of minor aches, ailments, and the discomfort of fever. (4) Although many aspirin products are on the market, most consumers do not realize that an aspirin tablet, regardless of its brand, is still aspirin. (5) All tablets contain a small quantity (five grams) of aspirin as the active ingredient the remainder is a filler. (6) The various brands differ only in the fillers they range from clay to chalk to sugar and tend to dissolve at slightly, but not significantly, different rates. (7) Phenacetin, another mild analgesic, is used either alone or in combination with aspirin and other drugs caffeine is also frequently mixed with aspirin, phenacetin, or both, as a stimulant to make a person feel better. (8) There is not reliable evidence, however, that caffeine improves the effect of aspirin. (9) These combination preparations are merely given fancy names and high prices they are widely advertised as super pain relievers, sleeping aids, and help for menstrual cramps even though their main ingredient is still aspirin. (10) A study by the Federal Trade Commission examined two brands of aspirin, one brand of buffered aspirin, and two APC (aspirin, phenacetin, and caffeine) products it showed no significant difference in effectiveness or speed in these pain relievers, in spite of advertising claims and significant differences in price. (11) Unless one is allergic to aspirin, therefore, the best way to relieve a headache and minor muscular and joint pains is to take the cheapest brand of plain aspirin.

P R A C T I C E   7 B

Eliminating Comma Splices

DIRECTIONS: Read the following paragraph. Some of the numbered word groups are complete sentences; others contain comma splices. Copy the paragraph, correcting the comma splices as you write. Use each of the five patterns outlined in the chapter to correct the comma splices. Check your work carefully.

Talking Apes

(1) In trying to discover how language is learned, psychologists have experimented with teaching human language to animals. (2) In addition, researchers have tried to evaluate the intelligence of nonhuman animals, they have also tried to train animals to communicate with human beings. (3) One of the most celebrated subjects was Washoe, a female chimpanzee, who was "spoken" to extensively in American Sign Language (ASL), she succeeded in learning 38 signs in her first two years of training. (4) The researchers taught her the signs by physically shaping Washoe's hands, they used a reward method to train her. (5) For instance, to encourage learning, the experimenters tickled Washoe when she used a sign appropriately, consequently, she became a tickling addict. (6) By her third year, Washoe had mastered 85 signs. (7) More importantly, she categorized objects associated with one another under one name, for example, the sign for *dog* also became a sign for a picture of a dog or the sound of a bark. (8) In addition to the results of the Washoe experiments, surprising results have been observed in research with gorillas, which for years were considered incapable of learning human language. (9) Koko, a female gorilla, for example, was taught ASL, in twenty-nine months she learned more than 200 signs. (10) Koko proved her intelligence by combining these signs correctly and meaningfully, she also invented new combinations for unfamiliar objects. (11) For example, she called a mask an "eye hat," she gave the name "white tiger" for zebra. (12) Furthermore, she "talked" to herself constantly when she played. (13) By the end of the experiment, she had mastered 375 signs, she was able to respond to a number of commands she had learned. (14) All this research does not prove that these apes can acquire human speech, it does suggest, however, that perhaps one day humans will be able to communicate with animals.

P R A C T I C E 7 C

Eliminating Run-ons and Comma Splices

DIRECTIONS: Read the following paragraph. Some of the numbered word groups are complete sentences; others are run-ons; still others contain comma splices. Copy the paragraph, correcting the run-ons and comma splices as you write. Check your work carefully.

Learned Behavior

(1) For a long time, psychologists and researchers have studied what makes people act the way they do. (2) Scientists learn about human behavior by studying conditioning, it is a process in which a response to specific circumstances or stimuli is learned. (3) The distinguished Russian psychologist Ivan Pavlov made lasting discoveries about conditioning, he is especially known for his work in classical conditioning. (4) In Pavlov's best-known experiment, a dog is placed in a harnesslike device. (5) The dog can get food powder in one of two ways, it can either eat food from a dish or receive an injection in the mouth. (6) Either method causes salivation this is an automatic response that all normal dogs have when they see or smell food. (7) This automatic behavior is called an unconditioned response, it results from an unconditioned stimulus. (8) Next in the experiment, Pavlov's dog, still in its harness, is injected with food powder at the same time that a buzzer sounds. (9) The procedure is repeated a number of times the buzzer sounds every time food powder is injected into the dog's mouth. (10) In the final step of the experiment, the researcher sounds the buzzer without providing any food powder, the dog still salivates. (11) The animal has finally been conditioned to respond to a buzzer by salivating, therefore, the buzzer is called a conditioned stimulus. (12) The response of salivating at the sound of the buzzer is a conditioned response. (13) The dog has learned to substitute one stimulus for another, as a result, it has made an association between a stimulus and a response. (14) Thus, the response of Pavlov's dog to the new stimulus is not a reflex, it is a learned behavior. (15) From these and other experiments, psychologists and researchers have discovered much about human behavior and look forward to making accurate descriptions of how humans learn.

O N   Y O U R   O W N

Ideas for Guided and Open Writing

GUIDED WRITING EXERCISE: In 1981 at the Lakeview Medical Center in Danville, Illinois, a woman gave birth to Siamese twins. The twins were attached at the waist and also joined by a severely deformed leg. In addition, they shared part of the circulatory system as well as intestines and genitals. Doctors determined that the twins could never be surgically separated. The parents of the twins and their doctors agreed that the babies should not be kept alive. In fact, the babies' incubator had a sign posted, "Do not feed, in accordance with parents' wishes." Some people believed that depriving the twins of food was an act of murder on the part of the parents. Other people were sympathetic to the plight of these parents, stating that the children could never lead normal lives and that the parents would always suffer financially and emotionally. A bitter court battle followed to determine whether the state should take custody of the babies, thus determining the future of the twins.

What do you think about the issue of allowing severely deformed babies to survive? In a well-developed paragraph of approximately 100–150 words, write a letter to the editor of a local newspaper that has recently reported this issue concerning the twins. State your opinion about this topic. You might begin your letter with "In this particular case the parents of these Siamese twins are justified (or are not justified) in their decision." As you write your letter, consider whether or not the parents have the right to decide to end their child's life. If the parents do not have the right, who should make the final decision? Offer specific reasons to support your belief. Check your work carefully to see that you have not made any comma-splice or run-on errors.

OPEN WRITING IDEAS: The following topics are suggestions for open writing exercises to help you practice the structures presented in this chapter. Develop these ideas into paragraphs of 100–150 words. Focus your attention on proper punctuation between clauses.

1. Some attorneys get clients by calling accident victims and offering to represent them in a lawsuit. What is your opinion of such a practice for acquiring clients? Give reasons for your opinion.

2. "Pumping iron" is a frequently used term to describe the sport of weight lifting. In fact, more and more Americans are going to gyms to lift weights. Why are so many Americans turning to weight lifting?

CHAPTER 8

Correcting Sentence Fragments

A fragment of anything is a part broken off or detached from a whole. It is something incomplete, such as a fragment of broken glass that was once part of a whole window. A *sentence fragment* is also something incomplete: It is a part broken off from a sentence and misleadingly punctuated as a complete sentence.

> Our vacation was a disaster. *Because our car broke down halfway there.*
> *Instead of celebrating my birthday.* We had to stay home and babysit my little brother.

Because our car broke down halfway there and *Instead of celebrating my birthday* are fragments.

Recognizing Sentence Fragments

Suppose you had written the following two word groups in one of your compositions. Both word groups are punctuated as sentences, but are they really sentences?

> The weary group returned to the bus. After five hours of climbing the pyramids.

In order to answer the questions, you need sentence-sense. Sentence-sense is the ability to recognize a complete sentence. A good way to develop sentence-sense is to read each word group from period to period. Then ask yourself the following questions:

> Does the word group have a complete subject and verb?
> Does the word group make sense by itself?

Read the first group of words aloud, and ask yourself the sentence-sense questions.

The weary group returned to the bus.

A *subject* is the performer of an action. A *verb* tells what the action is. You can usually discover the subject by asking *who* performed the action. This word group does have a complete subject and verb. *Group* is the subject, and *returned* is the verb; the word group also makes sense by itself. Next cover the first group as you read the second group aloud and ask yourself the sentence-sense questions.

After five hours of climbing the pyramids.

This word group does not have a subject or verb, and the word group does not make sense by itself.

Because a sentence fragment is a part broken off from a complete sentence, it usually follows or precedes the sentence it belongs with. To correct a fragment, simply attach it to the complete sentence.

The weary group returned to the bus after five hours of climbing the pyramids.

Common Forms of Sentence Fragments	**FRAGMENT**	The main lawn of the university is full of noisy frisbee enthusiasts. *Between the early afternoon and early evening hours.*
	CORRECTED	The main lawn of the university is full of noisy frisbee enthusiasts between the early afternoon and early evening hours.
	FRAGMENT	Antonio Ruiz finally accomplished his lifelong desire. *To see his birthplace in Mexico.*
	CORRECTED	Antonio Ruiz finally accomplished his lifelong desire to see his birthplace in Mexico.
	FRAGMENT	The police discovered a large, rusty shotgun. *Buried under an old wreck.*
	CORRECTED	The police discovered a large, rusty shotgun buried under an old wreck.
	FRAGMENT	The child was fascinated at the sight of the yak. *A stocky Tibetan long-haired wild ox.*
	CORRECTED	The child was fascinated at the sight of the yak, a stocky Tibetan long-haired wild ox.

FRAGMENT	The young man deliberated for fifteen minutes. *And then decided against buying a calculator.*
CORRECTED	The young man deliberated for fifteen minutes and then decided against buying a calculator.
FRAGMENT	*Whenever the barometric pressure changed.* He had severe headaches.
CORRECTED	Whenever the barometric pressure changed, he had severe headaches.
FRAGMENT	All the customers at the pet store seem to be interested in Sam's cockatoo. *Which says, "That's ridiculous."*
CORRECTED	All the customers at the pet store seem to be interested in Sam's cockatoo, which says, "That's ridiculous."

Fragments — Incomplete Sentences

The most difficult kinds of sentence errors to correct are those incomplete sentences that are not parts of following or preceding sentences. Some of these sentences are incomplete because important words have been left out. Usually the writer forgets part of a verb or the subject of a sentence because of the writer's eagerness to get his or her thoughts down on paper. Using the sentence-sense test, read the following sentence:

Poor Mr. Zukowski who had never changed a flat tire.

This sentence is incomplete. It has a subject — Mr. Zukowski — but it needs a verb to make the idea complete. *Who had never changed a flat tire* is a dependent clause. If you take out *who had never changed a flat tire*, all you have left is *Poor Mr. Zukowski*. Try to correct these incomplete sentences in the following practices and in your own writing.

PRACTICE 8A

Eliminating Fragments

DIRECTIONS: Read the following paragraph. Some of the numbered word groups are complete sentences; others are fragments.

Copy the paragraph, correcting each fragment as you write. As you rewrite the paragraph, leave out the sentence numbers. Check your work carefully.

The Tax Penalties of Marriage

(1) Each spring Americans participate in an annual ritual. (2) Which involves sorting sales receipts, cancelled checks, bank statements, and other records of income and expenses. (3) These citizens are preparing their income tax returns. (4) Unfortunately, as many as three out of four people who figure their own tax returns will overpay their taxes. (5) The reason being that these taxpayers do not take advantage of all the legal deductions available to them. (6) One peculiar section of the tax law, for example, allows two fully employed people filing individual returns to receive a larger deduction than a married couple, each fully employed and filing a joint return. (7) Thus, if two persons are living together without being married and each files an individual return. (8) They will pay significantly lower taxes than if they marry and file a joint return. (9) For example, in 1979 even if both persons worked full-time, the difference in deduction allowance between two individual returns and one joint return ranged from $1,300 to $2,000. (10) Depending on the income bracket of the individuals and on the form filed. (11) This discriminatory law led some couples to divorce each year in December. (12) And to remarry in January. (13) Because the Internal Revenue Service ruled in 1976 that this intentional avoidance of taxes was illegal. (14) Some couples have divorced and remained divorced but continue to maintain a common residence. (15) With no one but their tax accountants aware that they are no longer married. (16) Other couples have decided not to marry. (17) So that they will not have to pay the higher tax. (18) Unfortunately, as people face the yearly responsibility of having to pay taxes, many couples look to any solution, no matter how extreme, to help them save. (19) In many respects, the income tax laws are a mystery. (20) Although none is more puzzling than this government tax penalty on marriage.

P R A C T I C E   8 B

Eliminating Fragments

DIRECTIONS: Read the following paragraph. Some of the numbered word groups are complete sentences; others are fragments. Copy the paragraph, correcting each fragment as you write. As you rewrite the paragraph, leave out the sentence numbers. Check your work carefully.

Sickle-Cell Anemia

(1) Approximately 9 percent of all Blacks in the United States, and a much lower percentage of whites, carries a recessive gene for sickle-cell anemia. (2) This 9 percent is heterozygous with respect to this gene. (3) Meaning that 1 out of every 10 Blacks has one normal and one abnormal gene. (4) Another 0.25 percent of the Black population is homozygous for sickle-cell anemia. (5) Which means that 1 out of every 400 Blacks carries two defective genes. (6) Heterozygous parents are not likely to suffer from the disease. (7) Whereas any of their children carrying both defective genes will suffer. (8) In fact, individuals homozygous for this gene frequently die in childhood. (9) Or are extremely sick throughout life. (10) For example, they are usually anemic. (11) From complications caused by jaundice, a disease that affects the liver, complicating their condition. (12) In addition, these victims may have difficulty breathing and may suffer from severe stomach pains, sharp muscular aches, and acute bone discomforts. (13) All often complicated by high temperatures and other signs of infection. (14) People with this disease have red blood cells that are sickle-shaped, or crescent-shaped. (15) Instead of having typically circular red blood cells. (16) These abnormally shaped cells tend to clot together. (17) Causing a shortage in the supply of oxygen to the tissues. (18) Unfortunately, the sickle cells multiply as a result of lack of oxygen. (19) Therefore, the less oxygen available, the more sickle cells develop. (20) Thereby reducing the amount of oxygen even more. (21) The development of the disease, then, unfortunately follows an ugly cycle. (22) Although researchers have made great advances in detecting this hereditary disorder in fetuses. (23) They still look forward to the day when sickle-cell anemia will no longer be an incurable threat to many people.

PRACTICE 8 C

Eliminating Fragments

DIRECTIONS: Read the following paragraph. Some of the numbered word groups are complete sentences; others are fragments. Copy the paragraph, correcting each fragment as you write. As you rewrite the paragraph, leave out the sentence numbers. Check your work carefully.

Public Relations: Learning from the Past

(1) Most of the uses modern society has found for public relations, or PR, are not new. Modern PR practitioners having learned much of what they know by studying the experts of the past. (2) In 1095 Pope Urban II used PR to promote a war upon his Muslim neighbors to the east. (3) Strategically organizing an informal network including cardinals, archbishops, bishops, and parish priests. (4) He filled the hearts of the common people with one thought. (5) To serve God by fighting in this holy war and earn forgiveness of sins. (6) Fighting in the war also offered the Christians another benefit. (7) Having the once-in-a-lifetime chance to visit the holy shrines. (8) As a result, the response by the people was overwhelming. (9) Even though the Crusades were not entirely successful. (10) Another public relations expert of the past was Stephen Langton. (11) Who was Archbishop of Canterbury in 1215. (12) Langton used PR tactics to support a political cause. (13) He convinced an influential group of barons to stand up for their rights against King John. (14) And to force the king to sign the Magna Carta. (15) A model document for many governments. (16) Later, in the fifteenth century, Niccolò Machiavelli put his PR talents to use to support a political party in power. (17) Still studied today are his famous works *The Prince* and *Discourses*. (18) Which discuss how people can be governed firmly and effectively. (19) Machiavelli's political psychology, in fact, is still referred to today. (20) Many of the uses of public relations, then, have existed throughout world history. (21) With vivid examples serving as references for modern PR practitioners.

O N   Y O U R   O W N

Ideas for Guided and Open Writing

GUIDED WRITING EXERCISE: An old Mexican proverb states, "Tell me whose company you keep, and I'll tell you who you are." Do you think this is true? In a well-developed paragraph of approximately 100–150 words, explain why this proverb is or is not timeless and accurate from your experiences. You might use the following to begin your paragraph: "The kinds of friends a person has are (or are not) an accurate reflection about him or her." To develop the paragraph, reflect on specific times when this saying did or did not apply. Describe those concrete examples to support your argument. Consider, for example, the dates that you have had. Would you have gone out with them if you had met their friends first? Or, after having gone out a few times, did you know your dates better after having met their friends? What example can you think of to support or oppose the idea that a person is known by the company he or she keeps? Concentrate on writing complete sentences in your paragraph.

OPEN WRITING IDEAS: The following topics are suggestions for open writing exercises to help you practice the structures presented in this chapter. Develop your ideas into paragraphs of 100–150 words. Focus your attention on writing in complete sentences.

1. The United States government and private agencies have often constructed time capsules to preserve items representing our society. What five items representing today's American civilization would you include in a time capsule that is two feet by four feet and that is to be opened one hundred years from now? Briefly state why you would include each item.

2. How many regulations should we allow in our lives, particularly when those regulations interfere with personal choice? For instance, although people can move anywhere, they still have to follow rules. Some of these rules are important to personal safety, but others seem meaningless. Certain neighborhood associations, for example, have rules about the overall appearance of a house—that is, color of the house, upkeep of the lawn, and maintenance of the exterior. In fact, one neighborhood association in California permits its residents to paint their houses only certain colors. Do you believe these kinds of regulations are reasonable for a neighborhood? Why or why not?

CHAPTER 9

Maintaining Parallel Structure

One of the rules of our language is that similar ideas should be expressed in similar structures. When we want to talk about a series of things, qualities, ideas, problems, processes, or feelings, we combine a word with a word, a phrase with a phrase, or a clause with a clause.

Three Levels of Parallel Structure

Parallel words

When a writer lists a series of words, the words in the series should be all nouns, all adjectives, or all adverbs, but not mixed.

MIXED   The young photographer was charming, witty, and a beauty.

Charming and *witty* are adjectives; however, *beauty* is a noun. For the sentence to be parallel, *beauty* must be in an adjective form.

PARALLEL   The young photographer was charming, witty, and beautiful.

Parallel phrases

A phrase is a group of words with no subject or verb. When a writer lists a series of phrases, all the phrases should be the same: all *-ing* phrases, all *to + verb* phrases, all *-ed* phrases, or all *preposition + noun* phrases.

MIXED   His goals for this vacation were *to meet new friends, to forget his job,* and *enjoying himself all the time.*

The sentence is nonparallel because two *to + verb* phrases (*to meet new friends* and *to forget his job*) are mixed with an *-ing* phrase (*enjoying himself all the time*).

PARALLEL   His goals for this vacation were *to meet new friends, to forget his job,* and *to enjoy himself all the time.*

Parallel clauses

A clause is a group of words that contains a subject and a verb. When a writer lists a series of clauses, all the clauses in the series should be the same.

MIXED   *What we say* and *the things that we do* are never quite the same.

What we say is not structured the same as *the things that we do.* *What we say* is a clause; *the things that we do* is a noun followed by a clause. In order for the two parts of the sentence to be parallel, *the things that we do* should become a clause.

PARALLEL   *What we say* and *what we do* are never quite the same.

Correcting Nonparallel Structures

Correcting nonparallel structures can sometimes involve more than just making sure that words or clauses function in the same way. For example, if you found the following sentence in a paper that you wrote, what would be the best way to correct it?

Every day after football practice, the team manager collected the football gear, had distributed the towels to the players, and would gather the dirty laundry.

Notice the three different types of verb forms used in the sentence:

collected the football gear (past tense verb)
had distributed the towels to the players (past perfect tense verb)
would gather the dirty laundry (*would* + verb)

How can you correct this sentence, making each verb form the same? The simplest way is to make all the forms match the first item by making them all past tense verbs.

> **PARALLEL**   Every day after football practice, the team manager *collected* the football gear, *distributed* the towels to the players, and *gathered* the dirty laundry.

Sometimes the second and following items in a series cannot be made parallel with the first:

> **NONPARALLEL**   Popeye's archrival Bluto is an *egotist, selfish,* and *rude.*

You can't change *selfish* and *rude* into nouns, but you can change *egotist* into an adjective and make the items parallel in this way:

> **PARALLEL**   Popeye's archrival Bluto is *egotistic, selfish,* and *rude.*

Sometimes you may have two alternatives. For example, the following sentence might be corrected in two ways:

> **NONPARALLEL**   Eloisa used the new luggage *to take* an overnight trip to her friend's house, *for storing* old clothes, and *when she went on a vacation to the Grand Canyon.*

The nonparallel parts can be changed into *to* + *verb* phrases or *-ing* phrases.

> **PARALLEL**   Eloisa used the new luggage *to take* an
> **TO + VERB**   overnight trip to her friend's house, *to store*
> **PHRASES**   *old clothes,* and *to go* on a vacation to the Grand Canyon.
>
> **PARALLEL -ING**   Eloisa used the new luggage *for taking* an
> **PHRASES**   overnight trip to her friend's house, *for storing* old clothes, and *for going* on a vacation to the Grand Canyon.

Parallel Combinations

These parallel words (that go together as combinations) include *not only ... but also, both ... and, either ... or, neither ... nor,* and *whether ... or.* These should connect parallel words, phrases, and clauses.

| NONPARALLEL | The woman was not only a *charmer* but also *intelligent.* |
| PARALLEL | The woman was *not only charming but also intelligent.* |

To be parallel, *not only . . . but also* must join similar constructions.

The woman was not only *adjective* but also *adjective.*

Study the following sentences. Note the difference between non-parallel and parallel constructions.

NONPARALLEL	Either *the executive director requested the order* or *made a mistake.*
PARALLEL	The executive director either *requested the order* or *made a mistake.*
NONPARALLEL	The President agreed either *to hold the press conference at Camp David* or *at the White House.*
PARALLEL	The President agreed to hold the press conference either *at Camp David* or at *the White House.*

P R A C T I C E   9 A

Writing Parallel Forms

DIRECTIONS: Read the following paragraph. The underlined words and groups of words are not parallel in form. Copy the paragraph, making the underlined words and phrases parallel. Check your work carefully.

**The Super
Revival of the
National Hero**

(1) The American heroes of the thirties are being resurrected <u>by</u> <u>curious children</u> and <u>by adults who seek adventure</u>. (2) Personalities such as Superman, Flash Gordon, Buck Rogers, Orphan Annie, and Wonder Woman were characters popular <u>during the devastating years of the Depression</u> and <u>when World War II occurred</u>. (3) They appeal to the need today for heroes who are <u>all-American types</u>, <u>clean-cut</u>, and <u>virtuous</u>. (4) They offer their audience <u>an escape not only from the problems of modern life but they also become role models</u>. (5) For the superheroes, the fight between <u>good forces and ones that are undeniably evil</u> always exists. (6) Although the monstrous, clever archenemies always seek <u>power</u>, <u>glory</u>, and <u>getting revenge</u>, the hero eventually wins. (7) Moreover, his or her usually brief encounters with evil generally end <u>happily</u> and <u>with optimism</u>. (8) The hero is <u>a person with extraordinary powers</u> and <u>someone who seeks to make the world a safe place for everyone to live</u>. (9) The American public <u>admires his courage in the face of danger</u>, <u>is always idolizing his strength and love of justice</u>, and <u>calls his enemies their enemies</u>. (10) The superhero seeks <u>a peaceful world</u> and <u>to make a better tomorrow for everyone</u>. (11) Thus, faced with anxieties such as <u>inflation</u>, <u>trying to save energy</u>, and <u>how to maintain a home</u>, the American public escapes temporarily into the magical world of superheroes, where they know all problems will be resolved.

P R A C T I C E   9 B

Writing Parallel Forms

DIRECTIONS: Read the following paragraph. The underlined words and groups of words are not parallel in form. Copy the paragraph, making the underlined words and phrases parallel. Check your work carefully.

More Than
the Blues

(1) Can some women blame their criminal behavior on the fact that they are women? (2) The argument is of critical importance to a great number of women, according to many members of judicial systems in Great Britain and France. (3) Recently, in fact, one woman in England was accused of stealing over twenty-six times, was sending threatening letters, and finally stabbed another woman. (4) Her main argument for her behavior was that she was suffering from a condition not experienced by men—that is, premenstrual syndrome (PMS). (5) The judge accepted not only her argument, but he also reduced her sentence from first-degree murder to manslaughter. (6) Apparently, the symptoms of premenstrual syndrome are powerful enough either to cause a woman to behave abnormally or to experience temporary insanity. (7) To feel deeply depressed, severe tension, and being extremely irritable are some of the worst psychological symptoms of PMS. (8) Physical signs of the syndrome include having swollen breasts, bloatedness, and getting acne. (9) Although many women have long insisted that these symptoms demand serious medical attention, gynecologists (doctors of the special conditions of women) and psychologists, mostly men, have believed that the women were overreacting to natural functions of the body or insane. (10) Now, however, many researchers, gynecologists, and psychologists are trying to understand the physical nature of the illness and hope to treat it. (11) Doctors suspect that women suffering from PMS lack sufficient progesterone, one of two female hormones released by the pituitary gland, a kind of command center in the brain. (12) Therefore, doctors prescribe periodic injections of this hormone. (13) These injections balance the amount of estrogen released and how much progesterone is in the body. (14) This balance is important because these hormones indirectly influence a woman's emotions and how she will act. (15) Thus, if a woman's level of progesterone is abnormally low, she may become nervous and be behaving violently just prior to her menstrual period beginning. (16) Therefore, researchers believe that premenstrual symptoms may cause such stress and antisocial behavior that some women should not be held completely responsible for behavior that is atypical of their normal behavior or even for criminal actions.

PRACTICE 9C

Writing Parallel Forms

DIRECTIONS: Read the following paragraph. Most sentences contain many nonparallel words and groups of words. Copy the paragraph, making the sentences parallel in structure. Check your work carefully.

New World Anesthesiology

(1) Long before anesthesiology, the science of making a patient unconscious before surgery, was formally introduced in Europe in the 1800s, the Aztec civilization had been using general anesthetics efficiently and with success for years. (2) In 1519, in fact, when Cortez and his troops invaded Mexico, they were astonished to discover that the Aztec physicians were not only excellent surgeons but that they knew the art of anesthesiology. (3) The Aztecs became experts in anesthesiology as a result of their religious practices. (4) The great abundance of native plants in the tropical valleys of central Mexico contributed to the Aztecs' knowledge of anesthetics. (5) Priests experimented on their sacrificial victims with narcotics made from these native plants. (6) In particular, the Aztecs used the crushed seeds, leaves that had dried out, and using liquified roots of native plants and flowers to induce a state of unconsciousness. (7) For example, physicians crushed *yoyotli,* a narcotic plant, to powder form and then would force the victim to inhale the powder. (8) Other plants of the species *datura,* such as the jimson weed, were administered to the person before sending him up the Great Pyramid, where his chest was cut open and he was being sacrificed to the gods.
(9) Hyoscyamine, scopolamine, solandrine, and adropine found in the *datura* plants were used by the Aztecs and are still being used in modern medicine. (10) The Aztecs used these plants to induce sleep or putting the patient in a stupor, thus causing him or her to become entranced and follow the orders of the Aztec priests. (11) Another anesthetic used before cutting open the victim's chest and when the heart was ripped out was marijuana. (12) The leaves were burned so that the victim inhaled the smoke rendering him or her unconscious. (13) Also psilocybin, a narcotic which causes hallucinations and that is found in a certain type of mushroom, was given to the sacrificial victim. (14) Another plant used as an anesthetic that was used in religious sacrifices was the mescal cactus, more commonly known as *peyote.*

(15) Mescaline, extracted from the cactus, not only was a narcotic sleeping medicine but also it had a stimulating effect on people. (16) It served to relieve pain and preventing spasms. (17) In their attempts not only to diminish suffering of their victims but to perform their sacrificial rites as well, the Aztecs learned a great deal about drugs and how they affect humans.

O N   Y O U R   O W N

Ideas for Guided and Open Writing

GUIDED WRITING EXERCISE: Pinball machines are losing popularity to new, computerized video games. First designed from computer programs, these video games now can be seen not only in arcades or recreational centers, but also in airport cocktail lounges, convenience stores, bus terminals, and bars. Many people compare the video attraction to the mesmerizing effects of television upon its viewers. Video enthusiasts, for example, think nothing of spending hours playing the same game. In a well-developed paragraph of 100–150 words, discuss the kind of person who would make a video game champion. You might begin your paragraph with "To be a video game champion requires ——, ——, ——." As you construct your paragraph, think of the people you have observed playing these games. What are some of the outstanding characteristics that have helped them win? Be sure to check for consistency in the constructions that are parallel in your paragraph.

OPEN WRITING EXERCISES: The following topics are suggestions for open writing exercises to help you practice the structures presented in this chapter. Develop these ideas into paragraphs of 100–150 words. Focus your attention on maintaining parallel constructions.

1. Freshman year is always a difficult period for many college students. Some people believe that since freshman year is traumatic enough, grades cause unnecessary frustrations for the student. Others believe that grades help motivate the new student to university life. What is your belief? Does getting grades help or hinder a freshman in adjusting to college life?

2. Beauty pageants for women and body contests for men and women have become a controversial issue in recent years. Do you think that these contests are worthwhile?

CHAPTER 10

Correcting Misplaced and Dangling Modifiers

Misplaced Modifiers

Modifiers are words or groups of words that describe other words. The following sentence is dull because it contains no modifiers:

The backpackers hiked.

With modifiers, the sentence contains detail and therefore is more interesting.

The five tired backpackers, feeling proud of their accomplishment, hiked enthusiastically down the last stretch of the mountain.

The modifiers are the adjectives *five* and *tired*, the phrase *feeling proud of their accomplishments*, the adverb *enthusiastically*, and the phrases *down the last stretch* and *of the mountain*.

Using modifiers contributes much to interesting writing; however, modifiers that are misplaced in a sentence can make a piece of writing unintentionally humorous.

The hostess gave the appetizers to her friends with olives in them.

The phrase *with olives in them* is a misplaced modifier. The sentence sounds as if the hostess's friends have olives in them. The phrase *with olives in them* describes *appetizers* and belongs directly after that word. Here is what the writer intended to say:

The hostess gave the appetizers *with olives in them* to her friends.

The most important point to remember about modifiers is that a modifier must be placed as close as possible to the word it is describing.

Certain types of misplaced modifiers occur more frequently than others. The following are some of the more common types:

1. Misplaced Words

Words such as *almost, only, just, even, hardly, nearly,* or *merely* should be placed immediately before the words they modify.

He said that he admired *only* me. (He admired no one else.)

He said that *only* he admired me. (No one else admired me.)

He said *only* that he admired me. (He said nothing else.)

He *only* said that he admired me. (He did not mean it.)

He said that he *only* admired me. (But he didn't actually like me.)

2. Misplaced Phrases

Phrases should be placed next to the words they modify.

MISPLACED PHRASE	The housesitter informed the woman that the dog had escaped *by phone.*
REVISED	The housesitter informed the woman *by phone* that the dog had escaped.
MISPLACED PHRASE	The campers were excited to see the kindling wood *climbing up the hill.*
REVISED	*Climbing up the hill,* the campers were excited to see the kindling wood.

Notice that the misplaced phrase in this latter example was corrected by moving it next to *campers,* the word it modifies. In certain sentences, a modifying phrase should follow the word it modifies.

MISPLACED PHRASE	*Buried at the bottom of his tool kit,* Mr. Zacharias discovered an old spark plug.
REVISED	Mr. Zacharias discovered an old spark plug *buried at the bottom of his tool kit.*

3. Misplaced Clauses

Clauses should be placed as close as possible to the words they modify.

MISPLACED CLAUSE	We bought a hamburger in an expensive French restaurant *that cost $17.* (This sentence sounds as if the restaurant, not the hamburger, cost $17.)
REVISED	We bought a hamburger *that cost $17* in an expensive French restaurant.
MISPLACED CLAUSE	She related exciting stories about her travels *while she had breakfast.* (This sentence sounds as if her travels took place while she was eating breakfast.)
REVISED	*While she had breakfast*, she related exciting stories about her travels.

4. Squinting Modifier

Another kind of misplaced modifier is called a *squinting modifier*. A squinting modifier is a modifier trapped in between two parts of the sentence. Notice the confusion a squinting modifier causes.

SQUINTING MODIFIER	Roberto said *on Sunday* to call him. (Did Roberto say this on Sunday, or did he say to call him on Sunday?)

Of course, the sentence could have two different meanings:

REVISED	On Sunday, Roberto said to call him.
REVISED	Roberto said to call him on Sunday.

Dangling Modifiers

Dangling modifiers are another problem that sometimes occurs when students write modifiers. A *dangling modifier* is a group of words that does not clearly and logically refer to some other word in the sentence. The following sentence contains a dangling modifier:

Getting into the car, my shoe broke in half.

Was the shoe getting into the car? Unlike misplaced modifiers, dangling modifiers cannot be corrected by putting the modifier in another part of the sentence. In the following sentence, the dangling modifier has been moved to another position in the sentence:

My shoe, *getting into the car,* broke in half.

It still sounds as if the shoe were getting into the car.

How do you correct a dangling modifier? You must add words to make the meaning clear and logical. There are two ways to do this: (1) You can change the wording of the main part of the sentence, or (2) you can rewrite the dangler.

1. Getting into the car, *I accidentally broke my shoe in half.*

2. *As I was getting into the car,* my shoe broke in half.

Here are some of the forms that dangling modifiers can take:

DANGLING PHRASE	*By cutting down on smoking,* one's chances of having heart problems are reduced. (This sentence sounds right, but is it? Who is cutting down on smoking? According to the sentence, one's chances are cutting down on smoking.)
CORRECTED	*By cutting down on smoking, one* can reduce the chances of having heart problems.
CORRECTED	*If one cuts down on smoking,* he or she can reduce the chances of having heart problems.
DANGLING -*ING* PHRASE	*Taking our seats,* the game started. (It sounds as if the game was taking our seats.)
CORRECTED	*Taking our seats, we* realized the game had started.
CORRECTED	*As we took our seats,* the game started.
DANGLING *TO* + *VERB* PHRASE	*To be a champion swimmer,* confidence is necessary. (It sounds as if confidence is trying to become a champion swimmer.)
CORRECTED	*To be a champion swimmer, a person* must have confidence.
CORRECTED	*For a person to be a champion swimmer,* he or she must have confidence.
DANGLING CLAUSE	*While in the kitchen preparing supper,* the telephone rang. (It sounds as if the telephone was in the kitchen.)
CORRECTED	*While in the kitchen preparing supper,* I heard the telephone ring.
CORRECTED	*While I was in the kitchen preparing supper,* the telephone rang.

P R A C T I C E   1 0 A

Using Modifiers Appropriately

DIRECTIONS: Read the following paragraph. The underlined words are either dangling or misplaced modifiers. Rewrite the paragraph, correcting the dangling and misplaced modifiers. Check your work carefully.

The First Minutes of the American Crisis in Iran

(1) Interrupted from his work, a loud blast surprised the American embassy secretary. (2) Looking out his embassy window, an angry mob pushed its way into the building with loaded rifles. (3) The secretary grabbed the thick folder under his desk that was marked "classified" and hid the folder under his jacket. (4) Quickly running out of his office, the secretary's abrupt warning to leave startled his staff members immediately. (5) Looking into his eyes, however, they knew his warning only meant one thing: religious militants of the country were invading the embassy. (6) Considering the disgust, anger, and negative feelings these militants had been expressing toward the United States, the invasion was not a complete shock to the Americans. (7) A revolution had been brewing for many months that would dramatically affect the lives of numerous people. (8) The staff realized the seriousness of this international conflict and followed the secretary without a second thought who had already disappeared down a hall. (9) Unfortunately, the group reached only as far as the hallway when they were stopped by two men just carrying one rifle each. (10) Outnumbering the militants yet realizing that the two gun-carrying men held great power, there was nowhere to run. (11) Thus began the imprisonment of over fifty Americans and an ordeal that would nearly last for fifteen bitter months.

P R A C T I C E   1 0 B

Using Modifiers Appropriately

DIRECTIONS: Read the following paragraph. All sentences, except number 6, contain dangling or misplaced modifiers. Rewrite the paragraph, correcting the dangling and misplaced modifiers. Check your work carefully.

Circus PR

(1) Years ago, advertising nearly was the most important part of the excitement of the circus. (2) Handouts, heralds, and posters, in particular, creatively were the media used to draw attention to this event. (3) The handouts, which were booklets, told the complete stories of the circus acts and performers imaginatively illustrated. (4) Anxiously awaiting the circus, the handouts were read with great interest. (5) The townspeople read the handouts, fascinated by descriptions of incredible circus feats. (6) The heralds were the most popular form of circus advertising. (7) These heralds listed all the acts, features, and performers printed on long, narrow sheets. (8) The heralds exaggerated frequently the circus acts in two ways: by listing performers twice and by lying about the performers' skills. (9) Finally, describing each one of the acts as magnificent, ferocious, or marvelous, it is no wonder that posters attracted the most people to the Big Top. (10) These posters decorated every available fence, billboard, barn, and wall, which brilliantly and sensationally depicted the circus. (11) These life-size drawings of exotically costumed men fascinated both children and adults taming wild creatures. (12) After seeing the posters, the tickets were gone in a matter of hours. (13) Drawn in by the three kinds of advertising, the circus overflowed with excited people. (14) The advertising was successful, and everyone was almost happy.

PRACTICE 10C

Using Modifiers Appropriately

DIRECTIONS: Read the following paragraph. It is filled with misplaced and dangling modifiers. Copy the paragraph, correcting the misplaced and dangling modifiers. Check your work carefully.

The Courtship of the Stickleback Fish

(1) To mate, natural instinct is followed by most animals; however, some animals have problems following their instincts. (2) For example, the male stickleback fish does not know whether to court his mate or to attack her during mating season. (3) Being very protective animals, the nests of the male stickleback fish are carefully guarded, especially during the mating season. (4) The fish recognize the invaders because the bellies during the mating season of the male stickleback fish turn red. (5) In addition, the red belly attracts a female stickleback, whose silver belly is swollen with eggs obviously. (6) Upon seeing the silver-bellied female, a surprising relationship of fighting and flirting is begun. (7) Normally, enemies invading the territory turn upward, showing their bellies and their intentions, who are looking for a fight. (8) The female also turns upward; however, seeing her swollen belly excites the male and stops his attack usually. (9) The male turns away to lead the female to his nest, following with her belly downward. (10) No longer being able to see her silver belly, the female is attacked. (11) She tries to stop his attack once again by showing her belly. (12) Continuing this flirting-fighting behavior, their zigzagging eventually brings them back to the nest. (13) After shoving her into his nest, the male trembles to make her deposit her eggs next to the female. (14) Then the male fertilizes the eggs, driving her away, and eventually protects the developing young. (15) Thus, despite having strange courtship problems, mating eventually takes place.

O N   Y O U R   O W N

Ideas for Guided and Open Writing

GUIDED WRITING EXERCISE: The traditional T-shirt with a school symbol or school name on it has been replaced by the T-shirt with a slogan or a personal message on it. Sayings from "Where the heck is Grand Forks?" and "I survived the Mt. St. Helens eruption" to "Hands Off" and "Available" now plaster the fronts and backs of thousands of T-shirts. Some people think these shirts are harmless and humorous; others think they are disgusting and tasteless. What do you believe? In a well-developed paragraph of approximately 100–150 words, discuss why people might wear a T-shirt with a "message." You might begin your paragraph with "People wear T-shirts with messages in order to ———." Consider some reasons that people wear these T-shirts: to draw attention to themselves, to make political statements, to be funny, and so forth. Offer specific descriptive examples to develop your paragraph. Be careful to avoid misplaced and dangling modifiers in your paragraph.

OPEN WRITING IDEAS: The following topics are suggestions for open writing exercises to help you practice the structures presented in this chapter. Develop these ideas into paragraphs of 100–150 words. Focus your attention on avoiding misplaced and dangling modifiers in your paragraphs.

1. The roles of an athletic coach are many. Think about the various activities and duties you may have seen a coach perform. Discuss the most significant or difficult task of a coach's job. Give at least three reasons for your choice.

2. Many people in the United States have become increasingly interested in searching for their ancestry, hoping to discover the answer to the question "Who am I?" Think about the reasons that a person might want to find out about his or her past and tell why someone would do so. Consider, for example, an adopted child, a dying person, and so forth.

UNIT A
REVIEW

Practicing Basic Skills

DIRECTIONS: Read the following paragraph. The sentences contain errors studied in this unit. Copy the paragraph, correcting the errors in *a* and *an*, capitalization, plural nouns, possessives, pronoun reference, pronoun agreement, pronoun case, and subject-verb agreement. Also correct run-ons, comma splices, sentence fragments, nonparallel structures, misplaced modifiers, and dangling modifiers. Each numbered item contains two of these types of errors. Check your work carefully.

Senet: An Egyptian Game for the Soul

(1) Board games, enjoyed for centurys by children and adults all over the world, are not only excellent sources of entertainment but also often represent fascinating aspects of a particular culture. (2) One example is a ancient egyptian game called *senet,* meaning "passing." (3) *Senet* is based on the Egyptian belief that a persons soul continues to live after their physical body dies. (4) Although the soul must travel through hell before they can live peacefully. (5) The game only needs two players: one who represents the soul and the other to hunt the soul. (6) The first player attempts to move seven pieces, called "dancers," across a thirty-square board, this movement is similar to the soul's journey after death, its' "passing" through the underworld. (7) The other player, whom plays the role of Seth, the rebel god of evil, moves their seven dancers in the opposite direction in an attempt to capture the soul. (8) The rules for moving and capturing is like those of backgammon, however, *senet* uses wooden sticks, called "fingers," not dice. (9) In addition, the dancers of Seth make two journies around the board then the game becomes very challenging. (10) Seth's

dancers are always planning strategies to stop the soul, however, even if each of the soul's dancers are in danger, the soul still has a possibility of completing its journey. (11) Although the soul has seven dancers, not every one of the seven need to cross the board only one of the dancers has to move entirely across the board in order for the soul to complete its journey and win the game. (12) Thus, being a game related to life after death, the world is given an unique picture of Egyptian religion. (13) In other words, the Egyptian emphasis of life after death can be traced back to the people in bydos, an important city on the Nile, who were playing *senet* as early as 3500 B.C. on sun-dried mud surfaces. (14) Moreover, because of their religious importance, Egyptians buried four *senet* boards with Tutankhamen, the young ruler whom the Egyptians thought was a god. (15) The reason being that Tutankhamen and them believed that a soul's passing from life to death should be accompanied by a game of passing. (16) The influence of this religious game is seen even today in fact, the rural Sudanese still play a variation of *senet,* living just south of ancient Egypt. (17) Thus, *senet,* perhaps the oldest board game in the world, is a extraordinarily simple game offering valuable understanding of a culture's religious beliefs and how the soul struggles after death.

UNIT B

Focusing on Time

CHAPTER 11

Using the Present Tense

The present tense indicates an action or activity that is usually done or is a habit, as in the following examples:

Martin *reads* the newspaper from top to bottom. (a usual action)
Isabella *makes* all of her clothes. (a usual action)
Mo usually *eats* yogurt for breakfast. (a usual action)

The present tense is also frequently used to express future time. Time expressions such as *next week* and *tomorrow* usually signal the future.

The President *arrives* in Washington *tomorrow*.
His plane *departs* at *noon*.

Other common uses of the present tense are to describe general truths and general states of being.

The sun *sets* in the west. (scientific truth)
An adolescent often *seeks* group acceptance. (a truism)
Ramon *is* an optimist. (general state of being)

Formation

Notice that the tense is the same for all persons, except for the third person singular. The third person singular must have an *s* added on to the base form of the verb.

I, you, we, they	like	Mexican food.
He, she, it	likes	Mexican food.

Special Use of the Present Tense

Books and articles about literature, drama, and film are usually written in the present tense, even though the poem, story, or movie is old. This use of the present tense is called the *historical present*, a tense that is used for writing about history and works of art. The historical present is based on the idea that the work of art lives forever.

> In *The Wizard of Oz*, the Lion, the Scarecrow, the Tin Man, and Dorothy all search for a solution to their individual problems.

Critical studies and reviews that discuss the techniques of the writer are also written in the present.

> In *Huckleberry Finn*, Mark Twain depicts Jim as a sensitive, rather wise human being.
>
> Mark Twain's characters represent the everyday people of America of the late 1800s.

P R A C T I C E   1 1 A

Working with Present Tense

DIRECTIONS: Read the following paragraph. It is written in the past tense. Copy the paragraph, changing the verbs to present tense. Keep sentence 1 as it stands. Check your work carefully.

Genetic Research: A Question of Morality

(1) Humanity's search to discover the origins of life has led to many difficult questions. (2) The experiments of Dr. Pierre Soupart of Vanderbilt University proved how difficult these questions could become. (3) Dr. Soupart carried out complex genetic experiments that involved human eggs that were artificially conceived. (4) He artificially joined female eggs with male sperm outside a woman's body, producing the embryos for his experiment. (5) After joining the eggs and the sperm together, he observed their development for six days; then he allowed them to die. (6) At that point, the ova were examined for chromosome defects and other problems resulting from artificial conception. (7) Dr. Soupart's experiment caused many people to ask questions about the morality of his research. (8) They asked, "Was it

right or wrong for Soupart to create life artificially and then to kill it later?" (9) Many argued that these embryos were "biologically alive" from the moment the egg and sperm were joined together. (10) These people believed that Dr. Soupart intentionally created life in order to destroy it. (11) On the other hand, others argued that the early embryo could not be considered a human subject. (12) Therefore, they believed that his experiments were morally right. (13) Consequently, the question of experimenting with human embryos continued to be a controversial one. (14) Many researchers agreed that Dr. Soupart's experiments could be helpful in the future, but the moral questions about his work were the greatest obstacles he faced.

P R A C T I C E   1 1 B

Working with Present Tense

DIRECTIONS: Read the following paragraph. It is written in the past tense. Copy the paragraph, changing the verbs to present tense. Check your work carefully.

Don Juan, the Lover

(1) *Don Juan,* a famous opera written in 1888 by Richard Strauss, was based on a well-known poem by Nicholaus Lenau. (2) This musical work was about Don Juan, a celebrated hero who searched for the perfect woman. (3) During his search he had affairs with many women. (4) Don Juan always felt disappointed with each affair because, of course, he could never find the perfect woman. (5) In addition, each time he ended a relationship to continue his search, he left the woman broken-hearted and miserable. (6) Don Juan finally recognized how much suffering he was responsible for, and he eventually stopped his sexual adventures. (7) He then grew so depressed about himself and his actions that he felt as if his life had no more meaning. (8) Just as Don Juan started to think about ending his life, he was challenged to a duel by Don Pedro, who was the son of a man murdered by Don Juan. (9) Both men fought hard, but Don Pedro was not as strong a fighter as Don Juan. (10) At the moment that Don Juan started to kill Don Pedro, Don Juan thought about his own unhappy life. (11) Because of his misery, he realized that beating Don Pedro could not bring him

happiness. (12) As a result, he let Don Pedro kill him. (13) In the end, Don Juan discovered that perfection was impossible to find. (14) This tragic story showed the problems of people living only for adventure, excitement, and sex.

O N   Y O U R   O W N

Ideas for Guided and Open Writing

GUIDED WRITING EXERCISE: Our culture is very youth-oriented. Much emphasis is placed on dressing, acting, and, in particular, looking young. In an effort to look and feel young again, many people are joining health spas and athletic clubs. In addition, many people, both men and women, have plastic surgery to improve their appearance. Furthermore, even in the business world "younger is better." In fact, some of the highest paid fashion models in magazines are barely teenagers. Do you agree that our society stresses dressing, acting, and looking young too much? In a well-developed paragraph of 100–150 words, discuss who suffers the most from the pressures to look and be young. You might begin your paragraph with "—— are the people who suffer most from the pressures to look and be young." For your paragraph, consider men and women in their forties who are beginning to show their age. Think also about the elderly or even young adults. Support your belief with three reasons. Illustrate your argument with concrete examples. Write in the present tense.

OPEN WRITING IDEAS: The following topics are suggestions for open writing exercises to help you practice the structures presented in this chapter. Develop these ideas into paragraphs of 100–150 words. Focus your attention on the present tense.

1. The ancient system of bartering, that is, trading one good or service for another, is being revived. For example, flea markets and swap meets are popular in many cities. In what way, if any, do you think that this system can be of benefit to society?
2. You have just established a new national holiday or tradition in the United States. Tell what that holiday or tradition is. Also tell when, why, and how it is celebrated every year.

CHAPTER 12

Using the Progressive Tenses

Use the progressive form of the verb to show that an action is ongoing or continuous. To show that the action or activity is happening right now, use the present progressive.

The clock *is striking*.

If the action or activity happened continuously in the past, use the past progressive.

Even during the rain, the farmworkers *were picking* carrots.

Formation   To form the present progressive, use the following: am, is, are + verb + ing

PRESENT	He usually *watches* television.
PRESENT PROGRESSIVE	He *is watching* television in the living room. (is + watching)
PRESENT	She *jogs* every afternoon at four.
PRESENT PROGRESSIVE	She *is jogging* to the beach right now. (is + jogging)
PRESENT	They *discuss* movies once a week.
PRESENT PROGRESSIVE	They *are discussing* the latest Fellini movie. (are + discussing)

To form the past progressive, use the following: was, were + verb + ing

PAST PROGRESSIVE	He *was watching* television. (was + watching)

PAST PROGRESSIVE	She *was jogging* at the beach. (was + jogging)
PAST PROGRESSIVE	They *were discussing* the latest Fellini movie. (were + discussing)

To form the present or past progressive form of *to be*, change the verb to its progressive form, *being*, and put *am, is, are, was,* or *were* in front of it.

She *is* a stubborn person.	She *is being* a stubborn person.
He *is* a defeatist.	He *is being* a defeatist.
They *are* adventurous.	They *are being* adventurous.
I *was* generous.	I *was being* generous.
They *were* aggressive.	They *were being* aggressive.

P R A C T I C E   1 2 A

Changing to the Present Progressive

DIRECTIONS: Read the following paragraph. It is written in the present tense. Change the verbs in the present tense to the present progressive tense. Do not change the italicized words in sentences 1 and 13. Check your work carefully.

The Natural Way to Beauty and Health

(1) *Because many people are unhappy with the high cost of commercial health and beauty aids and are afraid of the chemical ingredients in them,* they shop for natural products. (2) Instead of brushing their teeth with regular toothpaste, or sodium monofluorophosphate, every day, many people now brush with a combination of chalk, glycerine, carrageenan, and spearmint oil. (3) Others find good results by simply brushing with dolomite or baking soda. (4) Furthermore, people look for natural products to protect their skin. (5) They now substitute apricots, cucumbers, jojoba nuts, and coconuts for commercial creams and lotions. (6) When looking for natural products to improve their skin, they shop for such foods as

oatmeal, lemons, honey, cucumbers, eggs, and mint to make inexpensive, yet effective, facial masks. (7) Some find mud and clay facial masks a helpful and fun beauty aid. (8) Still others soak in tubs sprinkled with chamomile flowers, lavender or rose leaves, rosemary, or hops. (9) They condition and rinse their hair with ingredients such as chamomile, jojoba oil, lemon juice, vinegar, eggs, and beer. (10) People use these not only for cosmetic reasons but also for medical reasons. (11) They depend upon mint tea or chamomile instead of commercial medicines to relieve upset stomachs and to calm teething babies. (12) In addition, many people now turn to herb teas instead of pills to calm their nerves. (13) *Although these natural products may not be any better than the commercial products they replace,* many people recognize the benefits of using these natural ingredients.

P R A C T I C E   1 2 B

Changing to the Present Progressive

DIRECTIONS: Read the following paragraph. It is written in the present tense. Copy the paragraph, changing the verbs from the present tense to the present progressive. Check your work carefully.

Saving for the Future

(1) Many people recommend saving up, or stockpiling, food to help starving people in times of famine. (2) Others support the idea of not giving away food because this solution causes population growth. (3) No one disagrees about the advantages of giving food away to hungry people right now. (4) However, people opposed to stockpiling argue against doing this. (5) These people insist that giving food away now adds to the problem of starvation in the future. (6) These issues create a great controversy important for all nations and all peoples. (7) World leaders and researchers are asked to examine this controversy from both an economic point of view and a moral point of view. (8) Because of the conflict between these two points of view, leaders have difficulties arriving at merciful yet practical solutions. (9) Although many leaders agree to economic solutions, others call those

solutions inhumane—that is, not helpful to the people. (10) People who support stockpiling state that all hungry persons must be helped at any cost. (11) Those opposed to stockpiling argue in support of "survival of the fittest." (12) They state that giving food away to these people continues poverty, malnutrition, and disease. (13) Unfortunately, while worldwide organization leaders discuss these problems, millions suffer and starve.

P R A C T I C E   1 2 C

Changing to the Past Progressive

DIRECTIONS: Read the following paragraph. It is written mostly in the simple past tense. Copy the entire paragraph, changing the underlined verbs to the past progressive tense. Check your work carefully.

The Hostage Crisis

(1) During the 444 days that fifty-two Americans were held hostage in Iran, life in the United States continued as usual. (2) Few events at this time received the same attention that the hostage crisis got. (3) In fact, throughout this time the majority of the people in the nation came together in their deep concern for the captive men and women and their families. (4) Television and radio broadcast continuous coverage of the attempts to free the hostages. (5) Frustrations grew as negotiations continued to fail. (6) Many people praised President Carter's patience and his conservative approach to the crisis. (7) However, others demanded that he send in the military. (8) Feeling that all Americans were persecuted, most citizens united in angry protest. (9) Some citizens protested by voicing anger and hostility toward the Iranians; others protested by opposing American support of the Shah of Iran. (10) Americans looked for someone to blame. (11) Some Americans accused the Central Intelligence Agency (CIA) of not doing its job in Iran. (12) Others called for better protection of United States embassies overseas. (13) Political experts questioned whether the situation could have been avoided. (14) Other people condemned Muslims as fanatics; still others tried to understand why the revolution had taken place. (15) Across the nation, people wore

yellow ribbons as a symbol for hope and also <u>hung</u> yellow ribbons from buildings, billboards, car antennas, and mailboxes. (16) Although it was a stressful time for America, the hostage crisis <u>helped</u> bring people together as a nation.

P R A C T I C E   1 2 D

Changing to the Past Progressive

DIRECTIONS: Read the following paragraph. It is written mostly in the simple past tense. Copy the paragraph, changing the underlined verbs to the past progressive tense. Check your work carefully.

The Hippie Generation

(1) The late sixties and early seventies was a time when many people <u>experimented</u> with new life-styles. (2) These people, referred to as "hippies," <u>looked</u> for complete changes in themselves. (3) They <u>escaped</u> from rush-hour traffic, city living, typical nine-to-five jobs, traditional marriages, and processed junk foods. (4) Instead, they <u>chose</u> to live in tepees, tents, treehouses, and old buses. (5) They <u>moved</u> away from comfortable neighborhoods to rural farm communities. (6) They <u>talked</u> about going "back to the land" and <u>dreamed</u> about living close to nature. (7) Many people <u>established</u> communes, which were small communities in which people worked and lived together. (8) They <u>supported</u> themselves by making leather goods, bakery items, and other crafts. (9) Moreover, many of these people <u>became</u> very aware of their health. (10) They <u>ate</u> only "organic" foods, foods grown without chemical pesticides and fertilizers. (11) Moreover, they <u>supplemented</u> their raw food diets with natural vitamins, herb teas, and protein drinks. (12) In addition, they <u>looked</u> for new spiritual and religious understanding in their lives. (13) They, therefore, <u>experimented</u> with many "mind-expanding" and hallucinatory drugs such as LSD, peyote, and mushrooms. (14) In their efforts to create new lives for themselves, many people of this time <u>faced</u> and finally <u>solved</u> various problems.(15) Although finally all of these life-style changes were hard for some people to understand, American society has since learned much about itself because of these experiments.

O N   Y O U R   O W N

Ideas for Guided and Open Writing

GUIDED WRITING EXERCISES:

1. *Present Progressive.* Some professional athletes make more than one million dollars a year. Many people are angry about these high salaries. These people feel that professional athletics is paying more attention to profits than to the sports themselves. Do you believe that high salaries are ruining or improving sports? In a paragraph of approximately 100–150 words, support or oppose high salaries for athletes. Discuss athletes in only one sport such as football, baseball, soccer, and so on. You might begin your paragraph with "High salaries of ——— players are ruining or improving ———." (Name the sport in the blank.) Consider some of the following questions as you develop your paragraph: Why are athletes asking for so much money? Do they have a responsibility to their fans and to the sport? Are they living up to their responsibility to their fans? What arguments are owners, managers, or other officials of the sport presenting? Are high salaries making athletics too commercial? Are these salaries making fans pay ticket prices that are too high? Pay particular attention to what is presently occurring in sports. Use the present progressive in your paragraph.

2. *Past Progressive.* Imagine yourself five years from now talking to a group of high school seniors. A teacher has asked you to discuss your experiences during your senior year in high school—that is, what you were doing, thinking, and feeling. Write a 100–150 word paragraph in which you remember the highlights of your senior year. If you wish, begin your paragraph with the following: "Looking back on my senior year in high school, I realize that . . ." How were you feeling about going to school and working (or not working)? How were you feeling about graduating in a year? What were you planning to do after graduation? How were you feeling about all the responsibilities you were going to have to face after graduation? Remember that you will be speaking of actions that continued over a period of time in the past. Concentrate, then, on using the past progressive tense appropriately.

OPEN WRITING IDEAS: The following topics are suggestions for open writing exercises to help you to practice the structures presented in this chapter. Develop these ideas into paragraphs of 100–150 words. Focus your attention in question 1 on the appropriate use of the present progressive and in question 2 on the appropriate use of the past progressive.

1. *Present Progressive.* The role of television newscasters is changing. Once newscasters reported the news in a serious, straightforward way, just as the news is reported on the radio today. Now, however, many newscasters are presenting the news more informally. The news programs often have background music during the reporting, and the newscasters themselves have become "stars." Do you like this change? Why or why not?

2. *Past Progressive.* Think back to the time when you first learned to drive. Describe the scene as you took your first lesson. What were you doing that made the event memorable, comical, or even tragic? How were you feeling?

CHAPTER 13

Using the Past Tense

When you wish to talk about an action or an event that began and ended in the past, use the past tense. Changing from present tense to past is not difficult. In fact, the greatest problem with the past tense is that students seem to have trouble remembering that they are writing about the past. Once students decide that they are going to write in the past tense, they have only to remember to add *-ed* to regular verbs and to memorize irregular verbs.

Formation of Past Tense — Regular Verbs

wreck	wreck*ed*
clean	clean*ed*
end	end*ed*
smoke	smok*ed*
rave	rav*ed*

Formation of Past Tense — Irregular Verbs

Irregular verbs form the past tense in many ways. Some do not change at all; others change completely. Because there are so many different kinds of irregular verbs, they must be learned individually as you need them. However, many of the irregular verbs are similar. Perhaps the following classification will be helpful. Verbs have three main forms: present, past, and past participle. The past participle is used with *has* or *have*.

PRESENT	Doug and Chris *take* vitamins.
PAST	Doug and Chris *took* vitamins last year.
PAST PARTICIPLE	Doug and Chris *have taken* vitamins for fifteen years.

The following verbs are the same for the present form, the past form, and the past participle (has or have + verb).

PRESENT FORM	PAST FORM	PAST PARTICIPLE
bet	bet	bet
broadcast	broadcast	broadcast
burst	burst	burst
cost	cost	cost
cut	cut	cut
hit	hit	hit
hurt	hurt	hurt
let	let	let
put	put	put
quit	quit	quit
set	set	set
shut	shut	shut

PRESENT	Those balloons usually *burst* in the sun.
PAST	Those balloons *burst* yesterday afternoon.
PRESENT	Linda Alvarez and Ron Gordon usually *broadcast* the football games.
PAST	Linda Alvarez and Ron Gordon *broadcast* last night at midnight.

The present form and the past form of *beat* are the same, but the past participle is different.

PRESENT	PAST FORM	PAST PARTICIPLE
beat	beat	beaten (also beat)

The present form and the past participle of the following verbs are the same, but the past form is different.

PRESENT FORM	PAST FORM	PAST PARTICIPLE
become	became	become
come	came	come
run	ran	run

The past form and the past participle of the following verbs are the same.

PRESENT FORM	PAST FORM AND PAST PARTICIPLE	PRESENT FORM	PAST FORM AND PAST PARTICIPLE
bring	brought	lose	lost
build	built	make	made
buy	bought	meet	met
catch	caught	pay	paid
dig	dug	raise	raised
feed	fed	read	read
feel	felt	say	said
fight	fought	sell	sold
find	found	send	sent
get	gotten (also got for past participle)	shoot	shot
hang	hung	sit	sat
have	had	sleep	slept
hear	heard	spend	spent
hold	held	stand	stood
keep	kept	teach	taught
lay	laid	tell	told
lead	led	think	thought
leave	left	understand	understood
lend	lent	win	won

The present form, the past form, and the past participle of the following verbs are different.

PRESENT FORM	PAST FORM	PAST PARTICIPLE	PRESENT FORM	PAST FORM	PAST PARTICIPLE
arise	arose	arisen	know	knew	known
be	was	been	lie (to recline)	lay	lain
begin	began	begun	ride	rode	ridden
bite	bit	bitten (also bit)	ring	rang	rung
blow	blew	blown	rise	rose	risen
break	broke	broken	see	saw	seen
choose	chose	chosen	shake	shook	shaken
do	did	done	show	showed	shown (also showed)
draw	drew	drawn	sing	sang	sung

PRESENT FORM	PAST FORM	PAST PARTICIPLE	PRESENT FORM	PAST FORM	PAST PARTICIPLE
drink	drank	drunk	sink	sank	sunk
drive	drove	driven	speak	spoke	spoken
eat	ate	eaten	steal	stole	stolen
fall	fell	fallen	strive	strove	striven
fly	flew	flown	swear	swore	sworn
forget	forgot	forgotten	swim	swam	swum
forsake	forsook	forsaken	take	took	taken
freeze	froze	frozen	tear	tore	torn
give	gave	given	throw	threw	thrown
go	went	gone	wear	wore	worn
grow	grew	grown	weave	wove	woven (also weaved)
hide	hid	hidden	write	wrote	written

Two-word verbs such as *hand in, call back, point out,* and *try on* sometimes cause problems for students who forget to make them past tense.

hand in	hand*ed* in
call back	call*ed* back
point out	point*ed* out
try on	tri*ed* on
think over	*thought* over
do over	*did* over
give up	*gave* up
call on	call*ed* on

P R A C T I C E   1 3 A

Regular Verbs

DIRECTIONS: Read the following paragraph. It is written in the present tense. Copy the passage, changing the verbs to simple past tense. Check your work carefully. A researcher in the year 1950 discovered the first important research results from a study conducted in the 1940's on the language of bees. He reported the following to a group of scientists.

**The Language
of Bees**

(1) Karl von Frisch's research into the "language" of bees proves that bees possess a complex communication system. (2) His studies focus on the behavior of bees as they return to the hive after looking for food. (3) Once they return to the hive, they perform a "dance," which the other bees in the hive follow and obey. (4) The returning bee indicates to other bees both the direction and the distance of the food source. (5) For example, a "round" dance shows the food to be a hundred yards away; a "wagging" dance indicates a farther distance. (6) In addition, the length and rhythm of the dance reveal the amount of food discovered. (7) Frisch's research also suggests that some species of the bees dance differently from bees of other species. (8) For example, when a dancing bee communicates a message to bees of other species, the dance confuses them. (9) Thus, each species of bees in Frisch's experiments possesses its own communication system. (10) Although the findings of Frisch's experiments surprise many people, his findings offer interesting information about communication among animals.

P R A C T I C E   1 3 B

Irregular Verbs

DIRECTIONS: Read the following paragraph. It is written in the present tense. Copy the passage, changing the underlined verbs to the past tense. Add the following phrase to the beginning of the first sentence: "In the 1960's." Check your work carefully.

Car Trends

(1) Automobile experts <u>foresee</u> cars of the future that <u>are</u> bigger and bolder than ever and that <u>have</u> powerful new V-10 and V-12 engines setting popularity trends among buyers. (2) These experts <u>feel</u> that as people <u>become</u> dependent upon the automobile, and as the country <u>strives</u> to replace old highways, the auto industry <u>stands</u> to make a profit by increasing its production of larger and faster cars. (3) In addition, they <u>hold</u> the view that a greater demand for comfort and luxury <u>grows</u> out of the desire for extra weight, size, and speed. (4) Experts also <u>find</u> that as people <u>choose</u> to drive greater distances, they <u>seek</u> additional comfort. (5) These experts <u>know</u> that as the number of people who <u>spend</u> time in their cars <u>rises</u>, so <u>do</u> the demands for unlimited extras. (6) The trend in the future, they <u>say</u>, <u>is</u> toward cars that <u>are</u> fully equipped with conveniences ranging from televisions to kitchenettes with bars. (7) However, whether or not these predictions <u>are</u> to come true <u>is</u> in the hands of the consumers since they <u>buy</u> to suit their needs.

O N   Y O U R   O W N

Ideas for Guided and Open Writing

GUIDED WRITING EXERCISES: Name one person who influenced you greatly at some point in your life. He or she may be either someone you know personally such as a family member or a friend, or someone you know casually such as your family doctor or the cashier at your local grocery store. In a well-developed paragraph of approximately 100–150 words, briefly analyze how this person played an important part in your life. You might begin your paragraph with "(Name of the person) was one of the most important people in my life when I was ———." Did any particular event strengthen your relationship, or did the person influence you over a period of time? You might discuss how you met or how you grew to appreciate this person. Why were you drawn to him or her? Since you will be describing events from the past, use the past tense appropriately.

OPEN WRITING IDEAS The following topics are suggestions for open writing exercises to help you practice the structures presented within this chapter. Develop these ideas into paragraphs of 100–150 words. Focus your attention on using both irregular and regular verbs in the past tense.

1. People often are nostalgic when they remember the past. When were your "good old days"? Were they when you were in high school, when you were a child, or when you went on a family vacation? Describe a particular period in your life that you look to as "the good old days." Give specific descriptions of the period's clothing, music, fads, and so on.

2. Briefly describe an incident in your life or in someone else's life that helped you understand the meaning of one of the following statements:

   The love of money is the root of all evil.

   The squeaky wheel gets the grease.

   You're nobody 'til somebody loves you.

   It's better to have loved and lost than never to have loved at all.

   Where there's a will, there's a way.

CHAPTER 14

Using the Future Tense

The future tense indicates activities that will take place in the future. The future tense is formed in two ways.

1. Place *will* or *shall* before the simple form of the verb.

The astronauts *will* return to Earth at sunrise.

David *will* perform in the play tonight.

Shall is rarely used, except in very formal speech and writing. *Shall* is sometimes used for the first person singular and first person plural, whereas *will* is used for all persons.

I, we	will (shall)
you	will
he, she, it	will
they	will

For example, the following sentence comes from the speech of a politician:

We *shall* meet the challenges of the future.

2. Place a form of *be + going to* before the simple form of the verb.

The team *is going to* practice extra hours.

Many speakers and writers use *be + going to +* a verb to indicate future activities and reserve *will* to show determination or prediction, as in the following example.

PREDICTION	Real estate value *will* continue to rise in the next twenty years.
DETERMINATION	He *will* go to school even if he has to work nights.
TYPICAL FUTURE ACTIVITY	We *are going to install* an air conditioner next summer.

P R A C T I C E   1 4 A

Using will

DIRECTIONS: Read the following paragraph, which is written in the present tense. It is part of a congressional report predicting what cars will be like in the 1990's. Copy the paragraph, changing the verbs from present tense to the future tense. Use *will* to indicate future time. In sentence 1, change "This year's" to "Next year's." Check your work carefully.

Cars of the Future

(1) This year's automobile models have some surprising new features that are different from some of the old, familiar features. (2) The full-size luxury cars of the seventies are no longer in use. (3) The automotive industry continues to build smaller, lighter cars in order to help the buyer cut costs and save fuel. (4) However, in spite of pressures from both the government and the consumer to cut gasoline costs, the internal combustion engine is still the most common engine model available. (5) Nevertheless, many more engines run on diesel fuel than ever before. (6) In addition, turbocharged, rotary, variable displacement, and gas turbine models are also available. (7) Moreover, even a few electric cars are manufactured. (8) Because of the large demand for small, economical cars, manufacturers no longer produce the bulky V-8 and V-6 models, once considered the greatest achievement in automobile technology. (9) Instead, they are replaced by the smaller, more practical, and more dependable four-cylinder models. (10) Furthermore, future models include two- and three-cylinder designs in order to help the buyer save money in gasoline costs, to help reduce pollution, and to help conserve national resources. (11) When designing cars of the future, automobile manufacturers continue to meet the needs of the public.

P R A C T I C E   1 4 B

Using be + going to

DIRECTIONS: Read the following paragraph. It is written in the present tense. Copy the paragraph, changing the main verbs from the present tense to the future tense using *be + going to.* Check your work carefully.

The High-Powered Briefcase

(1) As a result of the increased violence in our society, many businesses develop equipment to protect executives and other important businessmen and women afraid of being kidnapped or assassinated. (2) Bulletproof cars, bulletproof clothing, and electronic tracking devices, only some of the protective equipment already in use, are more and more in demand. (3) In addition, these executives need extra protection for classified material carried in their briefcases. (4) Claiming to have designed the best personal protection equipment, one company produces an effective electronically monitored attaché case. (5) This case protects not only the material in the case but also the person carrying the case. (6) Although the case looks exactly like the typical thin, rectangular, leather briefcase, it is not typical in any way. (7) To many people it seems like an invention from a James Bond movie. (8) This model is constructed of very lightweight, bulletproof material. (9) It is equipped with an electronic transmitter, which is able to locate the owner regardless of the person's location. (10) This same transmitter is also able to detect wiretaps and telephone bugs in the owner's telephone. (11) In addition, the case is able to record conversations for up to six hours. (12) Moreover, a tiny light inside the case warns the owner of the presence of an electronic bugging device monitoring him or her. (13) Another feature of this briefcase is a built-in alarm system. (14) Upon being grabbed away from the owner, the briefcase sounds an alarm. (15) In addition, the case is able to flash a high-powered beam at an attacker, temporarily blinding and stunning the person. (16) The features in this briefcase are promoted by the manufacturer as offering the owner maximum protection. (17) Although this kind of protection seems frightening to many people, such a briefcase makes many executives feel safe.

ON YOUR OWN

Ideas for Guided and Open Writing

GUIDED WRITING EXERCISE: You are on a committee to select two people to establish a space colony. Choose two of the following candidates: a Native American male medical student, a fifty-year-old male plumber, and a thirty-year-old female architect. In a well-developed 100–150 word composition, tell whom you would send and why. What qualities will each person offer the space colony? How will his or her background and experience help the colony? If you wish, begin your paragraph with "—— and —— will contribute the most to establishing a new space colony." Be sure to discuss specific contributions that your choices will make. Use the future tense in your paragraph.

OPEN WRITING IDEAS: The following topics are suggestions for open writing exercises to help you practice the structures presented in this chapter. Develop these ideas into paragraphs of 100–150 words. Focus your attention on the future tense. Alternate between *will* + simple form of the verb and *be* + *going to.*

1. Given that almost one of every two marriages in the United States ends in divorce, discuss what you believe the average American family will be like in five years.

2. "The more things change, the more they stay the same." Considering one aspect of our society (for example, music, transportation, film, clothing, telephone communications, mail, and so on), describe what you think it will be like at some point in the future.

CHAPTER 15

Using the Perfect Tenses

The present perfect and the past perfect tenses indicate activities performed at some point in the past.

PRESENT PERFECT   I *have* always *had* a pet.

PAST PERFECT   I *had* never *taken* vitamins until last year.

The Present Perfect

The *present perfect* indicates an action that began sometime in the past, continues into the present, and may extend beyond the moment of speaking.

The United States *has been* a democratic republic since 1776. (The present perfect is used because the United States became a democratic republic in the past, is one today, and will continue to be one in the future.)

Formation

To form the present perfect, use *has* or *have* and the past participle form of the verb. See Chapter 13 for the past participles of irregular verbs.

| I, you, we, they | have seen | the Grand Canyon. |
| He, she, it | has seen | the Grand Canyon. |

The past participles of regular verbs are exactly like the past tense.

PRESENT   He *walks* home every day.

PAST   He *walked* home yesterday.

PRESENT PERFECT   He *has walked* home every day for the past five years.

Notice the basic differences between the *past tense* and the *present perfect.*

PAST TENSE	PRESENT PERFECT TENSE
The past tense describes a specific action in the past that was completed in the past.	The present perfect summarizes experience over a particular period of time that extends up to the present.
I *found* an interesting restaurant.	I *have found* many interesting restaurants.
The past tense uses many time signals:	The present perfect uses a few time signals indicating length of time and frequency:
last year ten minutes ago on June 9	for five years again and again since 1965 frequently already up until now yet thus far, so far

Many times the present perfect is used without time expressions of any kind. These sentences usually indicate that a particular experience is or is not part of the general past of a person, as in the following examples:

Yes, I have read *Jane Eyre.*

No, I have never been to Rome.

Remember that the past participle of the verb *to be* is *been.* When you convert a present tense sentence with *to be* to a present perfect sentence with *to be,* you must rewrite *is* and *are* as *been.*

PRESENT	PRESENT PERFECT
Buying and selling gold *is* a profitable business.	Buying and selling gold *has been* a profitable business.
One of San Francisco's most delightful attractions *is* its cable cars.	One of San Francisco's most delightful attractions *has been* its cable cars.

The Past Perfect

The *past perfect* is used to express an event that happened or existed before another event in the past. To understand the past perfect, study the following diagram:

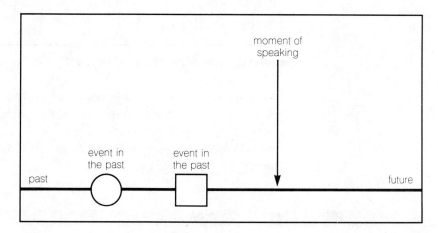

The circle indicates the event that occurred before the other event in the past (indicated by the square). Study the use of the past perfect in the following sentences:

I *had* just *washed* my hair when she walked in.

She *had* just *graduated* when I met her.

Maricela *had applied* to four colleges before she finished high school.

He *had been* very depressed *before* his accident.

Formation of the Past Perfect

To form the past perfect, use *had* and the past participle form of the verb. In the past perfect, *had* is used with all persons.

I
you
he, she, it   *had* never *walked* there before.
we
they

Remember to check Chapter 13 for the past participle forms of irregular verbs. When you change past tense verbs to the past perfect, change *was* or *were* to *been* and put *had* in front of it.

He *was* successful.   He *had been* successful before
                                        he became an alcoholic.

P R A C T I C E   1 5 A

Using the Present Perfect

DIRECTIONS: Read the following paragraph. It is written in the present progressive verb tense. Copy the paragraph, changing the verbs from the present progressive tense to the present perfect tense. Do not change sentence 13. In sentence 1, change Currently to During the past few years.

Saying No to Cars

(1) Currently, more and more questions are being raised about the financial and environmental problems created by the overuse of gasoline. (2) Hoping to find answers to these problems, many people are giving up cars as their main source of transportation. (3) In fact, a surprising number of people are using public transportation and joining car pools. (4) In addition, more people than ever before are deciding to ride bikes and walk wherever possible. (5) City, county, and state governments as well as corporations and schools are supporting the efforts of these people to reduce their dependence on car transportation. (6) These institutions are recognizing the need to conserve our natural resources. (7) For example, some major cities are sponsoring certain days as bike days in order to emphasize other possible kinds of transportation. (8) Moreover, many cities across the country are establishing certain streets as bike routes, and many of these cities are also creating separate lanes for bicycles and pedestrians. (9) Furthermore, large corporations are participating in efforts to reduce automobile use also. (10) A growing number of businesses, for example, are trying to boost carpooling among their employees by paying them according to the number of passengers riding in the car. (11) In addition, some larger corporations offer employees shuttle service to work in company-owned vans. (12) These steps to reduce the unnecessary use of cars are proving successful. (13) However, the final solution depends on the cooperation of individuals as well as institutions.

PRACTICE 15 B

Using the Present Perfect

DIRECTIONS: Read the following paragraph. It is written in the present tense. Copy the paragraph, changing the verbs from the simple present tense to the present perfect tense. Insert "Since its beginnings" at the beginning of sentence 1. Check your paragraph carefully.

Versatile Rock

(1) Rock music consists of a wide variety of musical styles. (2) Ranging from traditional to highly experimental sounds, rock appeals to many different kinds of audiences throughout the world. (3) Some rock, for example, follows a conventional ballad style. (4) For instance, certain songs of the Carpenters, Al Stewart, and even Kenny Rogers fall into this category. (5) Other rock borrows from classical music such as Mendelssohn's *Fourth Symphony,* Beethoven's *Fate Symphony,* as well as other classical pieces. (6) These pieces inspire groups such as Apollo 100; Tom Parker; and Emerson, Lake, and Palmer. (7) Another style known as "glam/fag/drag/theatrical" rock usually features male performers and groups wearing weird costumes, wigs, and heavy makeup. (8) Some of these performers included David Bowie, Alice Cooper, and KISS. (9) Social and political protest influence another style of rock music. (10) The songs of Bob Dylan, Joan Baez, and Helen Reddy often make people aware of their social responsibility to their fellow human beings. (11) Other rock, such as some of the songs by Linda Ronstadt, Judy Collins, and Simon and Garfunkel, takes its ideas from early English and American folk songs. (12) Another fairly recent style—new wave—bases its lyrics on drugs, sex, and violence. (13) Blondie, Devo, and other new wave groups represent the rebellious mood of some young people. (14) Because of these various styles, topics, and performers, rock continues to be the most popular music throughout the world.

PRACTICE 15 C

Using the Past Perfect

DIRECTIONS: Read the following paragraph. It is written mainly in the simple past tense. Assume that you are a sociologist writing in the 1990's about the events that took place in the past. Copy the paragraph, changing the underlined verbs from the past tense to the past perfect tense. Check your work carefully.

Dating in the Seventies and Eighties: Part I

(1) During the late seventies and early eighties, as a result of the continuing increase in divorces and the trend toward remaining single, forming male-female relationships <u>became</u> very complex. (2) In fact, people <u>grew</u> so frustrated in trying to meet new friends that they started to search for new ways of meeting potential spouses. (3) By the early eighties, because of the efforts of single people, new styles of dating <u>became</u> accepted. (4) Before then, single people looking for meaningful relationships <u>depended</u> on their family and friends to introduce them to new people. (5) However, as the years continued, such introductions <u>became</u> almost impossible because people constantly <u>changed</u> jobs and <u>moved</u> to new cities. (6) As a result, single people who <u>were</u> frustrated by not being able to meet new companions joined singles organizations and groups. (7) By the early eighties, some of these organizations <u>began</u> to cater to specific kinds of people such as tall singles, Christian singles, elderly singles, and middle-aged singles. (8) During these years, others <u>joined</u> special interest groups such as hiking clubs, gourmet clubs, and bridge clubs. (9) As a result of joining these clubs, many people <u>were able</u> to establish casual as well as intimate relationships. (10) Many of the others, who <u>were</u> unable to find compatible partners, looked at new approaches to dating.

P R A C T I C E   1 5 D

Using the Past Perfect

DIRECTIONS: Read the following paragraph. It is written mainly in the simple past tense. Assume that you are a sociologist writing in the 1990's about events that took place in the past. Copy the paragraph, changing the underlined verbs from the past tense to the past perfect tense. Check your work carefully.

Dating in the Seventies and Eighties: Part II

(1) Many people during the late seventies and early eighties grew unhappy with dating. (2) As a result, during those years these unhappy singles began to take new steps toward meeting new partners. (3) Some people who advertised for mates in newspapers and magazines found this approach to be an undependable and risky solution to the problem. (4) On the other hand, some women who referred to published guides of eligible bachelors found this a successful way to meet men. (5) Some men also were successful in using publications in order to meet foreign women. (6) Although these approaches were helpful for a portion of the singles population, these tactics failed for others. (7) Consequently, many of those who looked for other ways of meeting new friends began to use commercial dating services. (8) Many of these agencies that originally operated as small, personal dating services gradually expanded into large businesses that used computers to match clients. (9) Because these businesses recognized the need for people to meet one another, these dating agencies became popular. (10) In addition, dating services during that time started to match people according to astrological signs, biorhythms, and energy levels. (11) These new ways of meeting people seemed drastic until the eighties when they became more common.

ON YOUR OWN

Guided and Open Writing Ideas

GUIDED WRITING EXERCISES: Sexual activity among teenagers has been a constant concern of the American public. The majority of parents and teenagers believed for years that teenagers were not suposed to be sexually intimate. Today, however, many persons understand that many teenagers are sexually active. Instead of simply condemning teenage sexual activity, parents, as well as educators, are offering advice to help teenagers make responsible decisions regarding their sexual activity. For example, people are talking about sex more openly now. In addition, many secondary schools have started to offer courses discussing attitudes about sex, personal relationships, and family relationships. As a result of this honesty about the subject of teenage sexuality, the negative attitude toward sex among teenagers may have changed. At one time a teenager who had been sexually active was condemned by society; today, however, his or her actions are neither condemned nor condoned. Teenage sex is becoming more and more a part of life. In a well-developed paragraph of approximately 100–150 words, discuss whether or not you believe that this relaxed attitude toward sex has been beneficial to the individual. If you wish, begin your paragraph with one of the following sentences: "Today's relaxed attitude toward sex has encouraged casual sex among teenagers" or "Today's attitude toward sex has encouraged a necessary and beneficial sexual awareness among teenagers." Use present perfect and past perfect tenses in your discussion.

OPEN WRITING IDEAS: The following topics for open writing exercises are suggestions to help practice the structures presented in this chapter. Develop these ideas into paragraphs of 100–150 words. Focus your attention on the use of the present and past perfect tenses.

1. In order to satisfy moviegoers, Hollywood producers will continue to make certain types of movies until box office sales drop. Popular types of movies have been horror, fantasy, science fiction, and disaster movies. Pick one of these types of movies and discuss why the American public has liked it.

2. How have fast-food restaurant chains changed their images in the past few years? Choose one fast-food restaurant chain and discuss how its image has changed in the past five to ten years. Consider who its customers had been in the past and who they have been more recently. Also think about the kinds of food served as well as the appearance of the restaurant.

UNIT B
REVIEW

Focusing on Time

DIRECTIONS: Read the following paragraph. Some of the underlined verbs are written in the appropriate tense; other underlined
verbs are not in the appropriate tense. Copy the paragraph, correcting the verb tenses as you write. Check your work carefully.

The Wedding of the Century

(1) In a marriage celebration called the "Wedding of the Century," His
Royal Highness The Prince of Wales has married the Lady Diana
Spencer on July 29, 1981, in St. Paul's Cathedral, London, England.
(2) Not only has the wedding been a beautiful occasion, but it had also
been an important political event because it was bringing out people's
opinions about the monarchy. (3) Historians and politicians, who for the
last one hundred years notice the monarchy's decreasing popularity
since 1876, had watched the national response to the wedding
carefully. (4) Many of these historians are going to believe that the
positive feelings of the people toward the wedding have represented a
return to the traditional beliefs of the British. (5) This rebirth of faith in
England may, in the end, save England from its serious problems.
(6) Among those commenting on the grand event, Dame Rebecca
West says, "The royal scene has simply been a reflection of ourselves
behaving well. (7) If anybody will be honored, it is the human race."
(8) Another spectator at the wedding had stated "Over the years the
monarchy is helping give us a sense of self-worth and self-identity.
(9) It will be as though we are a part of an enormous, extended family."
(10) On the other hand, a small number of people are not believing that
the monarch still is going to unite the country. (11) Instead they will be
thinking that the monarchy would be a financial burden on the country.

(12) For example, leftist leader Cliff Fox, who previously <u>says</u>, "The royal family <u>was</u> a bloody parasite on the backs of the working class," <u>will be representing</u> the opinions of these people. (13) Another antimonarchist <u>is going to say</u>, "The crown is an expensive thing of the past." (14) In spite of the mixed feelings about the monarchy, the royal wedding <u>had been</u> a historic occasion that <u>had symbolized</u> a confidence in not only the past but also the future of a great nation.

UNIT C

Writing for a Specific Audience

CHAPTER 16

Choosing Appropriate Words

Writing an educated paper to an educated audience requires a writer to choose appropriate words. This chapter includes a glossary of usage, which lists words and explains their usage. This glossary distinguishes informal, colloquial, or nonstandard usage from usage appropriate for formal writing. Some of the words labeled as "informal," "colloquial," or "nonstandard" refer to words acceptable in spoken English in many informal situations. Words labeled "informal," "colloquial," or "nonstandard" are not generally acceptable in college writing.

Glossary of Usage

accept, except   These words are frequently mistaken for each other in writing. *Accept* means "to receive willingly." *Except* is most commonly used to mean "but" or "other than."

> I *accept* your kind offer.
> All the pastries *except* the apple turnovers were eaten.

ad   The shortened form *ad* and other shortened forms (*auto, exam, gym, lab, math, phone, photo, Xmas, nite,* and *thru*) are used in speech or advertising. However, the full form should always be used in formal writing.

> Joshua wants to be a researcher in a chemical *laboratory* [not *lab*].

advice, advise   These words are often confused. *Advice* is a noun, and *advise* is a verb.

Parents usually *advise* their children to continue their education.
The *advice* he gave her made sense.

affect, effect   Because these words sound very much alike, they are often confused. *Affect*, which is usually a verb, means "to influence." *Effect* is a noun meaning "result or influence."

The heckler's shouts did not *affect* the golfer's concentration.
What *effect* does insomnia have on people?

ain't   *Ain't* is used in nonstandard English as a contraction, or shortened form, for *am not, is not, are not, have not,* and *has not.* It is generally frowned upon unless it is used humorously.

all ready, already   The words have two different meanings. *All ready* is a pronoun plus an adjective that means "everyone and everything is prepared." *Already* is an adverb that means "by this time" or "before this time."

We were *all ready* to go swimming.
We had *already* eaten before they came.

alot, a lot   *Alot* is a misspelling for *a lot.* People very often use *a lot, a lot of,* and *lots of* to mean *many* and *much.* Avoid these colloquial phrases in formal writing. Use *many* and *much.*

COLLOQUIAL	Ruth baked *a lot* [not *alot*] of cookies for Christmas.
WRITTEN	Ruth baked *many* cookies for Christmas.

altar, alter   *Altar* refers to a "table used for sacred purposes," whereas *alter* means "to change" or "to modify."

The *altar* was covered with flowers.
The architect was hired to *alter* the plans.

amount of, number of   Use *amount* with nouns that cannot be counted as separate items; use *number* with nouns that can be counted as separate items.

a small *amount* of pudding	a small *number* of biscuits
a great *amount* of savings	a great *number* of traveler's checks

and/or   Use one or the other, but not both.

WORDY	This play is a success on stage *and/or* screen.
BETTER	This play is a success on stage *or* screen.

anyways, anywheres, everywheres, nowheres, somewheres   These words are nonstandard for *anyway, anywhere, everywhere, nowhere,* and *somewhere.*

Despite the drizzle, Joel went to the ball game *anyway* [not *anyways*].

around, about   *Around* is colloquial for *about* in expressions of time. Avoid *around*.

COLLOQUIAL	*Around* two years ago, Joanna played in her first piano recital.
WRITTEN	*About* two years ago, Joanna played in her first piano recital.

bad, badly   *Bad* is an adjective; *badly* is an adverb. In formal and informal writing, *bad* — not *badly* — is used after *be, appear, become, feel, look, seem, smell,* and *taste*. Don't be tricked into using *badly*.

Sal brought *bad* news.

We felt *bad* about the error.

We took the news *badly*.

Does Limburger smell very *bad*?

beside, besides   *Beside* (without the *s*) is most commonly used to mean "next to" or "by the side of."

The vase *beside* the door is from Italy.

Besides (with the *s*) means "except," "in addition to," and "moreover."

No one *besides* [meaning "except"] King Solomon knows the answer.

Besides [meaning "in addition to"] carrying a thirty-pound backpack, each geologist carried a load of rocks.

We didn't have enough money to go to the movies; *besides* [meaning "moreover"], the movie didn't look very interesting.

be sure and, come and, go and, try and   These are colloquial forms for *be sure to*, *come to*, *go to*, and *try to*.

> *Be sure to* [not *be sure and*] call me when you arrive.
> *Try to* [not *try and*] visit me soon.

between, among   *Among* refers to three or more people, places, or things. *Between* is generally used in referring to only two people, places, or groups.

> The property was divided *among* the four sisters.
> The traditional rivalry *between* the two state universities added to the excitement of the game.

busted   Avoid using *busted*. It is nonstandard for *broken* or *burst*, depending on your meaning.

> Our water pipe just *burst* [not *busted*].

buy   In written English, use *buy* with *from*, not with *off* or *off of*.

> **NONSTANDARD**   She bought the watch *off* (or *off of*) her neighbor.
>
> **STANDARD**   She bought the watch *from* her neighbor.

can, may   *Can* is used to express ability, and *may* is used to express permission, possibility, or probability.

> **ABILITY**   *Can* dogs hear high frequency sounds that people cannot hear?
>
> **PERMISSION**   You *may* not borrow books from that library without a card.
>
> **POSSIBILITY**   Hans *may* have to return to Germany this month.
>
> **PROBABILITY**   It *may* rain this weekend.

can't hardly, can't scarcely   Avoid these phrases. *Hardly* and *scarcely* have negative meanings and should not be used with the negative *not*. Use *can hardly* or *can scarcely*.

> I *can hardly* [not *can't hardly*] believe that we finished our nine-course dinner.
> Jerold *can scarcely* [not *can't scarcely*] get up from the table.

can't help but   This colloquial expression is common in everyday speech. However, it is not appropriate in writing.Use *can't help + verb + ing.*

COLLOQUIAL	Even so, I *can't help but* like him.
WRITTEN	Even so, I *can't help* liking him.

cite, site, sight   *Cite*, a verb, means "to indicate or mention"; *site*, a noun, means "a place where something is, was, or is to be"; *sight*, a noun or verb, has to do with vision.

CITE	Regina *cited* the death of the Equal Rights Amendment as another example of male dominance in America.
SITE	This is the *site* for the new city library.
SIGHT (NOUN)	Wearing contact lenses may improve one's *sight*.
SIGHT (VERB)	Was Leif Ericson the first explorer to *sight* the New World?

complement, compliment   These words are often confused. A *complement* is something that completes or something that makes a whole. A *compliment* is flattery or praise. Both words can be used as nouns or as verbs.

NOUN	In a right triangle, a thirty-degree angle is the *complement* to a sixty-degree angle. Lee accepts *compliments* graciously.
VERB	A brown tweed jacket *complements* a variety of outfits. Ernest *complimented* Carmen on her fine lecture.

conscience, conscious   *Conscience*, a noun, means "a knowledge or feeling of right and wrong"; *conscious*, an adjective, means "aware or alert."

Rachel's *conscience* was bothering her.

Mark was *conscious* of his acne problem.

could care less   This phrase is nonstandard for *couldn't care less*. Informal speech drops the *n't*; thus, the phrase says the opposite of what is meant and is illogical.

Moira *couldn't care less* [not *could care less*] if she doesn't ever see another rabbit in her garden.

could of, might of, should of, would of   These are common misspellings for *could have, might have, should have,* and *would have.*

You *could have* [not *could of*] seen her if you had been here earlier.

counsel, council   *Counsel* is a verb that means "to give advice to"; it is also a noun that means "advice" or "advisor." *Council* is a noun that means "an official group of people."

Counselors should *counsel* students to go to college.
The students needed the *counsel* given to them by the seniors.
The neighborhood *council* meets once a month.

course, coarse   *Course* is a noun that means "a school class," or "a way or path" as in his *course* in life. The expression "of course" means "without a doubt." *Coarse* is an adjective that means "rough or harsh" or "crude or unrefined."

COURSE	Are you signing up for a Spanish *course* this semester? Jake's only *course* of action was to pay the fine. *Of course* he wants to go to the Rolling Stones concert.
COARSE	Burlap is a *coarse* cloth. The guests were shocked by their host's *coarse* behavior.

desert, dessert   These words are often confused. *Desert*, with the accent placed on the first syllable, is a noun that means "a dry, sandy area." *Desert* (the same spelling but with the accent placed on the second syllable) is a verb that means "to leave or to abandon." *Dessert* is a noun that refers to the sweet food eaten at the end of the main meal.

DESERT (NOUN)	Honey made from cactus and other *desert* plants is delicious.
DESERT (VERB)	Hank decided to *desert* the sinking ship.
DESSERT	Chocolate mousse is one of my favorite *desserts*.

different   The adjective *different* is generally followed by *from*. In both speech and writing, *different than* is becoming common before a clause.

> Susana's character is *different than* I thought it was.
>
> The cockatiel is *different from* the cockatoo primarily in size.

disinterested, uninterested   A distinction is generally made between these two words. *Disinterested* is used to mean "having no selfish interest or personal feelings in a matter and, therefore, no reason or desire to be anything but strictly impartial"; *uninterested* is used to mean "not interested."

> The ideal juror is someone *disinterested* in the case.
>
> Zelda was *uninterested* in going to Laurie's ballet recital.

due to   *Due to* was originally used only as an adjective, and in formal English it is still generally restricted to this use.

> The argument between the boys was *due to* Sid's bad mood.

In informal English *due to* has come to be used also as a preposition meaning "because of." However, despite its commonness, some people still object to the use of *due to* as a preposition. You might be wise, therefore, to avoid this use when you are writing for readers who prefer rather formal language. "Because of" or "owing to" can be substituted.

> *Because of* [not *due to*] an engine malfunction, the plane had to land at a different airport.

due to the fact that   Avoid this wordy phrase. Use *because*.

> *Because* [not *due to the fact that*] our dog was very sick, we had to put him to sleep.

enthuse   *Enthuse* is colloquial. In formal speech and writing, use *to be enthusiastic*.

> Jannelle is *enthusiastic* [not *enthused*] about being on the student council.

etc., and etc.   *Etc.* means "and so forth"; therefore, *and etc.* means "and and so forth." Do not use *and* and *etc.* together *Etc.* is appropriate in reference and business usage but is out of place in both formal and informal writing, which generally avoid abbreviations.

NONSTANDARD   For their skiing trip, the Baxters bought skis, ski jackets, ski boots, ski pants, *and etc.*

STANDARD   For their skiing trip, the Baxters bought skis, ski jackets, ski boots, ski pants, *etc.*

everyone . . . their   Although this phrase is common in speech, it is not acceptable in formal writing. Use *everyone . . . his* (or *her*).

COLLOQUIAL   *Everyone* should see *their* dentist at least once a year.

WRITTEN   *Everyone* should see *his* or *her* dentist at least once a year.

formally, formerly   Because these words are similar in spelling and pronunciation, they are often confused. *Formally* indicates the manner in which something is done—that is, "in a formal way." *Formerly* refers to time; it means "in the past; some time ago."

The gentleman bowed very *formally*.
What is now Arizona was *formerly* Mexico.

had ought, hadn't ought   These are nonstandard for *ought* and *ought not*. To avoid problems with *ought*, use *should* instead.

Victoria *ought* [not *had ought*] to enjoy herself more often.
You *ought not* [not *hadn't ought*] to eat so much.
You *should not* eat so much.

hisself, ourself, theirself, theirselves   These words should be avoided. They are nonstandard for *himself, ourselves,* and *themselves*.

Because he received an "A," Chuck was pleased with *himself* [not *hisself*].
The council members voted for a larger salary for *themselves* [not *theirselves*].

imply, infer   The close relationship between *imply* and *infer* causes confusion. *Imply* means "to suggest, hint, indicate without saying outright, or express indirectly." *Infer* means "to draw a conclusion by reasoning or to conclude from something known or assumed."

His sad face *implied* his true feeling about the case.

I *inferred* from Shirley's tone of voice that she was angry.

A person *implies* something by his or her actions or words; a person *infers* something from what he or she has seen, heard, or read.

incidence, incidents   *Incidence* refers to the number of times something happens, whereas *incidents* are the things that happen.

Poor sanitation increases the *incidence* of hepatitis.

There have been too many *incidents* of violence this year.

instance, instants   *Instance* means an "example or illustration," whereas *instants* refers to short time units such as moments.

For *instance*, Rudy always contributed his time to good causes.

A few *instants* after the shot was heard, we heard the alarm.

into, in   *Into* generally shows movement from outside to inside, and *in* shows location.

The children jumped *into* the pool.	They played happily *in* the pool.
The ship disappeared *into* the fog.	It wandered aimlessly *in* the fog.

invite   *Invite* is a verb. Never use it as a noun; use *invitation*.

Julie sent twenty *invitations* [not *invites*] to her party.

irregardless   Because of the suffix *-less*, *regardless* already has a negative meaning: "without regard to." Adding the prefix *ir-*, meaning "not," makes a double negative. Avoid *irregardless*; use *regardless*.

Regardless [not *irregardless*] of her past attitude, Amie will be a fine group leader.

is when, is where   In speech, people sometimes use the phrase *is when* or *is where* in defining a word. In writing, however, definitions like these sound awkward and should be avoided. A better way to define a word in formal writing is (1) to delete *when* or *where* and (2) to give its class and its general characteristics.

INCORRECT	Paleontology *is where* you study fossils.
CORRECT	Paleontology (the word being defined) is *the study* (the general category it belongs to) *of fossils of plants and animals* (characteristics that make it different from other studies).

it's, its   These words are confused because they are both pronouns. *It's* is a contraction, or shortened form, for a pronoun and a verb—*it is*. On the other hand, *its* is a possessive pronoun.

It's (It is) a gloomy day.
The lion licked *its* paws hungrily.

kind of a, sort of a   These phrases are common in speech. In formal writing, however, drop the *a*.

That is the *kind of* [not *kind of a*] house we'd like to buy.
What *sort of* [not *sort of an*] instrument does he play?

lay, lie   These verbs are often confused. To *lay* means "to put" or "to place." To *lie* means "to be in a resting position."

Lay the book on the table.
The German shepherd *lies* peacefully near its master.

	PRESENT	PAST	PAST PARTICIPLE
to lay	lay (lays)	laid	laid
to lie	lie (lies)	lay	lain

less, fewer   In formal English *less* is used with nouns that cannot be counted as separate items, and *fewer* is used with nouns that can be counted as separate items.

Mo sent *fewer* [not *less*] valentine cards than usual.
The *less* [not *fewer*] television I watch, the more I read.

like, as   In speech *like* is commonly used as a conjunction, but in formal writing *as, as if,* and *as though* are used as conjunctions to introduce clauses.

Mayor Abalo won the election *as* [not *just like*] the reporters had predicted.

The Barlettas look *as if* [not *like*] they were in a hurry.

In both formal and informal English *like* — not *as* — is used as a preposition in phrases of comparison.

The cats meowed *like* [not *as*] newborn babies.

The house stood *like* [not *as*] a fortress against invaders.

loose, lose   *Loose* is an adjective that means "not firmly fastened"; *lose* is a verb that means "to mislay or to be deprived of."

Al's clothes are *loose* on him now that he's lost twenty pounds.

The team can't afford to *lose* one more game.

most, almost   *Most* is often used colloquially for *almost*. However, unless a conversation is being reported, this usage is not appropriate in writing. Use *almost, almost always, almost all, almost anyone*.

The bowling alleys are *almost always* [not *most always*] busy.

Luke inherited *almost all* [not *most all*] of his aunt's fortune.

Almost anyone [not *most anyone*] here qualifies for the scholarship.

off, off of, from   In nonstandard English, *off* or *off of* are often used for *from*. In formal writing, use *from*.

Frieda borrowed the coat *from* Erika [not *off of* Erika].

presence, presents   *Presence* means "the condition of being present," and *presents* are gifts.

The queen's *presence* at the theater was a surprise to everyone.

Children often are satisfied with simple *presents*.

principle, principal   These words are often confused. *Principle*, a noun only, means "an essential truth or rule." *Principal* is an adjective that means "primary"; *principal* also is a noun that means "the head of a school."

The *principle* he lived by was the Golden Rule.

Kim's *principal* interest in the contest was money.

Ms. Martinelli will be the new *principal* at Lewis High School.

reason . . . is because, reason . . . is on account of, the reason why   These expressions are widely used in informal speech and often in informal writing. However, in formal writing use *the reason . . . is that*.

The *reason* he came *is that* I called him [not *is because I called him*].

The *reason* the car stalled *was that* the carburetor flooded [not *was on account of the carburetor flooded*].

The *reason* he failed *was that* he was not motivated [not *the reason why he failed was . . .*].

respectively, respectfully   *Respectively* means "each one in the order mentioned"; *respectfully* means "in a way that shows respect or honor."

The three men were sentenced to life imprisonment in March, April, and June, *respectively*.

The young woman greeted her grandmother *respectfully*.

stationary, stationery   *Stationary* means "fixed," and *stationery* refers to writing paper.

A *stationary* bicycle provides good exercise.

That engraved *stationery* is attractive.

than, then   Because *than*, spoken rapidly and without emphasis, sounds like *then*, careless writers confuse them. *Then* is an adverb of time, and *than* is a conjunction in comparisons.

Then Mark danced.

Mark is a better piano player *than* dancer.

there, they're, their   *There* is an adverb that refers to location; *they're* is a contraction that means "they are." *Their* is a third person plural possessive pronoun.

I remember seeing an abandoned gold mine over *there*.

They're being sent to an air base in Nebraska this summer.

Rupert and Omar both received blue medals for *their* science projects.

these kind, those kind　　These are nonstandard forms. *Kind*, a noun, must agree in number with the adjective modifying it. For standard formal usage, write *this kind* or *that kind* for singular and *these kinds* and *those kinds* for plural.

> *This kind* of homework is boring; *that kind* is practical.
> *These kinds* of shoes are uncomfortable; *those kinds* are expensive.

to, too, two　　*To* is a preposition that refers to direction; *too* is an adverb that means "also" or "excessively"; *two* refers to the number 2.

> I am taking a train *to* Santa Fe in the morning.
> Unfortunately, the rock band played *too* softly.
> *Two* baseball players were injured in yesterday's game.

used to, supposed to　　Although the *d* is usually not pronounced in these phrases, it should not be omitted in writing.

> People *used to* [not *use to*] believe that man would never fly.
> Jo was *supposed to* [not *suppose to*] buy a loaf of bread for me.

weather, whether　　*Weather* is a noun that refers to storms or breezes or to rain or sunshine; *whether* is a conjunction used before clauses to introduce an alternative.

> The *weather* in Tampa Bay is often balmy.
> Marlene didn't know *whether* to write a letter to her congressperson or to send a telegram.

where . . . at, where . . . to　　Although *at* and *to* are used after *where* in speech, they are generally omitted in written English.

COLLOQUIAL	*Where* are the encyclopedias *at*?
WRITTEN	*Where* are the encyclopedias?
COLLOQUIAL	*Where* has the exchange student gone *to*?
WRITTEN	*Where* has the exchange student gone?

who, which, that　　In standard English *who* is most commonly used to refer to people.

Thomas is an architect *who* designs solar houses.

Are those the children *who* were just rescued?

Which refers to things (including animals). It is nonrestrictive; in other words, it provides information not necessary for the sentence to make sense. Therefore, *which* clauses are surrounded by commas.

My coffee grinder, *which* belonged to my grandfather, is an antique.

Roadrunners, *which* are native to the Arizona desert, are carnivorous.

That refers to people or things. It is restrictive; in other words, it provides information necessary for the sentence to make sense. Therefore, *that* clauses do not need commas.

Is she the secretary *that* types 140 words per minute?

Cinder and Peanut are the dogs *that* are being sold.

Whose refers to ownership by a person or group of people. It may be either restrictive or nonrestrictive.

The man, *whose* hair was peppered with gray, looked distinguished.

Were they the ones *whose* daughter won the award?

When the possessive pronoun refers to a thing rather than a person, either *whose* or (more formally) *of which* is used.

They lived on a ranch *whose* backyard was a thousand acres.

A young boy discovered some earthen pots, the contents *of which* were the famous Dead Sea Scrolls.

-wise   Avoid using created words such as *marketwise, customerwise, gradewise, pricewise,* and *percentagewise.* Adding *-wise* to nouns is needless. Use the original noun.

COLLOQUIAL	*Healthwise*, my grandfather will probably do well this year.
WRITTEN	My grandfather will probably enjoy good *health* this year.

P R A C T I C E   1 6 A

Choosing the Best Expression

DIRECTIONS: Read the following paragraph. Copy the passage, choosing the appropriate word or words for college writing from each parentheses. Check your work carefully.

The Controversial Biorhythm Theory

(1) A controversial (principal, principle) that (alot, a lot) of people have faith (in, into) is the biorhythm theory. (2) This theory states that three repeating cycles (affect, effect) people's lives. (3) A twenty-three-day cycle governs the physical abilities of people—(strengthwise, endurancewise, and energywise; in terms of their strength, endurance, and energy). (4) In addition, a twenty-eight-day cycle is (suppose, supposed) to influence the emotions of individuals and determine (there, they're, their) moods and creativity. (5) (Beside, Besides) the first two cycles, a thirty-three-day cycle also has an (affect, effect) on people. (6) The final cycle is different (from, than) the others (due to the fact that, because) it (most, almost) always determines the intellectual lives of individuals and (affects, effects) (there, they're, their) reasoning power, memory, and intelligence. (7) Beginning at a person's birth, these three cycles all (complement, compliment) each other continuously throughout that person's life. (8) In addition, if charted, biorhythms can (imply, infer) (what kind of a day, what kind of day) a person will have according to his or her cycles. (9) Thus, a person can expect to have a miserable day (around, about) the time that all three of his or her cycles are in negative phases. (10) On the other hand, if all cycles are extremely positive, (than, then) the individual (can't help but have, can't help having) a marvelous day. (11) Although many people are (enthused, enthusiastic) about the benefits of charting their biorhythms, others (couldn't care less, could care less) and are even suspicious of the theory. (12) In fact, these people (cite, site, sight) strong evidence suggesting that the theory is false. (13) (Irregardless, Regardless), many individuals wishing to (alter, altar) their behavior according to their "good and bad" days will, no doubt, continue to (accept, except) the biorhythm theory.

P R A C T I C E   1 6 B

Choosing the Best Expression

DIRECTIONS: Read the following paragraph. Note that the underlined words are not used appropriately for a formal college composition. Copy the passage, changing the underlined words to the
appropriate level of language. Check your work carefully.

American Folk Dance: Part I

(1) Just like the flamenco is to Spain and/or the Bon-odori, a harvest
dance, is to Japan, so the square dance is to the United States. (2) It is
the only truly American folk dance, if one does not consider the dance
fads who have come and gone since the pioneer days. (3) During the
nation's early years, dancing use to be frowned upon. (4) Acting as the
conscious of young America, the church was greatly concerned that a
person never loose spiritual control of hisself or herself and adviced
against close physical contact when possible; thus, dancing was
considered a course activity. (5) Attitudes changed, however, and the
European quadrille, a sort of a dance done in squares, eventually
became popular in the United States. (6) It was gradually excepted by
some religious groups and finally evolved into today's square dance.
(7) Around the middle of the 1800's, the format for the dance became
fixed: introduction, basic dance sequence, break, and ending. (8) As
this dance became popular, different regions slightly altared dance
styles, calls, music, and costumes. (9) In many rural areas for instants,
the barn style, which is when people form one large circle to dance,
was preferred. (10) Other areas followed the western style, which is
where the entire group divides into sets of four couples each. (11) In
addition, although certain calls like "allemande" and "do-si-do"
became principle terms for any square dancer, other calls differed as
much as the regional language of the dancers theirselves. (12) These
kind of regional variations were so distinctive that if square dancers,
who had all ready mastered all the steps in one area, traveled to
another part of the country, they might of felt lost when they first tried
and danced their. (13) These differences, however, ain't as prominent
anymore, and many aspects of the folk dance such as costuming,
calls, and style have been standardized. (14) Thru this standardization,
the popularity of square dancing has spread, less people shy away
from this traditional dance then ever before, and more people look to
this art form not just as a way to enjoy theirself but as a way to meet
new friends wherever they go.

P R A C T I C E   1 6 C

Choosing the Best Expression

DIRECTIONS: Read the following paragraph. Much of the language in it is inappropriately used for a formal college composition. Most numbered items have one, two, or three problems with inappropriate words. Sentence 4 has five problems. Copy the paragraph, choosing appropriate words as you write. Check your work carefully.

American Folk Dance: Part II

(1) According to a lot of enthusiastic square dancers, the reason for square dancing is having fun and making friends. (2) Many Americans, in fact, are enthused about the typical characteristics of this traditional dance. (3) Today, for example, no matter where a square dancer goes to, he or she can expect not only alot of fast dancing but also lively music to. (4) A square dancer most anywhere can also expect to see women and men, respectfully, dressed in full skirts, pants, boots, and etc., parading formerly onto the dance floor and remaining stationery until the caller begins the dance. (5) The site of the square dancers' bright costumes, then, is common from one region to the next as are the calls, which determine how the dancers move. (6) However, the amount of calls in a particular dance can change from one caller to the next. (7) Because the calls make the dance enjoyable, a good caller, which has in his repertoire anywheres from at least sixty-five calls on, will make creative changes as he or she sings out and cues the dancers. (8) Each dancer has to try and remain conscience of these changes; otherwise, everyone dancing in the square will lose their place. (9) Because of all the constant changes in the dance steps and the calls, a person can't help but get alot of exercise. (10) A dancer, in fact, may easily put in twelve miles on the dance floor during one nite of continuous twirling, shuffling, and swinging. (11) All these features appeal too enthusiastic square dancers, but a person need not be a professional to receive an invite to dance. (12) Most anyone can learn this kind of a dance; in fact, square dance enthusiasts advice that "if a person can walk, he can dance." (13) More and more people seem to be excepting this slogan because the incidents of people joining square dance clubs and programs is increasing. (14) In fact, Americans among the ages of six and ninety-six, weather they live in the city or in the country, are square dancing with such excitement that they are organizing annual road trips, regional festivals, and national conventions. (15) Because of the great interest in this art form, who is

steeped in tradition, square dancing can't hardly be said to be dying. (16) Indeed this popular interest is the reason why square dancing is likely to live on as America's true folk dance.

ON YOUR OWN

Ideas for Guided and Open Writing

GUIDED WRITING EXERCISE: Children's literature is becoming "reality literature"—that is, tragedy, suffering, divorce, drug addiction, loneliness, and death are depicted. Many parents, teachers, and psychologists believe that children benefit from seeing life "as it is" through realistic situations in literature. Such literature, they believe, helps to prepare children to face problems in their own families. These people believe most children's literature does not depict reality; in fact, it sometimes encourages children to have unrealistic ideas about life. Other people, however, condemn reality literature for children, saying that it is too depressing and too sad for children. These teachers, psychologists, and parents say that reality literature does not make children feel secure because these stories do not always have happy endings. Do you think that reality literature is good for children? In a well-developed paragraph of approximately 100–150 words, defend or attack exposing children to reality literature. You might begin your paragraph with "Exposing children to reality literature is harmful (or is not harmful) to children." Consult the usage glossary in this chapter for help with usage.

OPEN WRITING IDEAS: The following topics are suggestions for open writing exercises to help you practice the structures presented in this chapter. Develop these ideas into paragraphs of 100–150 words. Focus your attention on using appropriate language.

1. From stamps to rocks, from campaign buttons to matchbooks, from ticket stubs to paintings, many people greatly enjoy collecting things. Describe an interesting or unusual collection you have seen, and discuss why people would keep such a collection.

2. Selling liquor on college campuses has been a controversial issue for a long time. Whereas some people believe that selling liquor is harmful to students, others feel that students should be able to choose where to buy their liquor. Support or attack selling liquor on campus.

CHAPTER 17

Maintaining a Consistent Point of View

An important aspect of good writing involves an understanding of how to maintain a consistent point of view in writing. Point of view refers to the way a writer discusses his or her subject. A shift in point of view occurs when there are inconsistencies in person and number. *Person* refers to the form a pronoun takes to indicate who is speaking, who is being spoken to, and who is being spoken about. *Number* refers to the singular or plural form of a noun or pronoun.

I	first person singular (speaker or writer)
we	first person plural (speaker or writer)
you	second person singular and plural (listener or reader)
he, she, it	third person singular (topic of talk or writing)
they	third person plural (topic of talk or writing)

For example, if you are writing about an experience and you want your reader to know that you were personally involved, you take the *I* or first person point of view.

FIRST PERSON SINGULAR POINT OF VIEW   *I* could not believe the news when *I* heard that the Pope had been shot.

If you want your reader to know somebody else's response, you take the third person point of view.

THIRD PERSON SINGULAR POINT OF VIEW   *My brother* could not believe the news when *he* heard that the Pope had been shot.

151

THIRD PERSON PLURAL POINT OF VIEW	*All the people* in the theater could not believe the news when *they* heard that the Pope had been shot.

That the Pope had been shot is the event, but it is discussed from three different points of view: *I, my brother,* and *all the people. I* is first person singular, *my brother* is third person singular, and *all the people* is third person plural.

Unnecessary changes in the person or number of the subject are confusing to the reader. The reader not only loses the focus of the sentence but also wonders about the knowledge of the writer.

INCONSISTENT	The *theatergoers* cannot follow the plot very well because *you* get lost in the number of scene changes. (The subject, *theatergoers*, suddenly shifts to *you* — a shift from third person singular to second person.)
CONSISTENT	The *theatergoers* cannot follow the plot very well because *they* get lost in the number of scene changes.
INCONSISTENT	If *someone* calls the store too early, *they* get a recording. (The subject, *someone*, third person singular, changes to *they*, third person plural.)
CONSISTENT	If *someone* calls the store too early, *he or she* gets a recording.
INCONSISTENT	*Students* usually return a library book on time because *you* are fined if *you* do not. (The subject, *students*, third person plural, changes to *you*, second person plural.)
CONSISTENT	*Students* usually return a library book on time because *they* are fined if *they* do not.

Readers are also confused by a shift in point of view between sentences in a paragraph or composition.

INCONSISTENT	*One* rarely sees anyone at the library on a Saturday night. *You* would be shocked if *you* did. (*One* changes to *you*.)
CONSISTENT	*One* rarely sees anyone at the library on a Saturday night. A *person* would be shocked if *he or she* did. (*One, a person,* and *he or she* are consistent.)

Choose your point of view at the beginning of your paragraph and continue with that point of view throughout.

When you choose a point of view, carefully consider how you want to discuss your subject. If you want a message to sound personal and informal, use *you*, or the second person, throughout. Using *I*, or the first person, is also quite informal and very personal. If, on the other hand, you wish the message to be formal — if you do not want your readers to think that you are being too casual about your subject — then use the third person. Use *one, a person, a consumer, people, most Americans,* or a similar expression. The point of view a writer chooses contributes to the tone of a paper. Tone has to do with how a writer discusses a subject and how the reader feels when he or she reads the paper. Note the differences in tone that the following different points of view create:

I	*I* should try to be on time for classes so that *I* won't miss any of the lectures.
YOU	*You* should try to be on time for classes so that *you* won't miss any of the lectures.
THIRD PERSON SINGULAR	A *student* should try to be on time for classes so that *he or she* won't miss any of the lectures.
THIRD PERSON PLURAL	*Students* should try to be on time for classes so that *they* won't miss any of the lectures.

In formal writing, third person singular or plural is preferred, but overusing *one* may make your writing sound stiff. You can begin a paragraph with *one* and then substitute *he or she* and *him or her*.

One can earn much money if *he or she* invests in savings bonds.

If *one* gets a flat tire on the freeway, *he or she* should drive *his or her* car gradually to the side of the road.

You could also use a specific noun instead of *one*, and refer to that noun with *he or she* and *him or her*, as in the following examples:

When a *student* is going to be absent, *he or she* should inform *his or her* instructor.

A *person* who shows psychotic behavior often doesn't recognize *his or her* own symptoms.

A middle-aged person in our society is painfully aware of *his or her* age.

P R A C T I C E   1 7 A

Working with Point of View

DIRECTIONS: Read the following paragraph. It is filled with shifts in point of view within and between sentences. Copy the paragraph, correcting all shifts in person and number. Check your work carefully.

Dreams According to Sex

(1) Dreams have interested people for centuries. (2) For a long time, many people have believed that a person's dreams are determined by your hopes, anxieties, and fears. (3) Now, however, researchers have found that dreams are also influenced by one's gender. (4) In other words, whether someone is a male or female often determines the kinds of dreams they have. (5) A man, for example, might dream that in a chase scene they are the pursuers. (6) Yet, if a woman dreams about a chase scene, you would most likely be the one pursued. (7) In addition, in the man's dream, they would focus attention on how large their car is or how fast they are traveling. (8) However, when women dream, she probably will not pay attention to details of size or speed but to details of color or fashion. (9) Thus, lights, shadows, the brightness of the sun or moon, and other such details of color will catch the attention of women. (10) These differences between the dreams of males and females reveal important information about our social attitudes. (11) Men's dreams, for example, show that a man is trained to be an aggressive leader. (12) In addition, a man's attention to size and speed reveals their concern about performing and competing successfully in your daily life. (13) Women's dreams, on the other hand, reflect her traditional passive role. (14) In other words, females have been trained not to begin actions but to have things done to you or for you. (15) A woman is also taught to focus their attention on color, fashion, and the family. (16) Therefore, research has shown that a person's gender does affect what they dream about. (17) However, as men and women find their roles changing, the content of our dreams may change also.

P R A C T I C E   1 7 B

Working with Point of View

DIRECTIONS: Read the following paragraph. It is filled with shifts in point of view within and between sentences. Copy the paragraph, correcting all shifts in person and number. Check your work carefully.

Healthy Breathing

(1) Almost everyone knows that breathing is a process by which their body absorbs oxygen into one's cells. (2) In the cells the oxygen helps your body burn the proteins, fats, and carbohydrates that he or she needs to produce energy. (3) It also helps someone to purge—that is, cleanse—your body of carbon dioxide. (4) Many scientists and medical doctors are now beginning to look at other facts about breathing known by ancient philosophers and medical practitioners. (5) The way someone breathes can greatly affect their emotional as well as their physical health. (6) For example, research shows that whether you breathe quickly or slowly or whether one breathes shallowly or deeply may cause them certain mental and physical problems. (7) In addition, whether people breathe through their nose or one's diaphragm often affects his or her state of health. (8) We often think of breathing as a simple automatic function; however, one can control their breathing. (9) For example, when a person is uncontrollably upset, they can calm themselves by taking a deep breath. (10) Stress, fear, or trauma makes people breathe rapidly and shallowly. (11) When persons breathe this way, he or she loses precious oxygen, which, in turn, puts further stress on their bodies. (12) In contrast, when we are relaxed or at rest, your breathing is slow, even, and deep. (13) As a result, many scientists, psychologists, and researchers are studying how people can learn to control one's breathing. (14) Thus, the way one breathes can have a positive effect on their mental and physical health.

PRACTICE 17C

Working with Point of View

DIRECTIONS: Read the following paragraph. It is filled with shifts in point of view within and between sentences. Copy the paragraph, correcting all shifts in person and number. Check your work carefully.

**Mnemonics:
Remembering
Made Easy**

(1) A student may help improve their memory if one uses several well-known strategies and techniques. (2) Some of the most effective techniques you can use are called *mnemonic devices*, which include rhymes, patterns, acronyms, and acrostics. (3) For example, when people recite the simple rhyme "Thirty days hath September . . . ," he or she is using a mnemonic device so that one can remember the number of days in each month. (4) Moreover, patterns as mnemonic devices help us to recall information. (5) For example, it is easier for one to remember their Social Security number as 526-78-7952 than as 526,787,952. (6) In other words, separating the number into small units can help improve our memory. (7) In fact, numbers that repeat themselves in a pattern, such as the Social Security number 225-80-2255, may be even easier for him to recall. (8) Another mnemonic device that persons use to help him remember material is the *acronym*, a grouping of letters such as NATO, NASA, and UNESCO to help them recall somewhat complex material. (9) For example, he can recall the name of the National Aeronautics and Space Administration easily if he remembers NASA. (10) Someone uses another mnemonic tool, called *acrostics*, when we think of Roy G. Biv to recite the ordered colors of the rainbow: red, orange, yellow, green, blue, indigo, and violet. (11) Likewise, people use acrostics if they remember the sentence "Men very easily make jugs serve useful nocturnal purposes" when we want to recall the planets in order from the sun: Mercury, Venus, Earth, Mars, Jupiter, Saturn, Uranus, Neptune, Pluto. (12) In applying this mnemonic device, you take the first letter in each word of the phrase or sentence to represent specific items of information in a specific order. (13) Persons can use these and other more complex mnemonic devices to help one remember material better. (14) These strategies are not only effective in helping you retrieve, or bring to mind, certain information but are also creative and fun.

ON YOUR OWN

Ideas for Guided and Open Writing

GUIDED WRITING EXERCISE: Have you ever asked for advice from parents, counselors, and friends about how to choose a compatible roommate — that is, someone who is easy to get along with? Write a paragraph of approximately 100–150 words in which you offer advice to someone who is looking for a roommate for the first time. You might begin your paragraph with "Selecting a roommate requires careful planning." In your discussion consider the study habits, housekeeping routines, sleep habits, and religious influences of the potential roommate. Does the person smoke or drink? What kind of music does he or she prefer? Does this person work? Who are his or her friends? Is this individual a vegetarian? Is he or she moody, responsible, neat? Concentrate on maintaining a consistent point of view in your paragraph.

OPEN WRITING IDEAS: The following topics are suggestions for open writing exercises to help you practice the structures presented in this chapter. Develop these ideas into paragraphs of 100–150 words. Focus your attention on maintaining consistency in the appropriate point of view.

1. Discuss the characteristics of a typical spectator you might find at a particular event such as a football game, a rock concert, an opera, and so forth. Describe his or her actions, clothing, and speech.

2. Examine the various people driving on your city streets. Classify at least three types of drivers and briefly discuss the characteristics of each type.

CHAPTER 18

Maintaining Tone Through Appropriate Language

Besides maintaining a consistent point of view, a writer should try to maintain an appropriate and consistent tone. The tone of a composition has to do with the way it sounds and the way it makes the reader feel. The tone of a composition expresses the author's attitude toward the subject he or she is writing about. An author's attitude can range from contented to unhappy, from thankful to bitter, or from light to sad.

Of course, maintaining tone requires using a particular kind of language for a particular topic. To understand the importance of maintaining consistent tone, consider the following situation:

A student is writing a serious paper about "the severe problem of crime in this country." He continues by offering this general statement: "Unfortunately, robbery is an increasingly common crime on many of our city streets." Then, illustrating the statement with a personal story, he says he was "ripped off by some dude."

Obviously, the tone of this essay is inconsistent because the language used is inconsistent. The first two sentences sound formal; the last one sounds casual. Instead of being impressed by the seriousness of the subject, the reader is puzzled by the inconsistency and begins to question the knowledge of the author.

When writing any letter, paragraph, or essay, a writer should decide how he or she feels about the subject before he or she begins to write. Then, after the writer has written a draft, he or she should review it for consistency in tone and language.

Three kinds of tone are generally recognized: light, middle, and serious. College writing usually is middle tone, although tone always depends on how the writer feels about the subject, how the writer discusses the subject, and how the writer wants the reader to feel. Read the following examples and decide which is light, middle, or serious tone.

Paragraph 1

Eating at health food restaurants is always a memorable experience. From the minute you walk in to the moment you taste the last bean sprout, you know that you'll be healthy — whether you want to or not. The menu is overloaded with raw, natural, organic, vegetarian, nonfatty, energizing, vitamin-filled foods that would delight the taste buds of anyone who is tired of the appetizing traditional meal of meat and potatoes. After choosing what seems to be the most normal food on the menu — spinach salad smothered with grated tofu and bean sprouts — you hope that you can at least wash it down with a coke. But, no chance! The waitress then asks self-righteously if you'd prefer papaya juice or a mango protein yeast shake. Waiting for the food, you notice the thin, healthy, beautiful people obviously enjoying their vitamin plates, and you begin feeling better and better about your coming spinach. Finally the dish comes — complete with its vitamins, minerals, and sprouts — and you dig in, dreaming of the Big Mac you could have had.

Paragraph 2

The Kiuakiutl Indians are aggressive and violent above all else. Their social rank is determined at birth; with high social rank, they inherit not only the prestige that accompanies superiority but also a sacred obligation to enslave, mistreat, and terrorize those of lower rank. In this culture, it is common for young boys of high social rank to stone, beat, and otherwise abuse those of lower rank. Murder is commonplace and socially accepted. Not only is it accepted, but it is rewarded inasmuch as all of the possessions and titles of the victim are inherited by the murderer.

Paragraph 3

As a result of the increase in political terrorism, equipment to protect executives and other prominent businessmen who fear kidnapping or assassination has been developed. One of the most recent attention-getting devices is an electronically monitored briefcase. Bulletproof cars, bulletproof clothing, electronic tracking devices, and other James Bondian devices have now become part of the executive wardrobe. Although this briefcase looks like any other standard, thin, leather model, it is, in fact, a personal security system. Not only is the briefcase made of lightweight, bulletproof material, but it is equipped with a transmitter that is able to detect wiretaps and telephone bugs.

The first paragraph is written in a light tone. The language — *no chance, from the minute you walk in, the menu is overloaded with* — is light, chatty, and a little humorous. In addition, contractions such as *you'll* and *you'd* help keep the tone light. A reader can immediately sense that the author does not take the subject particularly seriously.

The second paragraph is obviously written in a serious tone. The author is concerned about the subject, and the vocabulary — *enslave, mistreat, terrorize,* and *commonplace* — indicates a serious tone. Another element of the serious style is complex sentence structure and long sentences.

The third paragraph is neither light nor serious; it is a middle tone. It is the kind of tone a college student would probably use for most writing. The author approaches the subject neither too lightly nor too seriously. The writer adds some of his or her own personality to the subject by referring to "James Bondian devices." Notice that the writer uses Standard English and chooses vocabulary from the middle level of diction, such as *device* (not *gadget*), *prominent* (not *big-time*), and so on.

When thinking about tone, consider: (1) the language (What kinds of words are used?), (2) the pronouns (Are they consistently third person? second? first?), and (3) the length of sentences (Longer sentences tend to identify more serious, formal writing).

In the following exercises you will be asked to change a mixed paragraph to a light one, or a mixed paragraph to a serious one. You may be asked to rewrite an inconsistent paragraph into a consistent middle tone paragraph. These exercises will help you to edit your own writing for consistency of tone and language.

P R A C T I C E   1 8 A

Understanding Tone

DIRECTIONS: Read the following paragraph. Some sentences are written in a serious tone, others are written in a light tone. Rewrite the paragraph, using only one tone. If you prefer a serious tone, assume that you are a team doctor writing to the Committee on College Sports. Your first sentence might read: "Although football has become one of America's favorite sports, it is quickly developing into one of the most dangerous games in the nation because of the high number of injuries among its players." If you prefer a light tone, assume that you are a team captain writing to a local news sportscaster. Your first sentence might read: "Even though football is becoming a really popular sport in America, it is getting to be pretty dangerous because the players are always getting hurt." Use language appropriate for the tone you choose in order to maintain consistency in your paragraph. Check your work carefully.

The Severity of Football

(1) Although football has become one of America's favorite sports, it is getting to be pretty dangerous because the players are always getting hurt. (2) Physical injuries such as concussions, lacerations, fractures, sprains, torn ligaments and the like, unfortunately, are common occurrences to football players. (3) Many of these injuries occur in other hard contact sports, but the amount and kinds of injuries in football are increasing. (4) Strangely enough, the most serious injuries are caused by one piece of safety equipment: the hard-shell football helmet. (5) Although the helmet really protects the player's head very well, it becomes like a weapon against the other guys. (6) A player can effectively knock out an opponent by using his own·headgear against the opponent. (7) Instead of ramming into the other guy with one's shoulders, for example, the player can use the helmet to block. (8) That kind of blocking is great, but it also knocks the other player entirely unconscious. (9) In fact, the force of the two players colliding with each other may be so bad that the guys need surgery to repair internal physical damages that they received during the collision. (10) Of course, tackles or blocks don't always end up hurting the guys so badly that they need to be operated on. (11) However, players get really banged up when they use their helmets for the purpose of blocking. (12) Furthermore, serious injuries occur when the guys don't even know how to use their helmets right. (13) Because the athletes can get really smashed up in this game, both officials and spectators of this contact sport should make the following demands to ensure the player's safety:

1. Sports gear should be super safe.
2. New regulations should reduce the opportunity for injury.
3. Coaches should drive home the importance of playing fairly and responsibly.

(14) If officials and spectators get things like they want them, perhaps the spectators and the athletes can enjoy the sport as they used to.

P R A C T I C E   1 8 B

Understanding Tone

DIRECTIONS: Read the following paragraph, which is written in a mixture of serious and light tones. Rewrite the entire paragraph, using a middle tone consistently. Sentence 1 is already written in a middle tone. Use it as a model for the rest of the paragraph. Pay particular attention to appropriate language. Check your work carefully.

Dying Tribes

(1) Recently, many people have been concerned about groups of animals dying out. (2) But not a whole lot of people seem to really know much about the millions of people that are being wiped out. (3) An estimated 200 million people from hunting and gathering tribes living primarily in remote areas of Brazil, Colombia, Vietnam, Afghanistan, and Australia are experiencing the same dangers of extinction that many animal species are experiencing. (4) Because these people live really far away from everybody and everything, they've ended up doing pretty much the same things for centuries. (5) Recently, however, government agencies and private corporations from large industrialized countries such as the United States, France, and the Soviet Union have entered into these regions to develop highways and industrial plants. (6) As a result, the tribal people must relocate to different regions where they must adjust to entirely new diets and new climates. (7) Many of these guys get really sick from eating weird foods they're not used to and from living in weather that's totally new to them. (8) In addition, they undergo the same problems as a result of wars,

which have been the cause of many of these tribal people having had to travel from their homelands to foreign areas. (9) Many of these people also get sick and end up dying after they've been around the people who've invaded their territory. (10) For example, numerous health disorders such as measles, which typically pose little threat to contemporary civilization, are new to tribal people and can frequently be fatal to them. (11) It's really too bad, but the governments and businesses are going to keep on doing what they're doing, and wars are going to be around a long time. (12) However, the tragic effects of progress as well as those of war will undoubtedly be lessened for these tribes if the public and the governments worldwide work together to help eliminate the suffering of these people.

P R A C T I C E   1 8 C

Understanding Tone

DIRECTIONS: Read the following paragraph, which is written in a mixture of serious and light tones. Rewrite the entire paragraph, using a middle tone consistently. Sentence 1 is already written in a middle tone. Use it as a model for the rest of the paragraph. Pay particular attention to appropriate language. Check your work carefully.

Camping

(1) Recently camping has become one of the most popular outdoor activities for Americans who like the rest, fun, and adventure camping provides. (2) Many people who want to get away from it all really have a good time sitting under a bunch of trees, seeing what's happening in nature. (3) They have the pure satisfaction of having raised a temporary canvas shelter and having reeled in delicate fish for their evening meal. (4) They think that the peace and quiet of nature is great, and they get a really good night's sleep. (5) To many campers one of the greatest pleasures is that the morning will present no challenges or responsibilities more difficult than rolling up sleeping bags and preparing breakfast. (6) Other persons, though, take off to the wilderness in huge R-V's and mobile campers that come with everything you could imagine in them. (7) Refusing to relinquish the

luxuries of home, these campers bring with them every possible piece of camping equipment available to modern consumers. (8) Sitting around in the middle of hundreds of other campers, they are ready to have a lot of fun. (9) If their choice is to experience the open wilderness, they frequently do so in convertible dune buggies or on motorbikes, motorcycles, and bicycles. (10) Also, those who just love the super quiet provided by lakes, rivers, streams, and other kinds of water go off in canoes, sailboats, and speedboats. (11) Thus, camping offers people the opportunity to experience the wilderness in a variety of ways.

O N   Y O U R   O W N

Ideas for Guided and Open Writing

GUIDED WRITING EXERCISE: Advertisements are created to attract different kinds of audiences. For example, manufacturers of sweet cereals usually attract children by using very colorful, cartoon-like advertisements with animal characters to sell their products. In addition, typically, commercials for women's perfume include soft music, handsome men, beautiful women, and romantic candlelight. If you could create a new product to sell, what would it be, and who would your audience be? In a well-developed paragraph of approximately 100–150 words, write a description, which will appear in a magazine, advertising a new product. Be sure that your advertisement is written for its appropriate audience. For example, if your product is a new acne soap, make sure you attract teenagers. If your product is for business people, write in a formal tone; your first sentence might be something like "The Abrams briefcase assures its owner the utmost in executive safety." If your product is a new educational game for people of all ages, you might write in a middle tone; your sentence might be like the following: "The Symptom Game helps players learn to make decisions and tests their knowledge of medical facts." If your product is a new kind of chip made from soybeans, you might write in a light tone; your topic sentence might be like the following: "Soy chip is the greatest chip ever made." Remember to keep your tone consistent throughout the paragraph.

OPEN WRITING IDEAS: The following topics are suggestions for open writing exercises to help you practice the structures presented in this chapter. Develop these ideas into paragraphs of 100–150 words. Focus your attention on maintaining a consistent tone that is appropriate for your audience and subject.

1. During court trials, reporters are allowed to sit in on proceedings. Recently, reporters with television cameras, which have not been allowed in the courtroom for years, have been permitted to televise hearings. Does the public have a right to view these hearings? Or do televised hearings interfere with the rights of the person on trial? Whose rights are to be protected here — those of the public, or of the person on trial? For a formal tone, you might consider your audience a senate committee reviewing this procedure. For middle tone, you might consider your audience the readers of a local newspaper. For a light tone, you might consider your audience a friend reading a letter from you.

2. Design a nightclub and tell who would like it and why. Consider your audience as you write. You might, for example, have architects, do-it-yourself types, or connoisseurs of the local "dives" as different audiences. Note that each audience will determine the tone of your paragraph.

CHAPTER 19

Avoiding Trite Language

In previous chapters you have learned about using language appropriate to the tone of your composition. In the usage chapter, you learned to distinguish between troublesome spellings or forms of words so that you would know the most appropriate word to use in your formal college writing. In this chapter, we will discuss trite language and the effect it has on your writing.

Trite language refers to timeworn expressions called *clichés*, which are expressions that we have heard many times such as the following:

white as a sheet	a blessing in disguise
food for thought	the plain truth
sharp as a tack	red as a beet
to be on pins and needles	old as the hills
ugly as sin	to keep a straight face
the one and only	pure and simple
the bitter end	bored to death
to vanish into thin air	crystal clear

Perhaps these expressions were once fresh and striking, but now they are so familiar and empty of meaning that we no longer pay attention to them. The use of these phrases causes a reader to feel that the writer is not saying anything new or worthwhile. The reader may also feel that the writer has thought little about the subject and has merely grabbed at words.

In this chapter, you will be editing trite language. Learn to recognize it so that you can omit it from your writing. Try to express your ideas freshly and creatively, without relying on old, worn-out phrases.

P R A C T I C E   1 9 A

Using Creative Expressions

DIRECTIONS: Read the following paragraph. The underlined words are overused phrases and clichés. Copy each paragraph, rewriting the clichés and using another word or group of words consistent with the language in the rest of the paragraph. Check your work carefully.

Home on the Range

(1) Although modern American literature glamorizes the western cowboy, his life was not all it was cracked up to be. (2) During the late 1800's soon after the Civil War ended, many pioneers dying to live on the wide, open range pulled up stakes to strike it rich. (3) Wet behind the ears, but willing to plunge out West, these pioneers became some of the first North American cowboys. (4) Although floored by the number of hard times they had to endure, these new cowboys never threw in the towel. (5) Instead they almost killed themselves trying to make it or break it in ranching. (6) Day in and day out they worked like crazy raising their cattle. (7) At the end of the day they were dead as doornails from a hard day's work, but their responsibilities as cowboys didn't let up. (8) As luck would have it, these rough and tumble men of steel had to travel across plains for what seemed like forever to get their cattle to market. (9) Traveling through untamed territories and weathering both droughts and blizzards made the trip last forever and a day. (10) Moreover, it bored the cowboys to tears. (11) Once in a blue moon when they reached a town along the trail, they could blow off enough steam to keep them going. (12) However, they still needed some way to kick up their heels on the cattle drive. (13) So, they got their kicks by testing each other's skills as cowboys. (14) Roping steers and riding broncos were two parts of the cowboy's work that really put them through the mill. (15) These activities separated the men from the boys. (16) These activities became the first events in what was later to become known throughout the land as the western rodeo.
(17) Eventually the fun and games of these contests spread like wildfire, and by the 1880's the rodeos made it to the big time in large towns. (18) The cowboy had found some way of putting pizzazz into his otherwise hard-as-nails existence. (19) Those were the good old days of the American cowboy.

PRACTICE 19B

Using Creative Language

DIRECTIONS: Read the following paragraph. The underlined words are overused phrases and clichés. Copy each paragraph, rewriting the clichés and using another word or group of words consistent with the language in the rest of the paragraph. Check your work carefully.

Hydroponics

(1) The many people who are fit to be tied over the aches and pains of gardening do not need to toss in the towel completely. (2) Those in the know believe that people who are fed up with traditional gardening should not become unglued just because they do not have a knack for gardening. (3) Instead, these garden experts have started to spread the word about hydroponics. (4) As a result, many people have started to become wrapped up in hydroponics, a method of growing plants without soil. (5) Scientists have known the inside scoop about this kind of gardening for a long time and have talked it over for years. (6) Slowly but surely, however, amateurs have gotten wind of this new concept and have taken a shot at learning the tricks of the trade. (7) They realize that growing gardens according to these new ideas is a snap, and it can bring them big bucks on top of it all. (8) In a hydroponics system, considered easy as pie, the grower anchors the plant roots in gravel or perlite. (9) He or she then shoots water and inorganic nutrient solutions through the gravel or perlite. (10) Gardeners growing flowers and vegetables hydroponically do not have to mess around with dirt in the house. (11) Also, if gardeners are really on the ball, they can control the number of plants that kick the bucket as a result of bacterial infections around the plant. (12) Moreover, people have been bowled over to find out that the run of the mill hydroponically grown vegetables not only taste up to par with soil-grown vegetables, but they sometimes grow up to 20 percent larger than their counterparts. (13) Hydroponics is not everyone's cup of tea, however. (14) People who get their kicks out of digging in the dirt or watching things grow in the earth would not be caught dead fiddling around with hydroponics. (15) Hydroponics may not set the entire world on fire, but it sure is what the doctor ordered for a growing number of people.

P R A C T I C E   1 9 C

Using Creative Language

DIRECTIONS: Read the following paragraph. Each sentence contains between one and three different overused phrases and clichés. Copy each paragraph, rewriting the clichés and using another word or group of words consistent with the language in the rest of the paragraph. Check your work carefully.

Siberian Meteorite

(1) For years scientists and astronomers have been wracking their brains to try to uncover the full scoop on the enormous ball of fire in the sky in Siberia on June 30, 1908. (2) The giant explosion wiped out an area way out in the boondocks of Russia. (3) The mysterious explosion—which blew apart trees for miles around, killed wildlife, practically knocked huts off the face of the earth, and sent shock waves felt around the world—has kept scientists in the dark for years. (4) They have been up to their ears in theories, and some of them have guessed that the explosion was caused by an alien spacecraft that had been blown to bits when it hit earth. (5) Other scientists believe that the explosion was caused by a mini black hole, or the head of a comet, traveling faster than light. (6) Still other scientists have simply been out in left field altogether. (7) Although they had left no stone unturned in their search for answers, and they had really put themselves through the mill trying to put two and two together, they were merely taking wild shots in the dark. (8) However, recently Soviet scientists have considered a fairly down-to-earth explanation. (9) After trying to fit all the pieces together, they have finally decided that the explosion was caused by a meteorite. (10) Most scientists had thought of this but had concluded it was hogwash because they could not find a lick of evidence of a meteor having crashed at that site. (11) However, when the scientists dug in the area, they couldn't believe their eyes when they found millions of tiny diamonds buried in the earth. (12) Keeping their noses to the grindstone, the scientists supposed that the diamonds had been formed by extreme pressures during a collision between celestial bodies. (13) Also what crossed their minds was that the meteorite, probably a stony type, exploded before it hit earth, causing the diamonds to form. (14) Even though they do not understand the whole picture, the Soviets are not down in the dumps; on the contrary, their heads are in the clouds over the fact that the meteorite most likely deposited between forty and eighty tons of diamonds in the area.

O N   Y O U R   O W N

Ideas for Guided and Open Writing

GUIDED WRITING EXERCISE: People often blame others for their own problems and inconveniences. Large oil companies pollute our environment; too many people crowd and dirty our cities; teachers do not teach students necessary skills; doctors overcharge their patients; used-car salespeople exploit and cheat their customers; movie theater managers make their customers pay high prices and wait in long lines; and so forth. All these inconveniences and problems are blamed on other people, yet should they be? In approximately 100–150 words, write a well-developed letter to the editor of your local newspaper as an angry citizen. In the letter, express your anger about people who do not take responsibility for helping solve social problems. Take only one issue, such as high electric bills, and express your frustrations about complainers who only blame others and do not see how they can solve the problem themselves. You might begin your letter with: "A person who worries about —— could help solve this problem by ——, ——, and ——." Offer some specific ideas people can follow to solve the problem. Pay attention to avoiding trite language as you write.

OPEN WRITING IDEAS: The following topics are suggestions for open writing exercises to help you practice the structures presented in this chapter. Develop these ideas into paragraphs of 100–150 words. Focus your attention on avoiding trite language.

1. Every year, on the day after Thanksgiving, the Christmas rush begins. Stores advertise holiday sales, Santa Clauses appear in shopping centers and on street corners, and "Rudolph the Red-nosed Reindeer" and "Frosty the Snowman" cartoons invade television. Is Christmas becoming a business holiday instead of a religious one? Defend or attack the idea that Christmas has become a commercial holiday.

2. Recently, women have been entering professions that were historically open only to men. For example, there are now women police and firefighters. Do you agree or disagree with women being allowed to enter these professions? Are there some jobs that women are not able to do? Defend or attack the idea that women should be able to enter any profession they choose.

CHAPTER 20

Avoiding Wordiness

Another problem for writers is *wordiness*, the unnecessary repetition of words and ideas. To avoid writing papers with wordy sentences, ask yourself the following questions as you are checking your work:

Do the same words or forms of words appear again and again?

Are there any expressions that you could replace with a single word?

Have you included any words or phrases that make sentences long but add nothing to the meaning?

Are any ideas repeated?

Have you used two sentences where one sentence with a compound subject or compound verb would do?

With these questions in mind, read the following sentence. Is it too wordy?

When the water is high in the early part of the month of November, attempting to try to cross the dangerous river at the Van Buren Bridge is a very hazardous danger.

First, *dangerous* and *danger* are forms of the same word; one of them should be removed. Second, the introductory clause can be cut, with no loss of meaning, to "When the water is high in early November." Next, cross out *very*, an overused intensifier that adds little to the meaning. Then take out *try to*, which repeats the idea of "to attempt." The sentence now is as follows:

> When the water is high in early November, attempting to cross the river at the Van Buren Bridge is a hazardous danger.

Although the sentence is much improved, it still has some extra words. Since the idea of "danger" is repeated in the two words *hazardous* and *danger*, one of these can be eliminated. *Attempting* can also be taken out, since the dangerous part is really the crossing. The final sentence is as follows:

> When the water is high in early November, crossing the river at the Van Buren Bridge is hazardous.

Notice that the sentence has been cut from thirty-one to seventeen words without interfering with the basic message being communicated.

When you are trying to tighten sentences in your own writing, look particularly for expressions and ideas that can be said in fewer words. Consider the following list. The phrases in the left-hand column can easily be replaced by the words in the right-hand column, which communicate the same idea in fewer words.

as anyone can see	clearly
at this point in time	now
heavy in weight	heavy
knelt on his knees	knelt
the week when exams are given	exam week
students who are in their last year of high school	seniors
a house that no one lives in anymore	an abandoned house
at the present time	presently
in our contemporary world of today	today
the ultimate conclusion	the conclusion
a customary habit	a habit (or a custom)
final results	the results
on account of the fact that	because
orange in color	orange
the city of Portland	Portland
shuttle back and forth	shuttle
new innovation	innovation

personal friend	friend
make contact with	meet
due to the fact that	because
advance planning	planning
set of twins	twins
share in common	share

P R A C T I C E   2 0 A

Being Concise

DIRECTIONS: Read the following paragraph, which is a wordy summary of a city council meeting. Copy the paragraph, eliminating unnecessary repetition of words and ideas. Refer to this chapter's list of wordy phrases to help you avoid wordiness. Check your work carefully.

Minutes of the Lake Santoro City Council Meeting

(1) The weekly meeting of the Lake Santoro City Council for last week was held last Tuesday evening at 7:30 P.M. (2) The most important principal issue that was discussed was the increasing popularity of local adult bookstores and theaters that were flourishing on account of the fact that more and more people were making these businesses popular. (3) The ultimate decision that was reached was to rezone those bookstores and theaters that were open for people who were interested in adult books and films and to move those bookstores and theaters to the district downtown where most businesses are located in the downtown area. (4) Almost all of the members who sit on the city council, however, were encouraged and heartened because of the fact that many citizens of the city arrived at the meeting and came to protest the number of adult bookstores and theaters that were growing and increasing day to day from Sunday through Saturday daily in the city of Lake Santoro. (5) Another issue that was discussed and talked about was the acceptance and welcoming of cable television companies to the city. (6) In spite of the fact that some of the members who are on the council wanted to allow cable television companies in the city by accepting such companies to organize in Lake Santoro, most of the other members did not like the idea and rejected the proposal for cable television. (7) The presiding vice-mayor, who

conducted the meeting, seemed to know parliamentary rules and regulations very well, and all of the members of the city council seemed to present important ideas and offer good input in the several fiery discussions about controversial subjects that are of debatable nature.

P R A C T I C E   2 0 B

Being Concise

DIRECTIONS: Read the following paragraph, which is a wordy discussion of the concerns of American big business. Copy the paragraph, eliminating unnecessary repetition of words and ideas. Refer to this chapter's list of wordy phrases to help you avoid wordiness. Check your work carefully.

The Bureaucratic Man

(1) Approximately two decades or about twenty years ago, William H. Whyte, Jr., wrote *The Organization Man*, in which he painted and depicted a rather gloomy, sad picture of how large organizations were affecting people's lives and how established associations were making an impact on the life-styles of many persons. (2) Americans have long followed and been guided by what has been called and referred to as the Protestant ethic—the philosophy, idea, and concept that hard work and competition are the ingredients for happiness and success. (3) This philosophy stresses the importance of the person or individual, rather than and instead of the group. (4) According to Whyte, a new philosophy, or way of life, is developing and is forming as a result and consequence of the rapid growth of big business. (5) At this point in time, the young person who is barely an adult looking for a job and trying to find employment believes that to make a living he or she must follow the orders of others and that, in order to survive, he or she must do what somebody else says to do. (6) The person learns to become less of an individual and more of a member of the group. (7) Therefore, creativity is disappearing and becoming increasingly less visible. (8) Instead, the individual or person becomes and begins to be an "organization man." (9) Thus and therefore, this organization man believes wholeheartedly and completely in the belongingness and

togetherness of the group. (10) The organization man, therefore, is an individual who imitates and tries to be like other organization men. (11) In fact, he comes to the ultimate conclusion that his personal and individual goals should be identically the same as the goals of the organization. (12) As anyone can see, people do not reject the system or go against it in any way; they cooperate with it. (13) Furthermore, the individual has so much faith and such a strong belief in the organization that he or she sees any problems, conflicts, and obstacles at the place of employment and job as his or her fault, not the company's. (14) Although Whyte presented and discussed his views and opinions of the organization man over and beyond twenty years ago, people still question America's worship of big business and people's reverence for large companies in the United States. (15) In fact, the individual in America in this contemporary world of today is affected and influenced by big businesses and large corporations more at the present time than he or she was twenty years ago when *The Organization Man* was written.

P R A C T I C E   2 0 C

Being Concise

DIRECTIONS: Read the following paragraph, which is a wordy discussion of social movement in the United States. Copy the paragraph, eliminating unnecessary repetition of words and ideas. Refer to this chapter's list of wordy phrases to help you avoid wordiness. Check your work carefully.

For and Against Abortion

(1) Social change, or change in society, is seldom and rarely rapid and quick, nor does social change happen overnight. (2) In addition, the effects of social change are seldom powerful and hard hitting. (3) In fact, changes in society develop and come about slowly and gradually over a long period of time. (4) An example of changes that are made in society involves and concentrates on the issue of abortion. (5) During the middle sixties about 1966, people believed and strongly felt that abortion should be legalized and not be considered illegal. (6) Pamphlets to citizens, letters to senators, and articles in newspapers and magazines made people aware of the issue and caught the attention of the public concerning the topic of abortion. (7) By early 1972, barely at the beginning of the decade of the seventies, sixteen states and the District of Columbia had changed their antiabortion laws and passed laws that legalized abortion and that no longer made abortion an illegal crime. (8) Then twelve months later, one year had passed, and in 1973 the U.S. Supreme Court overruled all state laws that prohibited or restricted women from having abortions during the first three months of pregnancy, and the Supreme Court allowed women three months pregnant to have an abortion legally in any state. (9) Disagreeing with the Supreme Court's action, people who were against abortion objected to the law. (10) These people began meeting together and uniting to form and establish groups such as "Right to Life." (11) These groups grew in strength and gained so much power and political clout that they were significant and important in the election and defeat of certain candidates for office in the late 1970's. (12) Whether this antiabortion movement will be forcefully powerful is doubtful and uncertain; however, if the strong reaction and feelings of the antiabortionists continue, the movement against abortion is not likely to be short-lived, nor will it have a quick death.

O N   Y O U R   O W N

Ideas for Guided and Open Writing

GUIDED WRITING EXERCISE: Whether or not foreign language should be a requirement in high schools and universities is a continuing problem. A large percentage of the American population cannot speak a foreign language very well, if at all. People from other countries often criticize Americans for not having an interest in learning another language. Americans, they say, expect everyone to learn English. As a result, these people from other countries believe that many Americans are egotistical about their own language and their country. What are the advantages or disadvantages of learning a foreign language? In a well-developed paragraph of approximately 100–150 words, discuss why Americans should or should not be required to learn a foreign language at some time during their years in high school or college. You might begin your paragraph with the following sentence: "Foreign language should (or should not) be a high school or college requirement for most Americans." Use any example(s) from your own experience or the experience of others to support your point. Avoid wordiness.

OPEN WRITING IDEAS: The following topics are suggestions for open writing exercises to help you practice the structures presented in this chapter. Develop these ideas into paragraphs of 100–150 words. Focus your attention on avoiding wordiness.

1. You are a bartender about to be interviewed on a local talk show about the typical customers who frequently come to your bar. Compare two types of customers you consider most interesting or unusual. Mention the kinds of drinks they order, their occupations, life-styles, dreams, and usual topics of discussion.

2. Chess, backgammon, and Scrabble are board games that are becoming popular once again. In fact, people who play these games have successfully started regional and national tournaments. Why do people play these games? Do these games offer anything more than entertainment? Do people learn anything from playing these games?

UNIT C REVIEW

Writing for a Specific Audience

DIRECTIONS: Read the following paragraph. It contains problems with point of view, tone, usage, trite language, and wordiness. Copy the paragraph, editing each sentence to eliminate these errors. Each sentence contains two types of errors studied in this unit. Check your work carefully.

Symbiosis in the Desert

(1) In the deserts of Arizona lays one of the clearest examples of *symbiosis*, a relationship in which two different organisms depend upon each other to live. (2) There, would you believe, is found the unique, one-of-a-kind relationship between the brown bat and the century plant. (3) The brown bat is known for it's long tongue and for its annual migrations between Arizona and the country of Mexico. (4) While in Arizona, these bats have one main primary food source: the century plant. (5) The century plant isn't really liked by most of your average desert animals. (6) In fact, the century plant's long, spiny, thick, fleshy leaves work like a charm to protect the plant against enemies and predators that are animals that want to eat the plant. (7) Another characteristic of these century plants that it blooms only once—usually when it is twenty to twenty-five years old—before it bites the dust. (8) When this kind of a plant is in full bloom, its stalk reaches a height of approximately twenty feet tall. (9) On the stalk you can see ten to twenty groups of flowers, each group consisting of a grand total of at least sixty tiny flowers. (10) Foodwise, these flowers, which bloom only at night, are the perfect attraction for the nocturnal brown bat, which runs around only at night. (11) These bats are blind, but knock on wood, they have good radar and sense of smell, so they

somehow get themselves over to the flowers. (12) The bat is drawn by the unmistakable musky odor that one would never miss that the century plant gives out, and it's love at first sight. (13) It's a trip that the brown bat knows which tiny flowers to skip over and which ones to get food off of. (14) At the same time that the brown bat is securing nourishment for itself, it helps these century plants to survive. (15) As this small mammal collects nectar from the flowery blossoms, it contacts pollen on its cerebral cortex. (16) And so, the rest of the other century plants that are left are pollinated as the little bat goes looking for something to eat. (17) Due to the fact that no other night animals consider the century plant as an integral element of their diets, the century plant relies on the brown bat for survival. (18) On the other hand, because the nocturnal century plant produces a lot of flowers, the nectar-feeding brown bat never loses a day's sleep about going hungry. (19) In a nutshell, this rare relationship between the brown bat and the century plant illustrates symbiosis in nature and the natural setting and environment on earth.

UNIT D

Incorporating the Ideas of Others

CHAPTER 21

Choosing Between Active and Passive Voice

When checking his or her work, the writer must judge the effectiveness of each sentence: Does the sentence have the effect I want it to have? Does the sentence emphasize what it should be emphasizing?

Sometimes a sentence may seem boring and poorly written. Perhaps this sentence has a problem with voice. When should a sentence be in the passive voice or in the active voice?

Active Voice

Most English sentences are written in the active voice. In active voice the subject does something to someone or something else, as in these examples:

SUBJECT	VERB	OBJECT
The boa constrictor	ate	the mouse.
Some teenagers	dislike	rock music.
Frederick	won	the pizza-eating contest.

These sentences are said to be in the active voice because the subjects of these sentences actively perform the actions of eating, disliking, and winning. Sometimes the word order is changed so that the object becomes the subject of the sentence, as in the following examples:

SUBJECT	VERB	BY PHRASE
The mouse	was eaten	by the boa constrictor.

185

SUBJECT	VERB	BY PHRASE
Rock music	is disliked	by some teenagers.
The pizza-eating contest	was won	by Frederick.

In these sentences, the subjects — the mouse, rock music, and the pizza-eating contest — are being passively acted upon by the boa constrictor, the teenagers, and Frederick. Therefore, these sentences are in the *passive* voice.

The original doers of the action are mentioned in the *by* phrase. The *by* phrase may be kept if the doer is important to the meaning of the sentence.

ACTIVE	The romantic young woman bought the four-poster bed in the window.
PASSIVE	The four-poster bed in the window was bought *by* the romantic young woman.

The active voice is natural and direct; therefore, it is used more than the passive voice. However, in certain situations the passive voice is more effective.

1. Passive voice is used when the doer of the action is unknown or unimportant. Consider the following situation: A bank has been robbed, but the robber is unknown. Which would be more appropriate — the active or the passive voice?

ACTIVE	Someone robbed the bank.
PASSIVE	The bank was robbed. (The performer of the action is unknown. The action is the important point.)

Consider this situation: John F. Kennedy was buried at Arlington National Cemetery by some unknown gravediggers. Who buried him is unimportant. Which would be more appropriate — the active or the passive voice?

ACTIVE	Some gravediggers buried John F. Kennedy at Arlington National Cemetery.
PASSIVE	John F. Kennedy is buried at Arlington National Cemetery. (Who buried him is unimportant.)

2. Passive voice is used when the writer wants to call attention to the receiver of the action.

PASSIVE	The four white rats were tested for cancer. (Who tested them is unimportant.)

PASSIVE	That china was left to me by my grandmother. (The writer wishes to emphasize the china.)
PASSIVE	Four of the five writing awards were given to University of Indiana students. (The writer is emphasizing how many writing awards were given to University of Indiana students.)

3. Passive voice is used when the speaker wishes to make a statement seem objective or impersonal. Be careful about this kind of construction; it is generally considered weak and vague.

PASSIVE	It is believed by many that the economic situation is critical.
PASSIVE	It is believed by members of the women's caucus that the bill will pass.

When changing from the active to the passive voice, remember to use a *by* phrase if who did it is important, or to leave out the *by* phrase if who did it is unimportant.

This restaurant is considered to serve authentic Mexican food.

In other situations the *by* phrase gives significant information.

This restaurant is considered *by local Mexican Americans* to serve authentic Mexican food. (In this case, the *by* phrase tells us who makes the consideration.)
Over 50,000 waterbeds were bought by the Japanese last year. (The *by* phrase tells us who bought 50,000 waterbeds.)

However, the omission of *by* phrases often creates sentences that are confusing on purpose. In these sentences, those truly responsible for an action are allowed to remain anonymous.

Seven million dollars of nuclear equipment was sold to the small underdeveloped country.

The preceding sentence is certainly much more pleasing (to President Reagan) than "President Reagan sold . . ." Thus, many times omitting the *by* phrase is done purposely in order to withhold information. Much political language avoids naming the doers of the action and therefore avoids accusing a specific person or group.

When changing from the passive to the active voice, one must keep the same tense. Study the following examples:

PASSIVE	The car *is rated* excellent by consumer advocates.
ACTIVE	Consumer advocates *rate* the car excellent.
PASSIVE	Five years ago, the car *was rated* excellent by consumer advocates.
ACTIVE	Five years ago, consumer advocates *rated* the car excellent.

An awareness of the form and effect of passive and active voices will help you improve your writing and revising. Understanding the appropriate use of the passive and active voices will help you say what you want to say in the most effective way. Although the following exercises ask you to write in the passive voice, in your own writing beware of the passive voice unless you have a definite reason for using it or wish to add variety to your sentence structure.

P R A C T I C E   2 1 A

Changing Active to Passive

DIRECTIONS: Read the following paragraph. It is written almost completely in the active voice. Copy the paragraph, changing the verbs to the passive voice. Drop the word <u>experimenters</u> when you rewrite the paragraph in the passive. Do not change sentences 1, 2, and 9. Check your work carefully.

Laboratory Report: The Ability to Avoid Certain Tastes

(1) Organisms are born with the ability to avoid substances that make them sick. (2) According to experiments done by researchers, both human and nonhuman animals can learn to avoid eating certain foods. (3) In one of these experiments, experimenters fed rats a particular food and then poisoned them. (4) Later on, the rats avoided this food and other foods tasting like it. (5) These experiments revealed two important facts: (a) The rats avoided the food when the experimenters included the poison in the food during the feeding and (b) the rats avoided the food when the experimenters gave the poison to the rats at some point after the feeding. (6) Not even severe brain damage affects

avoiding certain tastes. (7) In addition, as shown in other experiments, sights and sounds occurring at the time of the feeding do not affect the rats' avoidance of food. (8) As a result, flashing lights, buzzers, and other signals introduced with food do not influence the rats' avoidance behavior. (9) These and other observations of animal behavior may offer clues to the more complex behavior of humans.

P R A C T I C E   2 1 B

Changing Active to Passive

DIRECTIONS: Read the following paragraph. It is written almost completely in the active voice. Copy the paragraph, changing the verbs to the passive voice. Do not include the underlined words as you rewrite the paragraph. Check your work carefully.

Laboratory Report: The Ziegarnik Effect

(1) People call information remembered over long periods of time long-term memory. (2) Researchers refer to one important characteristic of long-term memory as the Ziegarnik effect, named because of the experiments of psychologist Dr. B. Ziegarnik. (3) In her experiments Ziegarnik presented the subjects with simple problems to solve, and then Ziegarnik later asked the subjects to recall the problems in order to test long-term memory. (4) The subjects could usually solve most of these problems if the experimenter gave them enough time. (5) However, during the experiment Dr. Ziegarnik interrupted the subjects before they had completed the task. (6) Later she asked the subjects to recall as many of the problems as possible. (7) Until this experiment most researchers believed that the subjects would remember the completed problems better than the uncompleted problems since the subjects had spent more time on the finished problems. (8) However, Ziegarnik found the opposite to be true; subjects usually remember the incomplete problems better than the completed problems. (9) Thus, psychologists consider the Ziegarnik effect important because it reveals the human tendency to recall interrupted activities.

PRACTICE 21C

Changing Passive to Active

DIRECTIONS: Read the following passage. It is written almost completely in the passive voice. Copy the paragraph, changing the verbs to the active voice. Do not change sentences 2, 4, and 10. Check your work carefully.

Buzkashi: The National Sport of Afghanistan

(1) Across the rough, barren land of Afghanistan, *buzkashi*, one of the most rugged, exciting, and treacherous games in the world, is played by horsemen called *chapandaz*. (2) The game is similar to a combination of football and polo, except that *buzkashi* is played with the beheaded and disemboweled carcass of a goat, sheep, or calf weighing up to 128 pounds. (3) Control of the carcass is sought by the *chapandaz*, much as control of the ball is sought by football players. (4) The carcass is placed in a shallow ditch in the middle of an enormous field, sometimes up to several miles in length. (5) It is then grabbed by a team member on horseback and carried across the field. (6) The carcass must be taken by the player to the end of the field, around a flag, and, finally, back to the center of the field for a score of three points. (7) Since the heavy carcass must be carried by the *chapandaz* such long distances, an extraordinary amount of strength and endurance is needed by these players. (8) In addition, a tremendous amount of skill and coordination are possessed by the *chapandaz*. (9) Many years of training are required by this fast and dangerous sport. (10) In addition, many players are hit, whipped, and knocked off their horses by other *chapandaz* anxiously pushing their way to the goal. (11) Not surprisingly, men trying to pick up the carcass are frequently killed by stampeding players on horseback. (12) Of course, the audience is excited by the fast pace and danger of *buzkashi*. (13) This action-packed game is rightfully claimed by Afghanistan, a strong nation of hearty, independent people, as its national sport.

P R A C T I C E   2 1 D

Changing Passive to Active

DIRECTIONS: Read the following paragraph. It is written almost completely in the passive voice. Copy the paragraph, changing the verbs to the active voice. Do not change sentence 8. Check your work carefully.

Poorly Designed Tools

(1) Most tools have not been designed by manufacturers with the user in mind. (2) For years concern has been expressed by orthopedic surgeons about health problems caused by poorly designed tools. (3) Stress, fatigue, and discomfort to muscles and tendons have been caused by the continued use of most everyday tools. (4) A particularly good example of a poorly designed tool is the typewriter. (5) The letters *E, T, O, N, A, D, R, I,* and *S* are used by typists more frequently than any other letters; however, most of the keys for these letters are placed by manufacturers on the left side of the keyboard. (6) As a result, an unnecessary amount of stress and fatigue is experienced by most typists, who are right-handed. (7) In addition, the weak, often inflexible little finger is required by the present keyboard to capitalize. (8) The little finger is also required by the present design of the typewriter to reach the numbers. (9) Because of these inconveniences to typists, new keyboard arrangements have been designed by inventors and manufacturers. (10) In fact, these new models have been successfully tested by typists. (11) Strain and muscle fatigue have been greatly reduced by the new typewriter designs. (12) However, no major efforts to promote these new typewriter models have been made by manufacturers. (13) A complete change of manufacturing procedures would be required by a new typewriter design, and this change is considered by business experts to be a financial risk. (14) Until the manufacturers are pressured by the workers themselves, the traditional models of typewriters will be used by everyone.

P R A C T I C E   2 1 E

Changing Passive to Active

DIRECTIONS: Read the following paragraph, which is part of a live football broadcast. It is written almost completely in present progressive tense of the passive voice. Copy the paragraph, changing the underlined verbs to active voice. Begin copying the paragraph with sentence 3. Your first sentence should read "The referee is starting the clock, and the fans are cheering the players on." Check your work carefully.

An Upset Victory

(1) It is the final quarter with four seconds remaining in the Jacksonville Sharks-Omaha Lancers game with the Lancers on the Sharks' thirty-seven-yard line. (2) It is fourth down and eight yards to go, and the teams are lining up. (3) The clock is being started by the referee, and the players are being cheered on by the fans. (4) On the sideline, Lancer defensive tackle John Reisling is being treated by the team trainer for minor injuries from the last play. (5) Meanwhile, back on the field, the ball is being snapped by the center to quarterback Royce Fonken. (6) Fonken, who is back to pass, is being protected by the Lancer line. (7) Still, Fonken is being heavily pursued by the blitzing Shark linebackers. (8) He manages to evade one tackle, but more men are being sent by the Sharks than the Lancers can block. (9) The ball is now being passed by Fonken, but he is immediately crushed. (10) The quarterback is down, but the high, lofty pass is being received by wide receiver Dave "Ham" Ricker. (11) The pass is being taken by Ricker on the nine-yard line, and he sprints into the end zone for a score. (12) Meanwhile, the quarterback Fonken appears shaken up on the play; he is being assisted off the field by team trainers. (13) Fonken reaches the sideline, where he is being congratulated by the normally unemotional head coach Stan Tims. (14) Confetti and streamers are being thrown in the air by the hometown fans, electrified with excitement, as the Lancers pull out a last-second victory over the Jacksonville Sharks, 21–20.

P R A C T I C E 2 1 F

Changing Active to Passive

DIRECTIONS: Read the following paragraph. It is written in the active voice in the past progressive tense. Copy the paragraph, changing the verbs from the active to the passive voice. Omit the underlined words. Your first sentence should read "At the moment Pope John Paul II was shot by a Turkish terrorist in St. Peter's Basilica in Rome on May 20, 1981, a highly efficient emergency system was put into action." Check your work carefully.

The Shooting of a Pope

(1) At the moment a Turkish terrorist shot Pope John Paul II in St. Peter's Basilica in Rome on May 20, 1981, security guards put a highly efficient emergency security system into action. (2) As Pontiff aides were protecting the Pope from possible further gunshots, the Vatican police were ordering the driver of the Pope's car to "move back and forth" to make the Pope a difficult target. (3) Vatican police and Swiss Guards assigned to protect the Pope were pushing back angry and confused crowds. (4) Aides were transferring the wounded Pontiff from his car to an awaiting ambulance. (5) At the same time, Papal officials were instructing attendants to follow standard emergency procedures by taking the Pope to Gemilli Hospital. (6) Meanwhile, at St. Peter's Square, officials were supervising the furious crowds. (7) Vatican police were treating two American women injured by the spray of gunfire. (8) At the same time, angry people from the crowds were helping Vatican security guards chase and capture the young assassin. (9) People were offering prayers for the Pope over loudspeakers, and a large group of people from John Paul's native country were singing hymns in Polish. (10) Around the world, heads of state were joining millions of shocked, grieving people in expressing deep sorrow over the violent act. (11) Television and radio newscasters worldwide were broadcasting continuous live news coverage of the incident. (12) Religious leaders were holding special prayer services on behalf of the wounded Pope. (13) By the end of the week, as the Pope's doctors were talking optimistically about the Pontiff's recovery, people everywhere were still expressing feelings of anger and helplessness about the violence in the world.

O N   Y O U R   O W N

Ideas for Guided and Open Writing

GUIDED WRITING EXERCISE: Not long ago, calculators were considered a fun toy used only by a small group of people in our society. Now, however, most people—from engineers to teachers, from homemakers to students—use calculators. So many people own calculators, in fact, that schoolchildren have even been encouraged to solve arithmetic problems using these machines. Although mathematics is still taught in elementary schools, many administrators have started to question the need for teaching addition, subtraction, multiplication, and division tables. Some teachers are starting to allow their students to use calculators in the classroom. In a well-developed paragraph of 100–150 words, support or attack the use of calculators in the classroom. You might begin your paragraph with the following: "Teachers should (or should not) encourage their students to use calculators in the classroom." Does relying on a calculator make students lazy, or does it allow them to concentrate on other subjects? Are there any advantages to students learning how to solve problems on their own? Are students learning by using the calculator? In your paragraph pay careful attention to voice. Use active and passive carefully.

OPEN WRITING IDEAS: The following topics are suggestions for open writing exercises to help you practice the structures presented in this chapter. Develop these ideas into paragraphs of 100–150 words. Focus your attention on the proper use of the active and passive voice.

1. Of the countless amusement parks in the United States, Disneyland and Disney World are the most famous nationally and internationally. Give at least two reasons why people are fascinated by these popular amusement parks. In your paragraph, include two sentences in the passive voice.

2. Consider a particular task you can do expertly such as mounting slides, tuning an engine, tuning a guitar, quilting, making wine or beer, and so on. Briefly describe the steps involved in this process. Be sure to write all the steps in the passive voice.

CHAPTER 22

Using Reported Speech

Writing about what people say is called *reported speech*. When you do not want to repeat people's exact words, you can report what they say by changing a direct quotation to reported speech.

DIRECT QUOTATION   The patient said to her doctor, "I need help."

REPORTED SPEECH   The patient told her doctor that she needed help.

Changing direct quotation to reported speech in the preceding example includes these steps:

1. Tell who is speaking.
2. Change *said to* to *told*.
3. Remove the quotation marks.
4. Add *that* before the quotation.
5. Change *I* (first person) to *she* (third person).
6. Change present tense *need* to past tense *needed*.

Here is another example:

DIRECT QUOTATION   The policewoman said to Carlo, "I *am going* to give you a citation."

REPORTED SPEECH   The policewoman told Carlo that she *was going to give* him a citation.

Notice that the present-progressive verb *am going* changed to past progressive *was going*. All verbs in present tense in the direct quotation change to past tense in the reported speech. In the following example, notice how the verb *can go* in the direct quotation is changed to *could go* in reported speech.

DIRECT QUOTATION	The customs agent said to the traveler, "You can go through the line."
REPORTED SPEECH	The customs agent told the traveler that he could go through the line.

When a direct quotation contains a time expression such as *tomorrow, yesterday, now, then,* it must be changed in the reported speech. Consider the following examples:

DIRECT QUOTATION	Nick said, "They left for Mexico City *yesterday*."
REPORTED SPEECH	Nick said that they had left for Mexico City *the previous day*.
DIRECT QUOTATION	Ahmed said, "I will fly home *tomorrow*."
REPORTED SPEECH	Ahmed said that he would fly home *the following day*.

TIME EXPRESSIONS	
Direct Quotation	*Reported Speech*
yesterday	the previous day; the day before
tomorrow	the next day; the following day
now	then
next (day, week)	following (day, week)
tonight	that night
this (month)	that (month)
here	there

For a question, changing from direct quotation to reported speech is different. Look at the following example and steps:

DIRECT QUOTATION	The policeman asked the driver, "Do you have a driver's license?"
REPORTED SPEECH	The policeman asked the driver if she had a driver's license.

1. Tell who is speaking.

2. Add *if* or *whether* before the direct quotation. (Do this only for *yes/no* questions.)

3. Change the question to a statement.

4. Change *you* (second person) to *she* (third person).

5. Change present tense *have* to past tense *had*.

When reporting speech, you have to be very clear that you are presenting someone else's words. Try to use words other than *told*, *said*, and *asked*. Use words that represent the way the words were originally spoken, such as the following:

QUESTION	asked if, questioned, how, wondered why, inquired when, considered when
EXCLAMATION	exclaimed, shouted, ordered, commanded
AGREEMENT	agreed, verified, conceded
DISAGREEMENT	disagreed, negated, argued
DIRECT QUOTATION	The husband said to his wife, "I think you *are* right about this problem."
REPORTED SPEECH	The husband *conceded* to his wife that she was right about the problem.

In this case, the word *conceded* gives a stronger and more accurate picture than *said*.

If the direct quotation is originally in the past tense, change the direct quotation to reported speech through the use of the past perfect.

DIRECT QUOTATION	Lamenting over his poor performance, Mark said to the officer, "I *failed* the driving test once before."
REPORTED SPEECH	Lamenting over his poor performance, Mark told the officer that he *had failed* the driving test once before.

Note that if the speaker information comes at the end of the quotation, it should be moved to the beginning of the reported speech.

DIRECT QUOTATION	"Don't say it, *John*," she said.
REPORTED SPEECH	*She told John* not to say it.

There are two cases in which the verb in the reported speech remains in the present tense: when factual information is being reported or when usual action is being reported.

FACTUAL INFORMATION

DIRECT QUOTATION   Columbus said, "The world is round."

REPORTED SPEECH   Columbus said *that* the world *is* round.

(Notice that the information is a truth and it still holds true; therefore, the verb is in the present.)

USUAL ACTION

DIRECT QUOTATION   Every time Noel picks up a cigarette, Anna says, "Why *don't* you quit smoking?"

REPORTED SPEECH   Every time Noel picks up a cigarette, Anna asks him why he *doesn't* quit smoking.

(Notice that Anna's action is usual; therefore, the verb is in the present.)

DIRECT QUOTATION   Every time Richard goes to the dentist, she asks him, "*Have* you *had* any pain in your gums lately?"

REPORTED SPEECH   Every time Richard goes to the dentist, she asks him if he *has had* any pain in his gums.

(Notice that the verb remains in the same tense because the question is a usual one.)

P R A C T I C E   2 2 A

Reporting What People Say

DIRECTIONS: The following is a copy of a lecture given to a college class called "How to Improve Reading Skills." Read the introduction; then read the questions following it. Copy the paragraph, beginning with the italicized sentence. Continue your paragraph, changing the twelve questions to statements of reported speech. The second sentence in the paragraph should read, "They should ask themselves whether their eyes frequently get tired or whether they often get headaches from reading." Begin each sentence with "They should ask themselves." Check your work carefully.

**Evaluating
Reading Skills**

Studies have shown that students entering college frequently have a great deal of trouble reading material required by their courses. Many students have developed poor reading habits throughout their school years. However, students can improve their reading habits and therefore improve their performance in school. To do so, they have to be aware of their reading skills. *To check their reading skills, students should ask themselves questions about their reading habits.*

1. Do your eyes frequently get tired, or do you often get headaches from reading?
2. Do you frequently have trouble concentrating on the material because your mind wanders while you read?
3. How often do your eyes jump back to previous words on the page?
4. Have you often felt that you read too slowly?
5. Have you ever had trouble understanding the main idea of a passage?
6. Can you usually recall important facts or details from the reading?
7. Have you often had difficulty in understanding an author's tone? Can you tell whether the author is being serious, light, or sarcastic?
8. Do you have trouble seeing the difference between fact and opinion?
9. Do you often have trouble finding the author's purpose for writing?
10. Do you consistently find it hard to follow the organization and development of a passage?

P R A C T I C E   2 2 B

Reporting What People Say

DIRECTIONS: The following is a copy of part of a television interview. In a paragraph, report the conversation between the two speakers. Begin your paragraph with the italicized sentence introducing the dialog. Then continue the paragraph by changing the direct speech to reported speech. The second sentence in the paragraph should read, "In an interview, Dr. Chang told Dr. Muldow that the World Health Organization estimated that approximately one million infant deaths a year worldwide were caused by the use of baby formula." Check your work carefully.

The Infant Formula Controversy

Dr. Lenore Muldow, a renowned pediatrician in child nutrition, and Professor Lee Chang, current Director of World Health at the World Bank, discuss the problems of using infant formulas in nonindustralized countries.

DR. CHANG

"Dr. Muldow, the World Health Organization estimates that approximately 1 million infant deaths a year worldwide are caused by the use of baby formula. In your recent travels, did you see any evidence of illness or death caused by the use of infant formula?"

DR. MULDOW

"Yes, in each country I visited, I witnessed many infant deaths that I diagnosed as being directly related to infant formula. I also saw and treated hundreds of cases of illnesses and malnutrition resulting from its use."

DR. CHANG

"The manufacturers of commercial formulas state that their baby formulas are safe and nutritious. In fact, their formulas have to pass strict USDA tests. If this is true, Dr. Muldow, then what has caused the large number of deaths and illnesses?

DR. MULDOW

"I am not questioning the nutritional value of infant formulas. In fact, women have bottle-fed their babies safely for years in many countries. The problem with infant formulas is that they are used in severely poor, nonindustrialized countries, where poor sanitation is one of the leading causes of death. Another problem is that 98–99 percent of the people in these countries cannot read; therefore, they don't know how to use baby formulas correctly."

DR. CHANG

"Are you saying that infants are dying from poor sanitation rather than from the formula itself?"

DR. MULDOW

"Yes, that's true. Mothers are mixing bottle formulas with contaminated water and then

giving this mixture to their babies in
unsterilized, frequently filthy bottles."

DR. CHANG

"Dr. Muldow, what, then, are your
recommendations to the President's Council
on World Health?"

DR. MULDOW

"Quite simply, it is my firm conviction that the
safest, most economical way to feed infants in
Third World countries is to breast-feed them."

P R A C T I C E   2 2 C

Reporting What People Say

DIRECTIONS: The following paragraph contains direct quotations.
Copy the paragraph, changing the words within quotation marks to
reported speech. Check your work carefully.

**Greetings from
Afghanistan**

(1) Typical everyday greetings among the people of Afghanistan,
whether between businessmen, strangers, close friends, or family
members are usually very long and elaborate. (2) In the United States,
of course, one simply says, "How are you?" (3) At that point, a simple,
positive answer is given in return, and the conversation usually
continues with one of the persons saying to the other, "What have you
been up to lately?" (4) Or, one of the persons will say, "Where have you
been lately?", opening up a discussion of recent events or activities in
each person's life. (5) In Afghanistan, however, changing the subject
from a person's health to another topic so quickly would usually be
considered rude and insensitive. (6) Instead, the questions about the
other person's health are repeated until neither speaker has any doubt
that everything is well with the other person. (7) For example, if a man
meets a distant female relative, he might ask her, "How are you?"
(8) She typically answers, "I'm fine, thank you." (9) She then might say
to him, "Are you well? Is your health good? Is everything all right at
home?" (10) He usually responds by saying, "I'm fine, thanks to God."
(11) He then usually continues by asking, "Are you in good health? Are
you really well? Is your family well? Are your children well?" (12) These

questions continue between the speakers until they have asked the questions in as many ways as possible. (13) Unlike American greetings, Afghan greetings focus mainly on the person's health and that of his or her family and children. (14) These lengthy greetings represent the hospitality and warmth of the Afghan people.

O N   Y O U R   O W N

Ideas for Guided and Open Writing

GUIDED WRITING EXERCISE: As people grow up, they often hear proverbs and sayings in response to some of their actions or behaviors. Some of these sayings are "Beggars can't be choosers," "The squeaky wheel gets the grease," "The early bird catches the worm," and "Every dark cloud has a silver lining." A popular magazine is searching for brief stories that tell how proverbs have been important in people's lives. This magazine has asked you to write a short paragraph about one instance in your past when you were reminded of a particular proverb. Develop your paragraph into 100–150 words. You might begin with the following: "Although the proverb '——' has existed for countless years, it still holds true today." As you write, briefly describe the incident. Report what the people involved had to say to you. Tell what your responses were. Use reported speech to describe conversations.

OPEN WRITING IDEAS: The following topics are suggestions for open writing exercises to help you practice the structures presented in this chapter. Develop these ideas into paragraphs of 100–150 words. Focus your attention on reporting all speech appropriately.

1. Many times when people think of a particular conversation they have had, they wish they had said something that they did not say. Think of a recent discussion you have had with a friend, relative, teacher, or businessperson, which you would have liked to have changed or added to. Describe the incident, as you wish it had occurred, reporting all important speech.

2. Gadgets such as scissors for left-handed people, staple removers, potato mashers, television remote-controls, automatic egg scramblers, doggie doors, and the like are simple devices designed to make everyday life easy. Although these and other gadgets are popular, people seldom think about the inventors of these devices. Assume that you have just seen a television interview with one of these inventors. Describe the content of that interview.

CHAPTER 23

Using Direct Quotations

When you want to report the words of a speaker exactly as they were spoken, use direct quotation. The following are examples of direct quotations:

SPEAKER INFORMATION BEFORE THE QUOTATION	Dale said, "The congressman will be able to see you in a moment."
QUOTATION INTERRUPTED BY SPEAKER INFORMATION	"The congressman," Dale said, "will be able to see you in a moment."
SPEAKER INFORMATION AFTER THE QUOTATION	"The congressman will be able to see you in a moment," Dale said.

Study these examples, and notice the following aspects about the punctuation and capitalization.

The first word of a direct quotation begins with a capital letter, whether the quotation comes at the beginning of the sentence or the end.

When the quotation is broken into two parts, as in the second example, two sets of quotation marks are used. Do not capitalize the first word of the second set of quotation marks.

Commas and periods come before final quotation marks.

The quotations are separated from *Dale said* with a comma or a pair of commas.

Question marks and exclamation marks can come before or after quotation marks. When the quotation is itself a question or an exclamation, the question mark or the exclamation mark comes before the final quotation marks.

"Do you believe a solution to this problem exists?" a reporter asked the politician.

"Stop that incessant mumbling!" commanded Ms. Bilby.

The young marketing representative happily exclaimed, "I sold my first computer today!"

However, when the question mark or exclamation mark punctuates the whole sentence, not just the quotation, the punctuation comes after the final quotation mark.

Who said, "Success is a journey not a destination"?

I can't believe she said, "You won"!

Suppose the person you are quoting says more than one sentence. If the two quoted sentences come together, use only one set of quotation marks.

"Don't forget what I told you. I'll be here if you need me," Susan assured her friend.

However, if the two quoted sentences are interrupted, each of the sentences should be enclosed in quotation marks.

"The fire is nearly under control," the fire chief reported. "Everyone is out of the building, and the fire has been contained to one room."

"How did you get into this building?" questioned the guard. "Do you have a building pass?"

When you report actual speech, remember to start a new paragraph each time the speaker changes.

"Do you believe in UFO's?" asked Robert.

"Yes, I guess I do. I can't believe we're the only civilization in the universe," answered Vicki.

Robert shrugged his shoulders and said, "You're probably right although, I hope I don't live to see any little green people!"

When you quote the actual words of a speaker inside of another direct quotation, use single quotation marks.

"I heard that President Reagan joked, 'I'd rather be in Philadelphia' after he had been shot," said Jenny.

Quotation marks are also used to indicate the titles of short stories, magazine and newspaper articles, essays, chapters of books, short poems, songs, and television and radio programs.

TITLES OF ARTICLES	"Know Your Children" by Benjamin Spock
TITLES OF SHORT STORIES	"The Lottery" by Shirley Jackson
TITLES OF POEMS	"The Raven" by Edgar Allan Poe
TITLES OF SONGS	"The Star-Spangled Banner" by Francis Scott Key
TITLES OF TV AND RADIO PROGRAMS	"The Johnny Carson Show" "The Top Forty Countdown"

Many times you may not want to use all the words of a speaker; you can keep the exact ones that you want by changing the direct quotation to reported speech and quoting only the word or words that are most significant.

DIRECT QUOTATION	The officer said, "This six-car accident is the most tragic one I have ever seen."

If you want to preserve only the main idea of the statement, you might report it in this way:

The officer commented that the six-car accident was the most "tragic" he had seen.

Here is another example of reported speech that preserves only the main point of the direct quotation:

DIRECT QUOTATION	Professor Sigworth said, "In the U.S.A. television is producing a society of dimwits who allow themselves to be controlled by the attitudes, opinions, and trends promoted on television."
REPORTED SPEECH	Talking about the effect television has on people, Professor Sigworth noted that the United States is turning into a "society of dimwits."

P R A C T I C E   2 3 A

Using Quotation Marks Correctly

DIRECTIONS: The following account is written in reported speech. Copy the paragraph, changing the reported speech to direct quotations. Begin the paragraph with sentence 4, which should read: "He began the interview by asking Ms. Justin, 'Did you witness the actual robbery?' " Check your work carefully.

Robbery Investigation

(1) Officer Richard Maxwell filed a report about the recent attempted bank robbery at the National Bank. (2) He interviewed both Ms. Justin, the branch manager, and a key witness named David Cano, who had been the only customer in the bank at the time of the attempted robbery. (3) Officer Maxwell arrived on the scene only minutes after the robbery attempt. (4) He began the interview by asking Ms. Justin whether she had witnessed the actual robbery. (5) Ms. Justin replied she had not. (6) She said she had been at the drive-in service window supervising a new teller at that time. (7) Officer Maxwell then asked her if she had been aware a robbery was going on at that time. (8) Ms. Justin answered that she had had no way of knowing it because she had been behind a soundproof partition. (9) Officer Maxwell then turned to Mr. Cano, who had been making a deposit as the attempted robbery took place. (10) The officer asked Mr. Cano to tell him all he remembered from the incident. (11) At that point, Mr. Cano stated that he had been at a teller's booth making a deposit when a tall, thin woman wearing dark glasses came up behind him and put a gun to his back. (12) Mr. Cano continued, saying it had taken him a few minutes to realize what was going on. (13) Then the woman had told him not to move and not to say a word. (14) Mr. Cano went on to say that the woman had told the teller to empty the drawer into a bag and to give it to her. (15) Just then, Mr. Cano continued, Ms. Justin had come from the service window, walked up behind the teller, and ordered him to take his lunch. (16) Mr. Cano then said that the tall woman standing behind him gave a sigh of disgust and ran out of the building as quickly as she could.

P R A C T I C E   2 3 B

Using Quotation Marks Correctly

DIRECTIONS: The conversation that takes place in the following interview is in reported speech. Copy the paragraph, changing the reported speech to direct quotations. Begin the paragraph with sentence 3, which should read: "At the beginning of the interview, Mariana shook hands with Mr. Perry and said, 'Hi, my name is Mariana Davis, and I want to thank you for taking the time to talk with me last week.' " Check your work carefully.

Interviewing for a Job

(1) Mariana Davis recently interviewed for a position as the Volunteer Coordinator for Public Services at St. Philip's Hospital. (2) She spoke with Mr. Harrold Perry, the supervisor for the Public Services Program at the hospital. (3) At the beginning of the interview, she shook hands with Mr. Perry, introduced herself and thanked him for having taken the time to talk with her by phone the previous week. (4) Mr. Perry said that he was impressed by her resume and especially by the amount of volunteer work she had done. (5) He then asked her if she had had a chance to read the material he had mailed her. (6) Mariana Davis said that she had finished reading the material and had a few questions to ask him. (7) First, she said, she was wondering whether the duties of the volunteer coordinator included writing the newsletter. (8) Mr. Perry responded that he didn't think so; however, the coordinator might have to be responsible for it at some point in the future. (9) He asked her if she had ever had any editing experience. (10) Mariana said that she had worked on the college newspaper as an assistant editor. (11) Then she asked him if he could tell her something about the vacation schedule. (12) He told her that she could take a total of two full weeks of paid vacation during the first year, but that she would have to arrange the dates during the summer and the fall. (13) Mariana then asked him whether she would be getting full insurance coverage. (14) Mr. Perry told her that she would be fully covered by the office group policy. (15) Mariana thanked him once again for his time, shook his hand, and asked when she would be told of his decision. (16) He said that he would phone her by the beginning of the following week.

P R A C T I C E   2 3 C

Using Quotation Marks Correctly

DIRECTIONS: The following paragraph is written in reported speech. Copy the paragraph, changing the reported speech to direct quotations. Check your work carefully.

A Minister's View

(1) In a recent talk show, the Reverend Stephen Mather, a Presbyterian minister, was interviewed by Ms. Leyla Trasoff. (2) Ms. Trasoff said that she would like to know what, in his opinion, was the major mood of society. (3) Reverend Mather responded by saying he believed that people continue to feel frustrated and anxious because of doubts and questions about the future. (4) Reverend Mather went on to explain that people were worried about the troubled economy, the possibility of nuclear war, crime, and pollution. (5) However, he said, people were becoming more optimistic. (6) Ms. Trasoff then asked him to identify the major problem in society. (7) Our society, he responded, is unfortunately still very self-centered. (8) He continued by saying that people too frequently considered others in the same way that they think of supermarket products—that is, the products either measure up or people change brands. (9) Reverend Mather then stated that Simon and Garfunkel had explained it well in an old song that went, "I like to sleep with the window open, you like to sleep with it closed—so good-bye, good-bye, good-bye." (10) Ms. Trasoff asked him what he saw as the attempts by the Church to help change people's focus. (11) Reverend Mather responded by saying that the Church had been trying to redirect attention toward service to others. (12) In closing, he also stated that the happiest people he knew were those who concentrated less on their own problems and more on the needs of others. (13) Ms. Trasoff thanked him for his time and thanked him for sharing his opinions.

O N   Y O U R   O W N

Ideas for Guided and Open Writing

GUIDED WRITING EXERCISE: Many people were treated with home remedies for common sicknesses as they were growing up. Spearmint tea for stomachaches, honey and lemon juice for coughs, and warm olive oil for earaches were among the home cures that existed in the past and still exist today. Senior citizens, including grandmothers, grandfathers, aunts, uncles, mother, fathers, and neighbors, are all rich resources of information about these home remedies, since they often had to be their own doctors. Do you remember any of these remedies or know anyone who would? Interview an older person and ask him or her about three of the most interesting, effective, or unusual cures he or she remembers. In a well-developed paragraph of approximately 100–150 words, write down your conversation with that person, using direct quotation. You might begin your paragraph with the following: "When I asked —— what his (or her) three favorite home remedies were, he (or she) replied, '——.'" Ask your interviewee how the remedies worked and why he or she liked them. Use different words to introduce the quotation. Vary the location of the speaker information: sometimes before the introduction, sometimes interrupting the quotation, and sometimes after the quotation.

OPEN WRITING IDEAS: The following topics are suggestions for open writing exercises to help you practice the structures presented in this chapter. Develop these ideas into paragraphs of 100–150 words. Focus your attention on reporting direct speech.

1. Think of one brand of particular product, such as cold medicine, chewing gum, shampoo, candy bars, aspirin, makeup, beer, motor oil, and so on. Ask three people who use that product why they like it. Ask them about the qualities and effectiveness of the product. Use direct quotations from these people.

2. Each year during the Christmas season thousands of shoppers invade stores and shopping malls to do their Christmas shopping. A familiar sight at these malls is Santa Clauses talking with children. Contrast the dialogs Santa Clauses have with children today with the dialogs they had with children twenty years ago. In your contrast, quote typical statements that the Santas and the children would make to each other.

CHAPTER 24

Using Reported Speech and Direct Quotations to Support Ideas

One of the most important writing tasks that students are asked to do is to support their ideas. Referring to experts and citing their opinions, research findings, and conclusions is an effective way to build strong supports. However, students often have a difficult time using the ideas of others to support their own ideas. Students may lack the skill and the practice necessary to carry out this task.

One way of using the ideas of others is through paraphrasing and summary. Learning to change direct speech to reported speech is a first step toward paraphrasing and summarizing. For example, if you are writing a paper about the treatment of the Jews during the Second World War, you might read a whole article written by a survivor of one of the concentration camps. Because you cannot include the entire article in your paper, you would *summarize* the entire article, or take only the significant facts and put them into your own words.

However, an even more useful skill is *paraphrasing*, or restating in your own words the thought or meaning expressed by someone else. In other words, you borrow an idea, opinion, interpretation, or statement from an expert and then rewrite it in your own language. Of course, you must give credit to the author by telling whose idea, opinion, interpretation, or statement it is. The following is an excerpt from *Anne Frank: The Diary of a Young Girl*:

> "Who has inflicted this upon us? Who has made us Jews different from all other people? Who has allowed us to suffer so terribly up till now?"

Although you want to use the information, you may not want to use her exact words. Therefore, you would change the direct quota-

tion to reported speech, being careful to change the author's original words into your own. Then you would incorporate the following
paraphrase into your paper:

> In her *Diary of a Young Girl*, Anne Frank repeatedly wonders
> what being has caused the Jewish nation among all groups of
> people to experience such extreme misery, pain, and sorrow.[4]

Notice that the ideas of the speaker have been kept, but her
words have been changed completely. Also note that the writer
acknowledges where the material comes from and footnotes the
paraphrase. The writer cannot be accused of *plagiarism*, which is
the unacceptable copying of another writer's words and ideas. Here
is an example of another student's attempt at paraphrasing. Unfortunately, the student has plagiarized Anne Frank's words.

> **PLAGIARISM**   In her diary, Anne Frank asked repeatedly
> who has inflicted that upon them and who
> had made the Jews so different from all
> other people. She asked who allowed Jews to
> suffer so badly.[4]

In this paraphrase the student uses some of Anne Frank's words
and phrases and clauses exactly, such as "inflicted," "who had
made the Jews so different from all other people," and "who has
allowed . . . to suffer . . ."

It is important to remember that another author's ideas, opinions, or words are his or her property protected by law. In order to
avoid plagiarism, follow these rules:

1. Tell whose ideas or words you are using in your paper. Introduce
the quotation or paraphrase by giving the name of the expert who
said it.

> *According to Dr. Victoria Vazquez, an eminent sociologist*, the fate
> of the world depends on "the conscious development and use of
> nuclear and solar energy."[2]

2. Put all quotations in quotation marks.

3. When you paraphrase, change the original words of speakers
into your own words.

4. Provide a footnote for each borrowed quotation or paraphrase.

**Introducing
Borrowed
Material**

When introducing short quotations and paraphrases, do not overuse a standard phrase such as "Dr. Ernesto Cruz says." Instead, change the way you introduce quotations as shown in the following list:

Ms. Hansing insists that . . .

Dr. Washington believes that . . .

Margaret Mead holds that . . .

According to Professor Yoshino, . . .

Dr. David Thomson stipulates . . .

Reverend Thweatt states . . .

The decline of literacy, according to Professor Rosaldo, is . . .

The National Rifle Association contends that . . .

The Society for the Prevention of Cruelty to Animals argues that . . .

**Combining
Paraphrase
and Quotation**

In some situations you may want to paraphrase some portion of a source and keep other parts of it in direct quotation. You may want to keep those words that are an especially important piece of information that shows the expert's opinion. The following quotation is taken from the writings of Professor Guy Lefrancois, an eminent psychologist:

> "The newborn infant has a simple, undeveloped personality, *consisting solely of the primitive urges that will be a lifetime source of psychic energy.* Freud's label for the child's earliest personality is *id*. Very simply, id encompasses the instinctual urges to which humans are heir; *id* is the level of personality that contains all human motives."

Since the quote is long, a writer would probably want to paraphrase it. If the writer wanted to keep the exact words of Professor Lefrancois's statement, he or she would include those words in a direct quotation. Notice that most of the statement is paraphrased, yet some of Professor Lefrancois's words have been quoted.

> According to Professor Lefrancois, newborn babies can be characterized by little else than their ids—reflexes and instincts. In fact, "primitive urges that will be a lifetime source of psychic energy" are the only elements that constitute the psychological and personal makeup of babies.[5]

P R A C T I C E   2 4 A

Using the Ideas of Others

DIRECTIONS: The following paragraph discusses the problems that are faced by family members of the mentally ill. The paragraph can be improved by additional support. The supports that follow the paragraph contain information that will become part of the paragraph. Read through the entire paragraph and all the supports. Then copy the paragraph, incorporating the right supports for sentences 4, 7, 9, 14, and 20, respectively. Paraphrase all of the non-underlined words in the support. Keep the underlined words exactly as they are written, and put them in quotation marks. Be sure to introduce the paraphrase or quotation with complete speaker information. Check your work carefully. Use the following examples of support A as models for your work:

SUPPORT A	Dr. Raul Bujanda, a specialist in mental disorders from the National Institute of Mental Health, says, "<u>Family members experience a tremendous amount of guilt</u>." Dr. Bujanda adds, "This overwhelming burden of self-blame for the misery of their loved ones torments the family incessantly."
VERSION 1	Dr. Raul Bujanda, a psychiatrist from the National Institute of Mental Health, says, "Family members experience a tremendous amount of guilt." Dr. Bujanda adds that all of this guilt about the unhappiness of their relative makes the family suffer constantly.
VERSION 2	Dr. Raul Bujanda, a psychiatrist from the National Institute of Mental Health, says, "Family members experience a tremendous amount of guilt." Dr. Bujanda adds that the family always feels miserable because they blame themselves for the problems of their family member.

Living with the Mentally Ill

(1) The family members of mentally ill persons experience as much stress and torment as the mentally ill themselves. (2) They feel guilty because they believe that they may have contributed in some way to the person's mental illness. (3) This has been especially true for parents, who have for years been unfairly held responsible for their children's behavior and happiness. (4) (Insert support A.) (5) The family, in addition, lives with the very heavy burden of wanting and needing to help the disturbed relative. (6) When their continued efforts bring no change in the person's behavior, the family members feel that they have failed miserably. (7) (Insert support B.) (8) In most cases they are simply reacting to their own feelings of helplessness. (9) (Insert support C.) (10) Many of these families have placed the mentally ill relative in a psychiatric institution where he or she could be cared for by those trained in the field of mental health. (11) In the most severe cases of extremely violent or self-destructive individuals, placing the person in an institution has, in fact, been encouraged. (12) However, whenever possible, specialists advise keeping the mentally ill person at home with the family so that the person can have a normal, healthy, loving environment. (13) Surprisingly, a large number of such mentally ill individuals do live at home. (14) (Insert support D.) (15) Although living at home is often beneficial to the troubled person, it nevertheless creates serious difficulties and stress for the families who care for the mentally ill relative. (16) The result is that the family members live with bizarre and unreasonable behavior, which eventually hurts the family. (17) They love the relative but at the same time do not enjoy being around him or her. (18) Everyone becomes a victim. (19) The solution is to involve the entire family in the therapy. (20) (Insert support E.) (21) Most importantly, family members should be counselled in order to help them reduce their feelings of guilt.

SUPPORTS

A: Dr. Raul Bujanda, a psychiatrist from the National Institute of Mental Health, says, "Family members experience a tremendous amount of pressure, blaming themselves for the misery of their loved ones, because there is no one else to blame."

B: Dr. Amelia Preston, a psychiatrist at the Southern Illinois Mental Health Center, states, "Repeated studies of the mentally ill demonstrate that all the family members of the mentally ill person become entangled in a self-destructive web of anger and resentment as a consequence of the ongoing frustrations they feel."

C: Dr. Preston stresses, "This condition is very much a negative circular pattern of resentment, anger, and guilt, each one reinforcing the other. Feelings of helplessness encourage <u>feelings of resentment and anger, which in turn perpetuate more guilt.</u>"

D: Dr. Sherry Robinson, a clinical psychiatrist at the Quinn Psychiatric Institute, notes, "<u>Two-thirds of all seriously mentally ill individuals live with their families.</u>"

E: Dr. Ariel Ballesteros, noted family psychiatrist at the Fielding Center for Mental Health Studies, says, "Mental health professionals now agree that everyone who lives with a mentally ill person is directly affected by his or her behavior. All close relations must <u>become familiar with the needs of the disturbed individual and the best methods for handling</u> his erratic behavior."

P R A C T I C E   2 4 B

Using the Ideas of Others

DIRECTIONS: The following paragraph discusses *garbology*, the study of garbage. The paragraph can be improved by additional support. The supports that follow the paragraph contain information that will become part of the paragraph. Read through the entire paragraph and all the supports. Then copy the paragraph, incorporating the right supports for sentences 4, 6, 8, 10, and 14, respectively. Paraphrase all of the nonunderlined words in the support. Keep the underlined words exactly as they are written and put them in quotation marks. Be sure to introduce the paraphrase or quotation with complete speaker information. Check your work carefully.

Garbology: Part I

(1) "You are what you eat" is a familiar saying known to most people. (2) However, according to a University of Arizona archaeologist who created the science of "garbology." in 1973, "You are what you throw away." (3) Known as "garbologists," the scientists and students of the University of Arizona Garbage Project, headed by Dr. William Rathje, study modern household garbage. (4) (Insert support A.) (5) Like traditional archaeologists, garbologists study particular groups of people and their way of life. (6) (Insert support B.) (7) A garbologist, like other archaeologists, studies the objects of a people in order to find out about their life-style. (8) (Insert support C.) (9) Garbologists can discover information about a society more accurately by analyzing people's garbage than by directly interviewing them about their daily habits. (10) (Insert support D.) (11) Most people, for example, are embarrassed about how much they waste, so they do not always give accurate information to interviewers. (12) In addition, people frequently underestimate the amount of alcohol they drink as well as the amount of junk foods, convenience foods, and sweets they eat. (13) However, waste reveals the facts. (14) (Insert support E.)

SUPPORTS:

A: Dr. Rathje comments, "As archaeologists of contemporary garbage, or garbologists, we 'excavate' modern household refuse from our 'site' of Tucson, Arizona, before it is deposited in landfills."

B: Dr. Rathje explains, "The majority of archaeologists focus on the observation and analysis of remnants of ancient civilizations; however, we garbologists carefully examine the refuse of our contemporary civilization. Therefore, the data we collect are a little fresher than most."

C: Dr. Rathje further states, "If archaeologists could use garbage in the past to reconstruct what was going on in ancient societies, we can use today's garbage to see what's going on in our society now."

D: Rathje notes, "Data provided by traditional methods of inquiry, such as questionnaires and polls, are inaccurate." "Garbage," says Rathje, "provides quantifiable evidence of what people actually did."

E: "It's all there in the trash," says Rathje.

P R A C T I C E   2 4 C

Using the Ideas of Others

DIRECTIONS: The following paragraph discusses *garbology*, the study of garbage. The paragraph can be improved by additional support. The supports that follow the paragraph contain information that will become part of the paragraph. Read through the entire paragraph and all the supports. Then copy the paragraph, incorporating the right supports for sentences 3, 6, 8, 11, and 14, respectively. Paraphrase all of the non-underlined words in the support. Keep the underlined words exactly as they are written and put them in quotation marks. Be sure to introduce the paraphrase or quotation with complete speaker information. Check your work carefully.

Garbology:
Part II

(1) University of Arizona garbologists study the garbage of people from various income levels and neighborhoods to try to understand what products they buy and use. (2) Garbologists hope that their findings will make people aware of how wasteful they are and eventually lead them to conserve the natural resources of our country. (3) (Insert support A.) (4) After examining the garbage of over 5,000 Tucsonans, Dr. Rathje and his team have been able to discover not only the buying and eating habits of these Tucsonans but also their recycling attitudes and habits. (5) Information gathered since 1973 reveals that approximately 15 percent of the food from the households was wasted. (6) (Insert support B.) (7) He also found that more than 80 percent of food wasted is in the form of large quantities of single items such as a chunk of steak, half a can of beans, or a whole apple. (8) (Insert support C.) (9) Moreover, these figures are probably much higher in reality, according to Dr. Rathje, because they do not take into account the amount of waste that goes to pets, fireplaces, compost heaps, and garbage disposals. (10) Another shocking discovery is that Americans think they are conserving; yet, in fact, they are are recycling less today than they have in the past. (11) (Insert support D.) (12) In addition, the average Tucson household throws away 500 whole glass bottles each year, and each of these bottles could have been either reused or recycled for making other bottles. (13) Very little recycling is done in any neighborhood. (14) (Insert support E.) (15) Therefore, analyzing people's garbage reveals much about what people buy, use, and waste, and this information should help motivate people to conserve resources in the future.

SUPPORTS

A: According to Dr. Peter Farrar, director of the Resource and Conservation Institute in Houston, "In addition to providing information about resource conservation, Dr. Rathje and the garbologists at the University of Arizona have provided scientific researchers with a superior means of investigating the haunting problems of disposing of nuclear waste and nonrecyclable products."

B: According to Dr. Rathje, "This means that Tucsonans waste more than 9,500 tons of food a year. The amount of food discarded in primarily middle-income neighborhoods may soar to figures as high as 20 percent of the total food purchased."

C: One garbologist stated, "If the figures we have found for Tucson are indicative of the overall food waste found in our society as a whole, then a nation that has as many people in it as Egypt or Canada could live on the amount of food thrown away annually in the United States."

D: "Today only 19 percent of all paper is recycled, which is a sharp contrast to the 35 percent that was recycled during World War II," according to Dr. Rathje.

E: Dr. Rathje comments, "Although more low-income families recycle aluminum cans than the average middle-income families, garbage pickup for low-income families still contains twice as many aluminum cans as middle-income pickups. Most people are untruthful about the extent to which they participate in recycling programs."

P R A C T I C E 2 4 D

Using the Ideas of Others

DIRECTIONS: The following paragraph discusses *dendrochronology*, the study of the growth of rings in trees. The paragraph can be improved by additional support. The supports that follow the paragraph contain information that will become part of the paragraph. Read through the entire paragraph and all the supports. Then copy the paragraph, incorporating the right supports for sentences 6, 8, 11, and 13, respectively. Paraphrase all of the non-underlined words in the support. Keep the underlined words exactly as they are written and put them in quotation marks. Be sure to introduce the paraphrase or quotation with complete speaker information. Check your work carefully.

Dendrochronology: Insights from Tree Rings

(1) Dendrochronology, the formal study of the growth rings in trees, was first established as a science in 1901. (2) Since that time, tree-ring research has provided much useful information about climate changes over hundreds of years, glacier formation and movement, and animal and plant life changes within entire regions. (3) In addition, growth rings give clues to dendrochronologists about man's past, present, and future impact on the environment. (4) These rings, which reveal so much about the environment, are directly affected by it. (5) Climate plays an especially important part in the growth and formation of these tree rings. (6) (Insert appropriate support.) (7) In fact, the use of these tree rings to learn about past climates has been the most significant area of dendrochronology in recent years. (8) (Insert appropriate support.) (9) Other important information that dendrochronology provides is about the amount of industrial pollution in a given period of time. (10) The amount of trace elements such as zinc, copper, mercury, and lead and the width of the growth rings show the amount of industrial pollution in a given year. (11) (Insert appropriate support.) (12) In addition, much information about the sun has been gathered through tree-ring research. (13) (Insert appropriate support.) (14) Tree-ring research continues to make important contributions in many areas of current science that will affect the general public.

SUPPORTS

David Harvey, a doctoral candidate at the University of Arizona, holds, "Smog reduces the ring width in trees." Harvey continues, "By examining the effects of this process, we will be better able to comprehend the future effects of air pollution on the development of forests. This could ultimately provide significant benefits to the conservation efforts being initiated worldwide."

According to Barbara Carper, a researcher in the field, "The influence of climatic stress is critical to the formation of growth rings. A wide annual growth ring forms in a good year, while a narrow growth ring results during a bad year."

Dr. Narish Darjeeling, a dendrochronologist from Colorado, reports, "The use of computers has enabled us to hypothesize about the climatic patterns and variations across the United States annually since 1600." Dr. Darjeeling goes on to say, "Dendrochronologists have been able to determine <u>past patterns and occurrences of precipitation, drought, as well as atmospheric and temperature pressure.</u>"

Dr. Luz C. Lopez, renowned dendrochronologist, says, "<u>Because solar activity greatly affects the radiocarbon content of tree rings,</u> the analysis of the presence of radiocarbon in tree rings has information about the sun's activity throughout specific periods of time. Projecting worldwide climatic variations <u>is a highly possible and promising result of this research.</u>"

O N   Y O U R   O W N

Ideas for Guided and Open Writing

GUIDED WRITING EXERCISE: Many people think politics is corrupt. Watergate, Abscam, and Billy Carter and the Libyan connection are some of the many examples of the corruption that has made people distrust politics and politicians. However, many people think that politics has not always been corrupt. They believe that inflation, crime, and social changes today have made politicians dishonest and politics immoral. However, throughout history, the honesty of politics and politicians has always been questioned; political corruption is not merely a twentieth-century phenomenon. Consider the following quotations:

The mind of man is fond of power; increase his prospects and you enlarge his desires. (Gouverneur Morris, 1787)

Political power is merely the organized power of one class to oppress another. (Karl Marx and Friedrich Engels, 1847)

Politics, as the word is commonly understood, are nothing but corruptions. (Jonathan Swift, 1706)

Politics is perhaps the only profession for which no preparation is thought necessary. (R. L. Stevenson, 1882)

That government is best which governs least. (Henry David Thoreau, 1849)

> The notion that politics is all a cheat and that politicians are no better than swindlers has subsisted ever since the beginning. (F. S. Oliver, 1930)
>
> People vote to throw a man out. They seldom vote to put a man in. (Charles Michelson, 1944)
>
> The less government we have, the better. (R. W. Emerson, 1841)

Assume the role of a campaign manager for a state senator. You are about to give a speech to local volunteer campaign workers to open the campaign. Incorporate three of the preceding quotations into a well-developed paragraph of approximately 150 words. Your objective is to promote enthusiasm among the campaign workers by attacking the ideas expressed in the quotations you select. You might begin your paragraph with the following: "Today, too many Americans believe what ——— said in ———, '———.' As loyal supporters of Senator ———, we are setting out today to prove that our candidate can make politics clean again." Keep one of your three selected quotations as direct quotation, and incorporate the other two into the paragraph as reported speech.

OPEN WRITING IDEAS: The following topics are suggestions for open writing exercises to help you practice the structures presented in this chapter. Develop these ideas into paragraphs of 100–150 words. Focus your attention on appropriately quoting direct speech to support your ideas.

1. Analyze one of the most appealing, offensive, or effective commercials on radio or television. Either quote directly or report what is stated to support your view.

2. Interview three older people such as your parents, relatives, or family friends about how times have changed since they were your age. You might ask them about education, dating, marriage, housing, economics, religion, or alcohol and drug consumption. Choose only one of these topics and discuss how times have changed. During the interview take notes. Incorporate direct quotations and reported speech to support your ideas.

UNIT D REVIEW

Incorporating the Ideas of Others

DIRECTIONS: Read the following paragraph. It discusses the adjustment problems of children within stepfamilies. The paragraph can be improved by additional supports. The supports that follow the paragraph contain information that will become part of the paragraph. Read through the entire paragraph and all the supports. Then copy the paragraph, incorporating the right supports for sentences 3, 7, 14, and 16, respectively, according to the instructions before each support. Be sure to introduce the paraphrase or quotation with complete speaker information. In addition, change sentence 6, which is written in active voice, to passive voice. Change sentence 15, written in passive voice, to active voice. Check your work carefully.

Adjustment Problems with Stepfamilies

(1) Until the early 1900's, stepfamilies, which are families consisting of a natural parent and a stepparent, were usually formed when one of the natural parents remarried after the death of his or her spouse. (2) Today, however, stepfamilies are usually formed after the divorce of the natural parents, instead of after the death of one of the parents. (3) (Insert item A.) (4) Stepfamilies have become one of the most common forms of family units in our society. (5) Because of the structure of these newly formed families, each family member must make many adjustments to the living situation. (6) However, the children usually experience the worst adjustment problems. (7) (Insert item B.) (8) Of course, this child often feels lonely when he or she loses a parent to another adult. (9) He or she often feels angry, depressed, resentful, and betrayed. (10) In addition, the child often competes for

the attention of the natural parent because the stepparent may seem to be a rival. (11) Moreover, when an only child suddenly shares a household with one or more stepbrothers and stepsisters because of the remarriage, he or she often feels very frustrated. (12) The natural child no longer has all of the parent's attention; instead, the parent must now be shared with other children. (13) On the other hand, a child who gains brothers and sisters through a stepfamily arrangement may also feel insecure because he or she may no longer be the oldest or the youngest child in the household. (14) (Insert item C.) (15) Although these problems are experienced by many children in stepfamilies, much work is being done by counselors to help these children. (16) (Insert item D.)

SUPPORTS

A: (Include three of the following statistics quoted from *The American Council on Stepfamilies*. Insert them in the paragraph as direct quotations.)

"Approximately 1 million divorces—one out of every two marriages—occur each year."

"Fifty percent of all marriages end in divorce."

"Fifty to sixty percent of all divorces involve children."

"Approximately 8 percent of all divorced people remarry."

"Forty percent of all remarriages end in divorce within four years."

"Over 13 percent of children under eighteen are living in stepfamilies."

"Over 15 million children are now living with a remarried parent."

B: (Change the underlined portion to direct quotation. Paraphrase the remainder of the passage.)

Emily B. Visher, Ph.D. and John S. Visher, M.D. of the Stepfamily Foundation of California, Inc. have stated that remarriage for the adults is a gain of an important adult relationship, but for the children, remarriage frequently represents a loss of a close parent-child relationship. As a result the youngster is no longer the dominant person in the parent's world. Therefore, the child must struggle to comprehend his or her new position in his parent's world.

C: (Paraphrase the following case studies; include only the most pertinent information, such as name of source.)

Dr. Maximillian Shensky, Director of the Portland Family Counseling Institute, cites the following example:

"At seventeen years of age, Myra assumed the role of the 'woman of the house' when she moved into her father's home subsequent to her parents' divorce. For seven years she had performed all the household chores and had prepared all the meals for her two younger brothers and her father. Upon the remarriage of her father, Myra struggled desperately to retain her role as 'the woman of the house.' However, she did not succeed, and she therefore had difficulty trying to understand her identity within the family."

D: (Change the following direct quotation to reported speech. Be sure to include the speaker information.)

Jeanna O'Brien from the Salt Lake City Family Health Sciences Center notes, "An understanding of the problems suffered by every person involved in the formation of the stepfamilies is probably the key to helping the entire family adjust to their new family arrangement."

UNIT E

*Combining Sentences
for Special Purposes*

CHAPTER 25

Combining for Description

This chapter focuses on combining short sentences to create smoother, more effective sentences. Writers sometimes have difficulty writing smooth and effective descriptive sentences. Consider the following sentences written by a student about his professor:

THREE SEPARATE SENTENCES Professor Dimwipple is tall. He is slim. He is well built.

During the revising process the writer may read these sentences and decide that they are too short and choppy. The first question the writer may ask is, "How can they be combined?" First, the writer should notice that the purpose of the three sentences is to describe Professor Dimwipple with the adjectives *tall, well built,* and *slim*. Since the adjectives are the essential pieces of information in these sentences, there is no reason to repeat the whole sentences.

COMBINED WITH ADJECTIVES Professor Dimwipple is *tall, slim,* and *well-built*.

The resulting sentence is more efficient and effective than the three original choppy sentences.

Using Appositive Phrases

Another way to combine descriptive sentences is to use *appositives*, noun phrases that describe nouns. Consider the following sentences. They seem disconnected and childish.

231

Antonio Pasos's painting is a colorful picture of a Yaqui ritual. The painting greatly impressed Professor Cabos. He is the judge of the Santa Rita Art Show.

What makes these sentences seem simple is not their shortness. By presenting three ideas as if they were equally important, the writer fails to make clear what point is being emphasized. Notice what happens when two of the sentences are made into appositive phrases.

Antonio Pasos's painting, *a colorful picture of a Yaqui ritual*, greatly impressed Professor Cabos, *the judge of the Santa Rita Art Show*.

Now the writer's message is clearer because the relationship between the important ideas and the details is better established. Now the writer's idea that Professor Cabos was greatly impressed by Antonio Pasos's painting is clear. When you are editing your first drafts, watch for sentences such as the following, which can be combined into one sentence by changing one of the sentences into an appositive.

Mt. St. Helens erupted in 1980. It is a famous volcano in Washington.

The first of the two sentences contains the writer's main idea. Therefore, it should not be made into an appositive. The second one, which gives added information about the volcano, can be made into an appositive.

Mt. St. Helens, *a famous volcano in Washington*, erupted in 1980.

However, consider the following sentence:

Bjorn Borg is a well-known tennis player from Sweden. He won many of the world's major tennis tournaments in the late 1970's.

The first sentence, which has a *be* verb, can be made into an appositive:

Bjorn Borg, *a well-known tennis player from Sweden*, won many of the world's major tennis tournaments in the late 1970's.

When there are two related sentences with *be* verbs, usually either one can be made into an appositive, depending on which idea you want to emphasize.

TWO SENTENCES	*Bless Me, Ultima* is Rodolfo Anaya's greatest work. It is a novel based on his boyhood in New Mexico.
COMBINED	*Bless Me, Ultima*, Rodolfo Anaya's greatest work, is a novel based on his boyhood in New Mexico.
COMBINED	*Bless Me, Ultima*, a novel based on Rodolfo Anaya's boyhood in New Mexico, is his greatest work.

Using -*ing or* -ed *Phrases*

Sometimes two sentences can be more efficiently and effectively combined by changing one of the sentences into a phrase beginning in an -*ing* or -*ed* word. (Such phrases are also called *participial phrases*.) This is especially true if the verb in the sentence you are inserting consists of a form of *be* plus an -*ed* or -*ing* word (for example, *was sleeping*). Consider the following sentences:

TWO SENTENCES	Lisa did not hear the blast. She *was sleeping* soundly on the couch.
COMBINED	Lisa, *sleeping soundly on the couch*, did not hear the blast.

A sentence changed into an -*ing* or -*ed* phrase can usually be placed either immediately before or immediately after the noun it modifies.

TWO SENTENCES	Carlos was saddened by the recent departure of his friend. Carlos decided to take a short vacation.
COMBINED	Carlos, *saddened by the recent departure of his friend*, decided to take a short vacation.
COMBINED	*Saddened by the recent departure of his friend*, Carlos decided to take a short vacation.

Again, depending on the idea you wish to emphasize, you can make either sentence into an -*ing* or -*ed* phrase, as shown in the following sentences:

TWO SENTENCES	The primitive tool was donated to the charity auction by a local antique collector. It is believed to be one of only ten of its kind in existence.

COMBINED   *Donated to the charity auction by a local antique collector*, the primitive tool is believed to be one of only ten of its kind in existence.

COMBINED   The primitive tool, *believed to be one of only ten of its kind in existence*, was donated to the charity auction by a local antique collector.

These -*ing* or -*ed* phrases are especially helpful when you want to describe simultaneous action. Consider the following sentences describing a baseball player. Both actions happen at the same time.

The rookie slid into home plate. The rookie shouted, "I made it."

You can emphasize the fact that these two events occurred at the same time by turning one of the sentences into an -*ing* phrase:

COMBINED   *Sliding into home plate*, the rookie shouted, "I made it."

COMBINED   *Shouting*, "*I made it*," the rookie slid into home plate.

Notice that in all of the examples with -*ing* or -*ed* phrases, the phrases have been surrounded by commas. Sometimes -*ing* and -*ed* phrases do not require surrounding commas. When the phrase is necessary to the meaning of the sentence, the phrase does not need commas. The following is an example of an -*ed* phrase not needing commas:

The student bought the text required for the course.

In this sentence the phrase *required for the course* is necessary to the meaning of the sentence. The student didn't buy any book; he or she bought the book required for the course. Notice that the phrase is not surrounded by commas.

Here is another example of a phrase without commas:

The woman *sitting in the corner* is a detective.

The participial phrase "sitting in the corner" tells specifically which woman is the detective.

**Using
Adjective
Clauses**

Not all descriptive sentences can be transformed into adjectives or phrases. Many sentences, however, can be transformed into adjective clauses, groups of words having a subject and verb, beginning with *which, that, who, whom,* or *whose.* Consider the following sentences:

That silk shawl is quite valuable to me. It was embroidered by my great aunt.

Because the second sentence provides more information about the shawl mentioned in the first sentence, it would make sense to combine the two statements. The second sentence can be transformed into a clause describing *shawl.*

That silk shawl, which was embroidered by my great aunt, is quite valuable to me.

Notice that the clause in this sentence begins with *which.* Notice that as in the case of *-ing* and *-ed* phrases, adjective clauses can be written with or without commas. If the adjective clause is necessary to the meaning of the sentence, it is not enclosed by a set of commas.

The man *who is wearing a brown tie* is the president of the university.

The clause *who is wearing a brown tie* is necessary to the meaning of the sentence. Therefore, it is not enclosed in commas. An adjective clause with commas provides extra information not necessary to the meaning of the sentence.

My videotape recorder, which I bought only six months ago, is already technically outdated.

The clause "which I bought only six months ago" is extra information that is not necessary to the meaning of the sentence. Therefore, it is enclosed by commas.

The following are the pronouns that begin adjective clauses:

Which refers to things (including animals), and a *which* clause is enclosed in commas.

The coffee, *which* is the worst I've ever tasted, is stale.

State fairs, *which* are a holdover from farming societies, maintain their appeal.

That refers to people or things, and a *that* clause is not usually enclosed in commas.

> This is the wrestling team *that* won several awards.
>
> Snoopy and Charlie Brown are the characters *that* are the most popular with preschoolers.

Who or **whom** refers to one or more persons.

> People *who* live in glass houses shouldn't throw stones.
>
> The man *whom* I will marry must be willing to share homemaking responsibilities with me.

Whose refers to ownership by a person or group of people.

> Our neighbors *whose* house was robbed moved away.
>
> The major, *whose* thirty-fifth birthday is tomorrow, is called the "old man."

Notice how the following sets of two sentences have been combined with *which, that, who, whom,* or *whose*.

TWO SENTENCES	During the Mexican American War in 1848, the northern Mexican territory was lost. The northern Mexican territory is now Texas, New Mexico, Arizona, California, and Colorado.
COMBINED	During the Mexican American War in 1848, the northern Mexican territory, *which is now Texas, New Mexico, Arizona, Califora, and Colorado*, was lost.
TWO SENTENCES	Marilyn Burns was the coach of the women's wrestling team. That team won several international competitions.
COMBINED	Marilyn Burns was the coach of the women's wrestling team *that won several international competitons*.
TWO SENTENCES	The Riveras took Ana to a restaurant specializing in barbecued meats. Ana is a vegetarian.
COMBINED	The Riveras took Ana, *who is a vegetarian*, to a restaurant specializing in barbecued meats.
TWO SENTENCES	Ernest Hemingway wrote *The Old Man and the Sea*. He had a passion for the sea.
COMBINED	Ernest Hemingway, *who had a passion for the sea*, wrote *The Old Man and the Sea*.

TWO SENTENCES	Mr. Patterns retired last year. Everybody at our school loved him.
COMBINED	Mr. Patterns, *whom everybody at our school loved*, retired last year.
TWO SENTENCES	Tamara Wycoff·always does well in biology. Her mother is a doctor.
COMBINED	Tamara Wycoff, *whose mother is a doctor*, always does well in biology.

Many times either of two related sentences can be made into an adjective clause, depending on which detail deserves more emphasis. Consider the following sentences.

TWO SENTENCES	Charlotte Stevenson now sings in the San Francisco Opera. She was a member of the University Opera Club.
COMBINED	Charlotte Stevenson, *who was a member of the University Opera Club*, now sings in the San Francisco Opera.
COMBINED	Charlotte Stevenson, *who now sings in the San Francisco Opera*, was a member of the University Opera Club.

Using Compound Subjects and Verbs

When describing a series of events in a situation, writers frequently produce sentences such as the following:

Raymond spotted the buck. He adjusted his rifle. Then he aimed.
Theresa got out of the car. She lifted the hood. She checked the battery.

Not only do these sentences sound short and choppy, but they are also repetitive. Because all these sentences contain the same or almost the same subjects, they can be combined with compound verbs in this way:

Raymond *spotted* the buck, *adjusted* his rifle, and then *aimed*.
Theresa *got out* of the car, *lifted* the hood, and *checked* the battery.

Compound verbs work well in these sentences for two reasons:

1. The subjects of the sentences in each group refer to the same persons (Raymond and Theresa).

2. The events presented in the sentences occur in chronological order — that is, in time order.

> **TWO SENTENCES**   Matilda is finicky about her appearance. James is finicky about his grooming.

Obviously these two sentences make identical or nearly identical statements about both subjects. Because of this repetition, the sentences can be combined with compound verbs in this way:

> **COMBINED**   Matilda *and* James *are both finicky.*

Now the one idea is much more efficiently and economically stated in one sentence rather than in two.

P R A C T I C E   2 5 A

Using Adjectives

DIRECTIONS: Read the following paragraph. Each numbered item contains a group of short, choppy sentences. Copy the paragraph, combining the sentences in each group to form one sentence. Use adjectives to combine these sentences. Check your work carefully.

A Gemstone for Every Month

(1) For thousands of years people have appreciated gemstones. They are beautiful. They are rare. (2) Some of these stones, known as "birthstones," have associations with the months of the year. These associations are traditional. They are, moreover, widely accepted. (3) For example, January's birthstone, the garnet, was so popular in England during the reign of Queen Victoria that ten thousand workers were employed on a full-time basis to mine and cut these stones. These stones are dark red. Also, they are semiprecious. (4) The amethyst, February's birthstone, is a purple stone associated with St. Valentine and with Bacchus, the Roman god of wine. Bacchus was famous for being passionate and wild. (5) The birthstone for March is the aquamarine. It is transparent. It is also bluish green. (6) A stone called the peridot, the birthstone for August, is mainly found on only one tiny island in the Red Sea. The peridot is also soft. This stone is yellowish green. (7) In addition, one of June's birthstones, the

"moonstone," glows with a light similar to that of moonlight. The light is pale. Moreover, it is bluish white. (8) Another of June's birthstones is the alexandrite, which changes color from a greyish green in daylight to a purplish red in artificial light. The alexandrite is brilliant and lovely. It is also fascinating. (9) Bad luck is often associated with the opal, October's birthstone. This birthstone is hard. It is also characterized as being brittle. (10) People think opals bring bad luck because the stones tend to crack suddenly in certain climates after losing some of their water. These climates are dry. (11) The ruby, which is July's birthstone, is a gemstone that ranges in color from deep red to pale rose. This gemstone is hard. It is extremely scarce and highly prized. (12) It is understandable that people continue to appreciate the beauty and magic of these markers of the months. These markers are ancient and spectacular.

PRACTICE 25B

Using Appositives

DIRECTIONS: Read the following paragraph. Most numbered items have sentences paired together. Copy the paragraph. Combine the paired sentences by changing one sentence in the pair into an appositive. For clarity in item 3 use dashes (—), not commas, to set off the appositive. Check your work carefully.

A Smoker's Disease

(1) Emphysema is a disease in which the lungs become dry and spongy. It causes its victims to suffer great pain when running, walking, and sometimes even breathing. (2) Emphysema is a severe, disabling disease. It is an enemy to many cigarette smokers. (3) In fact, certain conditions in early infancy or childhood can create in some persons a tendency for this disease later in life. These conditions include poor diet, chronic colds, and other respiratory ailments. (4) In addition, many who suffer from emphysema are born with an inability to form antitrypsin. Antitrypsin is a substance that slows down tissue-destroying substances. (5) These persons may, therefore, be at a disadvantage in fighting off respiratory infections when they do smoke. (6) When these people have a smoking habit, their health is

endangered. These people are individuals unaware of their serious condition. (7) The reason is that emphysema is a treacherous disease. It can develop slowly over twenty or thirty years. (8) However, very few people today seem to think much about what they will be doing twenty or thirty years from now or about what shape their bodies will be in then. (9) These smokers do not realize the danger of their actions. These smokers are the kinds of people who are not frightened by repeatedly coughing up mucous. (10) Nevertheless, the danger is not exaggerated: over one million Americans cause themselves as well as their families great pain and stress. These Americans are victims of emphysema. (11) By the time emphysema is detected, the damage to the lung is lasting. The damaged lung is tissue once thick and strong, now paper thin and brittle. (12) In fact, the disease is so deadly that once it has developed, almost nothing can cure the condition of an emphysematic. The emphysematic is an unfortunate victim of heredity and habit.

P R A C T I C E   2 5 C

Using Adjective Clauses

DIRECTIONS: Read the following paragraph. Most numbered items have sentences paired together. Copy the paragraph. Combine the paired sentences by changing one sentence in the pair into an adjective clause. Check your work carefully.

Moon Origins: Part I

(1) For centuries, people have tried to discover the origin of the moon. (2) The origin has always been a puzzle for scientists. Scientists are frustrated because they find problems with every major theory about the moon's origin. (3) The first theory is called the fission theory. It claims that a "daughter" broke off from the earth. (4) George Darwin proposed that the moon was actually part of the planet earth, not just located near it. George Darwin was one of the famous supporters of this theory. (5) In the last 1800's, in fact, Darwin hypothesized that forces of the sun and of the earth's rotation combined creating on the earth a huge bulge. He hypothesized that the bulge eventually broke away in a swarm of particles to form the moon. (6) The fission theory

was widely accepted at first. The fission theory was eventually attacked by other scientists. (7) It could not completely explain how such a bulge could have broken away from the earth. The bulge was being pulled on by the earth's strong tidal forces. (8) Another problem with the theory about the moon being formed from the earth is that elements in moon rocks have been found to be different from those in earth rocks. (9) A second theory is called the sister-planet theory. It states that a large amount of particles remained left over after the earth formed. (10) The sister-planet theory, like the fission theory, was attacked. The theory suggests that the particles gradually accumulated to form the moon. (11) Many scientists opposing this theory point out that Venus and Mars do not have moons. These moons would be expected if the sister-planet theory were true for all planets. (12) Although the fission theory and the sister-planet theory have problems, scientists still refer to these two theories. These scientists continue to do research. (13) Thus, researchers hope eventually to solve the puzzle of the moon's origin. Their new theories are taken from combinations of old theories.

P R A C T I C E   2 5 D

Using Participial Phrases

DIRECTIONS: Read the following paragraph. Most numbered items have sentences paired together. Copy the paragraph. Combine the paired sentences by changing one sentence in the pair into a participial phrase. Check your work carefully.

Moon Origins:
Part II

(1) Astronomers and other scientists are dissatisfied with the fission theory and the sister-planet theory. (2) Astronomers and other scientists continue guessing about the moon's origin. (3) A major theory claims that the moon came from somewhere in our solar system, was thrown into an orbit coming toward Earth, and then was captured into Earth's orbit. This explanation is known as the capture theory. (4) This theory explains why the moon contains elements that are not contained in the earth. This theory was once considered possible. (5) The capture theory is considered inaccurate because it describes unlikely conditions. The conditions occurred during the moon's approach to Earth. (6) Scientists are beginning to combine new and old theories about the moon's origin. These scientists have been influenced by results of Apollo missions. (7) One new theory, the collision-condensation theory, states that a large piece of matter from outer space collided with Earth. That piece formed an enormous cloud. (8) The cloud heated and broke into fine dust. It lost many of its elements through evaporation. (9) The leftover elements of the cloud began to cool and harden. These leftover elements gradually became the moon, a sister planet to Earth. (10) In another theory, one of many small bodies in the early solar system was captured into orbit around Earth. This theory is named the co-accretion theory. (11) That body eventually accumulated the last bits of earthlike material and became the moon. The earthlike material was remaining near the earth. (12) Because none of these theories has been proved, researchers will continue to examine lunar material in hopes of discovering more clues about the origin of the moon.

P R A C T I C E   2 5 E

Using Compound
Subjects and Verbs

DIRECTIONS: Read the following paragraph. Most of the numbered items have sentences paired together. Copy the paragraph, using compound subjects or compound verbs to combine the paired sentences. Check your work carefully.

**The First
Computer**

(1) Although computers have made a tremendous impact on modern business, they were practically unimaginable over one hundred years ago. (2) However in the early 1800's, Charles Babbage, a professor of mathematics at Cambridge University in England, designed a machine that could solve difficult mathematical problems. He experimented for years with the machine. (3) He hoped that the machine could calculate the results accurately. He hoped the machine could also record the results accurately. (4) His machine, called the analytic engine, contained all the main parts of a computer. His machine became the model for today's computer. (5) For twenty years Babbage had experimented on his computers. He had used up the government funding for his work. (6) By 1842, he needed money to help him continue his research. He also looked for interested people to help him continue his research. (7) At about this time, Babbage met Lady Ada Lovelace, a brilliant twenty-six-year-old woman. He was impressed by her accomplishments. (8) Lovelace had already published her translation of an article about Babbage's machine. Later she had written a paper in which she corrected some serious errors in Babbage's own work. (9) Lovelace soon joined Babbage's project as an assistant. She eventually became his partner. (10) Among other things, her suggestions about storing information helped improve the machine. Her ideas about the many possible uses of the computer helped also. (11) Unfortunately, Babbage was never able to build a successful model of the analytic engine. Lovelace was never able to build one with him. (12) Even if they had had enough money, and even if Lovelace had not died of cancer at the age of thirty-six, they probably would never have built one. They probably would never have perfected it. (13) The reason was that the special gears and shafts for the machine had not been developed. The equipment needed to make those parts had not been developed. (14) Nevertheless, Charles Babbage will be remembered for laying the foundation for computers in the future.

ON YOUR OWN

*Ideas for Guided
and Open Writing*

GUIDED WRITING EXERCISE: When people camp out in the wilderness, they often find that their peace and quiet is interrupted by noisy motorcycles, airplanes, boats, four-wheel-drive vehicles, dune buggies, and so on. To these persons, it seems as if quiet lakes and other isolated spots no longer exist. No matter how far they travel into isolated areas, they can never get away from noisy people. Should some places be kept off limits to people using motor vehicles? If so, how can people with health problems and physical handicaps enjoy these spots? Should people be allowed to enjoy the wilderness in any way they want? Or would the wilderness be ruined by people bringing cars, airplanes, and motorboats there? Should the wilderness be protected against these kinds of campers? In a paragraph of approximately 100–150 words, attack or defend using motor vehicles in the wilderness. You might begin your paragraph with the following: "Motor vehicles should (or should not) be prohibited in wilderness areas." In your discussion, pay careful attention to combining for description through the use of adjectives, adjective clauses, appositives, participial phrases, and compound subjects and verbs.

OPEN WRITING IDEAS: The following topics are suggestions for open writing exercises to help you practice the structures presented in this chapter. Develop these ideas into paragraphs of 100–150 words. Focus your attention on the appropriate use of combining for description.

1. Imagine the kind of home one of your college professors might own. Describe the style of furniture, the decorations, the kind of art, and so on that might be included in this house. In your description, tell why you imagine your professor to live in such surroundings.

2. Although setting world records in sports has long been a great interest of many people, within the last decade a growing number of persons have become interested in establishing world records in other areas. To set world records, these people gorge their mouths full of cigars, stay at the beach for hours building giant sand castles, and sit on top of flag poles for days. Why do you think people want to set these records? In your discussion, describe the kind of person who would want to set such an unusual world record.

CHAPTER 26

Expressing Time

Sometimes sentences can be improved by combining them to emphasize time. Words such as *before, after, as, while,* and *when* make the order of events clear and therefore help to communicate the main idea. Consider the following sentences. How can a time relationship between them be shown more clearly?

The band had played its last song.
The cheering crowd of teenagers reluctantly left the stadium.

The sentences could be combined with *once, as soon as, the moment that,* and *when,* which are some of the most familiar time words we use.

COMBINED	*As soon as* the band had played its last song, the cheering crowd of teenagers reluctantly left the stadium.
COMBINED	*The moment that* the band had played its last song, the cheering crowd of teenagers reluctantly left the stadium.
COMBINED	*When* the band had played its last song, the cheering crowd of teenagers reluctantly left the stadium.
COMBINED	*Once* the band had played its last song, the cheering crowd of teenagers reluctantly left the stadium.

To emphasize the time of one event in relation to the other event, use *after*, *before*, or *until*.

After the printing press was invented in 1500, books no longer had to be hand-copied.

Before the printing press was invented in 1500, books had to be hand-copied.

Until the printing press was invented in 1500, books were hand-copied.

As, *at the same time as*, *just as*, *when*, and *while* emphasize that two events occurred simultaneously. Consider the following sentences:

TWO SENTENCES	The parade marched by. The firecrackers brightly lit up the sky.
COMBINED	*As* the parade marched by, the firecrackers brightly lit up the sky.
COMBINED	*At the same time as* the parade marched by, the firecrackers brightly lit up the sky.
COMBINED	*While* the parade marched by, the firecrackers brightly lit up the sky.
COMBINED	*Just as* the parade marched by, the firecrackers brightly lit up the sky.
COMBINED	*When* the parade marched by, the firecrackers brightly lit up the sky.

P R A C T I C E   2 6 A

Using Time Words

DIRECTIONS: Read the following paragraph. Most numbered items have sentences paired together. Copy the paragraph, combining the paired sentences with the words or phrases in parentheses at the end of each pair. Check your work carefully.

Carnival Preparations

(1) The final preparations for the Iowa Springs College Spring Carnival was an exercise in cooperation for everyone involved. (2) One person was taking care of one part of a job. Two or three others worked to complete the rest of it. (as) (3) For example, Yolanda Moreno and her friends set up the booth for the beanbag basketball game. They were a very organized team. (when) (4) Yolanda balanced a large laundry basket up on a pole. Jeff Carter and Charlotte Brooks struggled to fasten it. (while) (5) The basket was finally in place. The three of them laid out a plan on the floor with electrical tape. (after) (6) The plan was being completed. Several other students were making the beanbags and collecting items to be given as prizes. (at the same time as) (7) In another part of the field, members of the drama club began to organize and decorate the inside of a fortune-telling booth. The dean and his assistant had worked with them to set up the tent. (after) (8) In addition, members of the International Students Club had barely finished making the barbecue pit. Ali Hassan and Rhadika Palajari ran over to fit the grill on the bricks and to place the charcoal in the pit. (before) (9) Everyone thought that the work was complete. It began to thunder. (just as) (10) The carnival chair heard the thunder. He yelled for everyone to pick up the thirty-five dozen donuts and bagels on the lawn and to put them away. (the moment that) (11) The food had been safely stored. Everyone went back to work. (as soon as) (12) They continued to work well into the afternoon. Most of the rides and booths had been set up. (until) (13) The planning committee organized the carnival. They did not realize how well everyone would cooperate. (when)

PRACTICE 26B

Using Time Words

DIRECTIONS: Read the following paragraph. Most numbered items have sentences paired together. Copy the paragraph, combining the paired sentences with the words or phrases in parentheses at the end of each pair. Check your work carefully.

Brazil's Gold Rush

(1) In 1980, Serra Pelada (Bald Mountain), located near the Amazon River in Brazil's Amazon jungle, became the site of one of the largest and most feverish gold rushes in the history of Brazil. (2) Genesio Ferreira da Silva, a farmer, discovered small amounts of gold on his land. He hired a geologist to analyze the gold and learned that he had a gold mine. (after) (3) Other people heard of the mine. As many as 23,000 prospectors started to search on his land and the surrounding property for the gold. (as soon as) (4) People continued to look for the gold day and night. They found huge nuggets, one of which weighed 15 pounds and was worth over $100,000. (as) (5) The Ferreiras had mistakenly believed that the mine was theirs. They realized that the Brazilian government owns all mineral rights. (until) (6) The government took control of the mine. The Ferreiras had been able to stake claims on what was found to be the richest part of the vein. (before) (7) Federal police were sent to the area to enforce strict regulations among the people prospecting for gold. The government realized the size of the gold deposit. (when) (8) The police arrived in the area. They registered all miners and prohibited liquor, gambling, and the presence of women in the area. (once) (9) The government realized that it needed the prospectors, however. It hired the workers and gave them free medical care. (when) (10) Genesio Ferreira da Silva found a fortune in his own backyard. Little did he realize that his discovery would be a boost for an entire nation. (when)

P R A C T I C E   2 6 C

Using Time Words

DIRECTIONS: Read the following paragraph. Most numbered items have sentences paired together. Copy the paragraph. Combine the pair of sentences, using the following words and phrases at least once: when, just as, until, while, before, after, once, as soon as, and at the moment that. Check your work carefully.

Victory for the Handicapped

(1) On July 3, 1981, nine brave handicapped persons accompanied by seven guides and two reporters set examples for disabled people all over the world. They climbed 14,141 feet to reach the snowcapped top of Mount Rainier in Washington. (2) These nine adventurers included five blind people using Braille maps, two deaf persons, a man with an artificial leg, and one epileptic. (3) These nine climbers reached the top one full day ahead of their Fourth of July goal. Their triumphant cheers and applause could be heard over the two-way radios of their families and friends. (4) Many supporters hugged one another in joy. Others were waving flags to celebrate the climbers' extraordinary accomplishment. (5) Thirty-six-year-old Richard Rose, an epileptic who had previously been involved in a Supreme Court case about the discrimination epileptics suffered in their jobs, safely reached the top. He exclaimed, "There's one for the epileptics!" (6) Going down the mountain was not too difficult for the climbers. They were about five minutes from the camp at Ingraham Flats, 11,500 feet high. (7) Some of the hikers first saw the camp. Enormous chunks of ice from the sun-warmed Ingraham Glacier crashed about 200 yards from the hikers, miraculously hurting no one. (8) The climbers could leave the icy area. One person tripped and fell. (9) Fred Noesner, one of the blind climbers, dropped his climbing ax. He lost his footing and stumbled for a number of feet. (10) The climbers thought that they were going to die. They finally reached a clear path and continued down to the foot of the mountain. (11) The excited but exhausted adventurers reached the lodge. Their families, friends, and other supporters, many of whom were disabled, celebrated the remarkable achievement of these nine determined people.

ON YOUR OWN

Ideas for Guided and Open Writing

GUIDED WRITING EXERCISE: In the seventies, more and more people began living together, and their legal rights as partners were not clear. An example of the problems that arise when these people separate was seen in the break between actor Lee Marvin and his ex-girlfriend. In the late seventies Marvin and Michele Triola Marvin, the woman he had been living with for eleven years, went to court in a very publicized trial. Michelle Triola felt that, although she and Marvin had lived together without being married, she should be awarded money for having given up her career for eleven years to support Marvin in his career. She asked for money also because she said that Marvin had made a verbal agreement to support her financially. Do you think that people who live together without marrying should receive alimony and property when they separate, just as married people do? In a paragraph of approximately 100–150 words, support or attack the idea of an unmarried person receiving alimony. You might begin your paragraph with the following: "When a couple decides to live together, each person has (or does not have) the legal right to receive alimony if the couple breaks up." Does length of time that the couple lives together influence the partners' rights? Does the kind of career the partners have affect their rights? Pay particular attention to the correct use of time expressions as you write.

OPEN WRITING IDEAS: The following topics are suggestions for open writing exercises to help you practice the structures presented in this chapter. Develop these ideas into paragraphs of 100–150 words. Focus your attention on expressing time.

1. Think of a product you once bought that you discovered was defective, or think of a company that provided you with poor service or that did not live up to its claims. Write a letter to the Consumer Affairs Commission, describing what happened with that product or company.

2. Describe an incident in which you learned the true value of friendship. Explain what happened.

CHAPTER 27

Making Comparisons

When comparing two people, objects, or ideas, a writer can show the comparison more effectively by using a particular word or phrase to combine the sentences. Depending on whether the writer wishes to show similarities or differences, he or she can choose certain words, phrases, or structures to combine the sentences.

Showing Similarities

When writers want to show how two things are similar, they sometimes put two sentences close together so that the reader will understand that the ideas in them are related. Often, however, the connection between the ideas could be shown more powerfully by using a word or phrase to join the sentences.

Suppose you are writing a paragraph about how all the schools in your city have adopted severe discipline procedures. In the course of your paragraph you write the following:

Fenster School sentences anyone caught smoking in school to two hours of hard labor on the grounds.
Macmillan School fines anyone who skips classes $5 a class.

Since both sentences give examples of severe discipline procedures, you could combine them with *and*.

Fenster School sentences anyone caught smoking in school to two hours of hard labor on the grounds, *and* Macmillan School fines anyone who skips classes $5 a class.

When you connect two sentences with *and*, always remember to put a comma before the *and*. Because *and* is such a familiar connecting word, however, people tend to use it too often.

Words and expressions such as *similarly, likewise,* and *in the same manner* frequently work better when you want to emphasize similarities between two things. When these connectors are used between sentences, they must be preceded by a semicolon and followed by a comma.

TWO SENTENCES	Uncooked meat begins to spoil on the third day in the refrigerator. Most vegetables begin to spoil within a week.
COMBINED	Uncooked meat begins to spoil on the third day in the refrigerator; similarly, most vegetables begin to spoil within a week.
TWO SENTENCES	Sunglasses help people to see in glaring light. Goggles help people to see underwater.
COMBINED	Sunglasses help people to see in glaring light; likewise, goggles help people to see underwater.
TWO SENTENCES	In words like *gnash* and *gnarl*, the *g* is silent. In words like *knead* and *kneel*, the *k* is silent.
COMBINED	In words like *gnash* and *gnarl*, the *g* is silent; in the same manner, in words like *knead* and *kneel*, the *k* is silent.

If the wording of two sentences is very similar, the relationship between them can be shown by joining them with a semicolon.

TWO SENTENCES	Television revolutionized communication in the 1950's. Computers are revolutionizing communication today.
COMBINED	Television revolutionized communication in the 1950's; computers are revolutionizing communication today.

The semicolon is enough to show that the following ideas are related, but the word *also* helps show the connection more strongly.

TWO SENTENCES	George Lucas, the creator of *Star Wars*, produces fine science fiction films. Gene Roddenberry, the creator of *Star Trek*, produces fine science fiction films too.

COMBINED	George Lucas, the creator of *Star Wars*, produces fine science fiction films; Gene Roddenberry, the creator of *Star Trek*, *also* produces fine science fiction films.

Another way to combine similar ideas is to rewrite two short sentences with *Just as* or *Just as . . . so*.

TWO SENTENCES	Football is the most popular sport in the United States. Soccer is the most popular sport in Mexico.
COMBINED	*Just as* football is the most popular sport in the United States, soccer is the most popular sport in Mexico.
TWO SENTENCES	The original inhabitants of California flavored English with Spanish expressions. The settlers of Georgia flavored English with Gullah expressions.
COMBINED	*Just as* the original inhabitants of California flavored English with Spanish expressions, *so* the settlers of Georgia flavored English with Gullah expressions.

Expressing Differences

To emphasize the *difference* between two things or ideas, use other combining words. For example, in a paragraph contrasting driving one's own car and carpooling, a student wrote the following sentences:

Driving one's own car gives a person privacy.
Carpooling restricts a person's privacy and time.

How can the contrast between the two ideas be emphasized? Using *but* is an effective way of showing contrast between these two sentences.

Driving one's own car gives a person privacy, *but* carpooling restricts a person's privacy and time.

Words and expressions such as *however, in contrast, in contrast to this*, and *on the other hand* also indicate differences. Because these are somewhat formal connectors, they sound best in long, rather formal sentences. When these connectors are used between sentences, these expressions are preceded by a semicolon and followed by a comma.

TWO SENTENCES	The solutions to the American inflation problem are clear. The solutions to American apathy do not seem to exist.
COMBINED	The solutions to the American inflation problem are clear; *however*, the solutions to American apathy do not seem to exist.
TWO SENTENCES	In the Western world, an overweight woman was once considered voluptuous. An overweight woman is considered quite unattractive today.
COMBINED	In the Western world, an overweight woman was once considered voluptuous; *in contrast*, an overweight woman is considered quite unattractive today.
TWO SENTENCES	The responsibilites of being a parent are many. The pleasures of being a parent are infinite.
COMBINED	The responsibilities of being a parent are many; *on the other hand*, the pleasures of being a parent are infinite.

For variety, place the connecting word or phrase after the complete subject of the sentence. This structure sounds best when the subject consists of only a few words.

TWO SENTENCES	Health enthusiasts claim that honey is healthier than refined, white sugar. Sugar manufacturers state that there is no difference between the two.
COMBINED	Health enthusiasts claim that honey is healthier than refined, white sugar; sugar manufacturers, *however*, state that there is no difference between the two.
TWO SENTENCES	Many Sioux are expert beadworkers. The Zunis are skilled silversmiths.
COMBINED	Many Sioux are expert beadworkers; the Zunis, *on the other hand*, are skilled silversmiths.

Notice that the sentences are separated by a semicolon and that the connectors are enclosed in commas.

Sentences showing differences can be combined with just a semicolon, particularly when the wording of the sentences is very similar.

TWO SENTENCES	Horse-and-buggy travel was popular in the 1800's. Supersonic jet travel is popular today.
COMBINED	Horse-and-buggy travel was popular in the 1800's; supersonic jet travel is popular today.

Notice in the following example how the words *was once* and *is now* also help to show the contrast.

TWO SENTENCES	Cotton *was once* considered Arizona's most important natural resource. Copper *is now* its most important resource.
COMBINED	Cotton *was once* considered Arizona's most important natural resource; copper *is now* its most important resource.

Connecting subordinators such as *while, whereas,* and *although* can be used effectively to show differences.

TWO SENTENCES	Roberto considers television entertaining. His twin sister Marisa finds it boring.
COMBINED	Roberto considers television entertaining *while* his twin sister Marisa finds it boring.

Notice that *while* is not preceded by any punctuation. However, if the *while* clause comes at the beginning of the sentence, it must be followed by a comma.

While Roberto considers television entertaining, his twin sister Marisa finds it boring.

Whereas and *although* are punctuated in the same way.

TWO SENTENCES	America's favorite fast food is the hamburger. Mexico's most popular fast food is the *burrito*.
COMBINED	*Whereas* America's favorite fast food is the hamburger, Mexico's most popular fast food is the *burrito*.
TWO SENTENCES	One of the highlights of the winter sky is Orion. The highlight of the summer sky is the Big Dipper.
COMBINED	*Although* one of the highlights of the winter sky is Orion, the highlight of the summer sky is the Big Dipper.

P R A C T I C E   2 7 A

Expressing Similarities

DIRECTIONS: Read the following paragraph. Most of the numbered items contain sentences paired together. Copy the paragraph, combining the paired sentences with the connector in parentheses at the end of each pair. Check your work carefully.

Christianity and Mithraism: Some Similarities

(1) During the first century A.D., many Romans, dissatisfied with their lives, looked for a religion that promised life after death. (2) They were attracted to Mithraism, based on the legend of Mithra, a Persian god, because it promised not only eternal happiness but protection by a powerful god. (3) Mithraism and Christianity shared so many similarities that they were rival religions for a period of time. (4) For example, Mithraism tried to explain the meaning of life. Christianity explained the purpose of man's life in relation to God. (similarly) (5) Mithra, a hero-god, was responsible for saving his people. Jesus, Christians believed, was the savior of the world. (in comparison) (6) Mithra, after taming a huge bull created by the high god Ahura Magda, "sacrificed" the bull, whose blood produces the animals and plants necessary for man to live. Christians believed that they were saved by the blood of Jesus when he was sacrificed on the cross. (;) (7) Another interesting fact about Mithraism is that Mithra ate a final dinner with his friends to honor the sacrifice of the bull. Jesus met with his apostles at the Last Supper before he was crucified. (likewise) (8) Mithra later rose into heaven and continued to guide his followers in their trials with the devil. Christians, believing that Jesus rose into heaven, claimed that he remained spiritually with them and influenced their daily lives. (in comparison) (9) Another strong element of Mithrasim was the feast of Mithra, celebrated on December 25. That date was celebrated by first-century Christians as Jesus' birth, even though the actual date was unknown. (also) (10) Thus, Mithraism promised immortality and help from a savior-god. Christianity offered its followers everlasting life through belief in Jesus Christ. (just as . . . so) (11) All of these similarities between Mithraism and Christianity made the rivalry strong. (12) As a result, some people believe that Mithraism influenced the development of Christianity, for instance, in declaring December 25 the date of Jesus' birth. (13) However, many other people, stressing that the story of Mithra is only a legend and that the story of Jesus is a fact, see the similarities just as interesting coincidences.

P R A C T I C E   2 7 B

Expressing Differences

DIRECTIONS: Read the following paragraph. It was written by a historian in 1994 looking at the Carter and Reagan administrations. Most of the numbered items contain sentences paired together. Copy the paragraph, combining the paired sentences with the connectors in parentheses at the end of each pair. Check your work carefully.

Differing Viewpoints: Carter vs. Reagan

(1) Although America's two major political parties both try to support the principles of the Constitution, their viewpoints about how to accomplish those goals are very different. (2) The Democratic party aims to improve the general well-being of each individual in society by establishing government agencies. The Republican party aims to improve the well-being of the individual in society by encouraging business growth. (while) (3) The administrations of Jimmy Carter and Ronald Reagan are good examples of the differences between these two parties. (4) Carter's foreign policy, for example, focused on the importance of human rights. Reagan's foreign policy concentrated on the importance of military strength. (;) (5) Carter, an outspoken world leader, favored limiting aid to countries that used cruel forms of punishment that imprisoned political rebels. Reagan, who gave aid to dictatorships, was not a world leader in those matters of human rights. (in contrast to this) (6) In addition, Carter was concerned with adopting a flexible, related approach to other countries. Reagan believed in adopting a firm, powerful approach. (whereas) (7) Carter did not consider having a strong U.S. military force very important. Reagan was concerned with making the United States a top military power internationally. (but) (8) The opposing ideas of the Democratic and Republican parties also could be seen in the economic policies of both the Carter and Reagan administrations. (9) Carter wanted to improve the condition of Americans by spending money on various social welfare programs. Reagan believed in cutting back unnecessary social welfare programs. (on the other hand) (10) For example, Carter encouraged programs for education, Social Security, and welfare. Reagan tried to save money for Americans by reducing the budget for these social welfare programs. (while) (11) Carter, in addition, believed in the need for government control in many areas. Reagan recommended reducing government control of business and reducing

price controls. (however) (12) As a result, Carter allowed gasoline prices to remain fixed until just before the 1980 election. Reagan removed gasoline price limits in order to encourage growth of big business. (while) (13) These actions, as well as many others, represent the very different but positive viewpoints of each party.

P R A C T I C E   2 7 C

Expressing Similarities and Differences

DIRECTIONS: Read the following paragraph. Most of the numbered items contain sentences paired together. Copy the paragraph, combining each pair of sentences. Use each of the following words at least once: similarly, likewise, in the same manner, just as . . . so, just as, however, in contrast, in contrast to this, on the other hand, while, whereas, and although.

Bed-and-Breakfast Homes

(1) For years Europeans have opened up their homes to overnight travellers. Many Americans are now opening up their homes to travellers needing a place to stay. (2) These homes, called bed-and-breakfast homes, are similar to motels. (3) Motels provide travellers with a comfortable place to stay overnight. Bed-and-breakfast inns provide people with a comfortable place to sleep overnight. (4) Motels usually offer their guests a small room that includes a television, a telephone, a bathroom, and a bed. Bed-and-breakfast homes usually offer the same comforts to their guests. (5) In addition, some motels provide guests with a free breakfast. Bed-and-breakfast homes include breakfast in the cost of the overnight stay. (6) Despite these similarities, motels and bed-and-breakfast homes have important differences. (7) For instance, motel rooms are usually cold and impersonal. Bed-and-breakfast rooms have a warm, friendly atmosphere. (8) Motel rooms generally look the same. Each bed-and-breakfast room is very different because of the different people who own the homes. (9) People staying in a motel usually stay in the business section of town and rarely get to see the neighborhoods of these towns. Guests in

bed-and-breakfast homes stay in the neighborhoods and can get a clear idea of what the town is like. (10) In addition, people who stay in motels seldom get to meet the residents of the town they are visiting. Travellers staying overnight in bed-and-breakfast homes have a chance to meet and get to know the people who own the homes. (11) People may stay in motels as long as they want. People cannot always stay in bed-and-breakfast homes for long periods of time. (12) Motels are located throughout the United States. Bed-and-breakfast homes cannot be found in every town since they are just starting to become popular. (13) Finally, motel rooms are usually very expensive. Bed-and-breakfast rooms are inexpensive. (14) Motels are still the most common and convenient places to stay. Because bed-and-breakfast homes have many advantages, they will probably become more and more popular in the future.

O N   Y O U R   O W N

Ideas for Guided and Open Writing

GUIDED WRITING EXERCISE: Many people look back on their childhood and remember the games they used to play, the toys they used to have, the clothes they used to wear, and the way their parents disciplined them. These people often talk about how times have changed. Think about your own childhood, and think about the lives today of children such as your younger brother or sister, a younger cousin or nephew, or a younger neighbor down the street. What kinds of games or activities do they play? What kinds of toys do they have? What style of clothes do they wear? How do their parents treat them? Do you see any important similarities or differences? In a well-developed paragraph of approximately 100–150 words, compare or contrast two elements of your childhood such as games, toys, clothes, or discipline with the same elements in the lives of children today. You might begin your paragraph with "Children's —— and —— today are similar to (or different from) the —— and —— I had as a child." Think about the recent trend of children wearing designer jeans. What did you wear as a child? Consider the electronic toys children play with. Are they similar to anything you played with? What were some of your favorite games to play? Do children still play those games? How were you disciplined when you misbehaved? Does the same thing happen to children today?

OPEN WRITING IDEAS: The following topics are suggestions for open writing exercises to help you practice the structures presented in this chapter. Develop these ideas into paragraphs of 100–150 words. Focus your attention on making comparisons.

1. Consider all the changes you have made in your writing since the beginning of the semester. What strengths did you have then? What weaknesses did you have then? What are your strengths and weaknesses now? Compare or contrast your writing skills at the beginning of the semester with those today.

2. Pick two comic strips that are in one of the following groups: comics about family life such as *Blondie, Family Circle, The Ryatts, Better Half,* or *Momma*; comics about children such as *Dennis the Menace, Peanuts,* or *Nancy*; comics about heroes or detectives such as *Spiderman, Steve Roper,* or *Kerry Drake*; comics about women such as *Mary Worth, Brenda Starr,* or *Apartment 3G*. Compare or contrast the main characters in these two strips, the kinds of problems the characters have, and their ways of solving problems.

CHAPTER 28

Giving Reasons

Another purpose for combining sentences to show the relationship between them is to show that one gives a reason for a result or a cause for an effect. Consider the following sentences. What is the relationship between them?

> In the last few seconds of the countdown, the takeoff was cancelled. The radio equipment was found to be faulty.

The first sentence tells that something happened: The takeoff was cancelled. The second sentence tells why it happened. Therefore, the first sentence is the result, and the second sentence is the reason. One way to show this result-reason relationship between the sentences is to combine them with *for*.

> In the last few seconds of the countdown, the takeoff was cancelled, *for* the radio equipment was found to be faulty.

The connecting word *for* is a signal for a reason. Notice that the two sentences are connected by a comma and *for*. Connecting the two sentences with *for* alone is not enough. A comma must come before the coordinating conjunction.

The subordinators *since* and *because* can also join a reason with its result. Notice that, as in the example with *for*, the reason follows the connecting word.

TWO SENTENCES   Desert plants require very little water to survive. They are particularly appropriate for plant lovers who have little time for watering their plants.

COMBINED	Since desert plants require very little water to survive, they are particularly appropriate for plant lovers who have little time for watering their plants.
TWO SENTENCES	The flood caused irreparable damage to hundreds of houses. The President declared the area a national disaster.
COMBINED	Because the flood caused irreparable damage to hundreds of houses, the President declared the area a national disaster.

Connecting words and expressions such as *therefore, thus, consequently, as a result,* and *for this reason* also show result-reason relationships. When you use one of these connectors, give the reason first and follow it with a semicolon. Then write the connector and place a comma after it.

TWO SENTENCES	The attempted assassination of the President was shockingly unexpected. The event made people concerned about increasing Presidential protection.
COMBINED	The attempted assassination of the President was shockingly unexpected; thus, the event made people concerned about increasing Presidential protection.
TWO SENTENCES	The price of raw materials and labor has doubled in the last ten years. Construction costs of new homes have increased dramatically.
COMBINED	The price of raw materials and labor has doubled in the last ten years; therefore, construction costs of new homes have increased dramatically.
TWO SENTENCES	The new renters were late with every month's rent. The owner asked them to leave.
COMBINED	The new renters were late with every month's rent; consequently, the owner asked them to leave.
TWO SENTENCES	The mayor reduced the number of hours people could water their gardens. Over 10 trillion cubic feet of water was saved in one summer.

COMBINED	The mayor reduced the number of hours people could water their gardens; <u>as a result,</u> over 10 trillion cubic feet of water was saved in one summer.
TWO SENTENCES	Microwave ovens leak a certain amount of radiation while in use. Persons wearing pacemakers should keep a safe distance from microwaves.
COMBINED	Microwave ovens leak a certain amount of radiation while in use; <u>for this reason,</u> persons wearing pacemakers should keep a safe distance from microwaves.

In the following practices, you will be asked to combine sentences using the various connectors that show reason and result. After practicing with them, try to use the connectors in your own writing.

P R A C T I C E   2 8 A

Showing Reason and Result

DIRECTIONS: Read the following paragraph. Most of the numbered items contain sentences paired together. Copy the paragraph, combining the paired sentences with the connector that is in parentheses at the end of each pair. Check your work carefully.

Harnessing the Sun

(1) The sun is a limitless and free energy source. Many Americans are seriously studying the advantages of this energy source. (as a result) (2) Solar energy is one of the safest and cleanest of all possible energy sources now thought of as a substitute for fossil fuels such as coal and oil. Solar power plants, for example, would not pollute the earth or the atmosphere. (because) (3) Solar energy can also be a practical energy source. Researchers estimate that only 15,000 square miles of Arizona and California desert set aside for solar power plants could meet the energy needs of the United States for several decades. (since) (4) However, how to use the sun as a source of energy is not yet completely understood and probably will not be in the near future.

Solar power will probably not become the main energy source in the United States very soon. (as a result) (5) Americans, for example, have depended almost completely on coal and oil. Most people have given little thought to searching for energy in other sources and other places until recently. (because) (6) Moreover, very few businesses such as natural gas and electric companies, large oil companies, and mining companies are interested in developing solar power. Providing solar energy would not bring them a big profit. (since) (7) If every home or building ran completely or partly on solar power, the country would use considerably less natural gas, coal, oil, and electricity. Utilities, oil companies, and the like would probably lose money. (for this reason) (8) These companies are not willing to pay for solar energy research. Until now, money for researching solar power has come mostly from groups and citizens concerned about the environment. (since) (9) These groups have made slow progress in developing cheap ways to use solar energy. Not many homeowners are willing to install solar heating. (consequently) (10) However, times and attitudes have begun to change. The Energy Research and Development Agency is beginning to examine the feasibility of solar power. (for) (11) In addition, some businesses are beginning to make and sell solar energy equipment for the home. The government and businesses are starting to cooperate about using solar energy. (therefore) (12) As a result of all these efforts, using solar energy may one day be a practical solution for meeting America's energy needs.

P R A C T I C E   2 8 B

Showing Cause and Effect

DIRECTIONS: Read the following paragraph. Most of the numbered items have sentences paired together. Copy the paragraph, combining the paired sentences with the connector that is in parentheses at the end of each pair. Check your work carefully.

***Destiny in
the Stars***

(1) Astrology claims to predict the future by studying the position of the planets and stars. It has been popular for over 3,000 years. (because) (2) It has been important in the lives of many people for so long. Astrology has an interesting history. (since) (3) Babylonian and Roman societies trusted astrology. They used it to help them predict events in the lives of the common people as well as in the lives of their leaders. (therefore) (4) One Babylonian king died a few days after an eclipse. The ancient astrologers said that eclipses predicted the death of kings. (consequently) (5) Later around 350 B.C., the Greeks honored their gods by naming constellations, or groups of stars, after them. Each constellation was said to represent the personality of that god. (as a result) (6) The Greeks believed that their gods controlled the fate of ordinary people. It was then easy for the Greeks to believe that the stars control the fate of humans. (since) (7) Astrology eventually became popular in Asia and Europe. (8) The Catholic Church there did not want its members to follow astrology. The Church criticized it. (because) (9) Many people pointed out that astrology made false predictions. (10) For example, astrologers believed that the sign of Libra was associated with the wind. When they saw a group of planets arranged in the sky near Libra in 1186, they predicted a terrible hurricane. (therefore) (11) However, this disaster never happened. (12) In 1524, people noticed a group of planets around Aquarius, associated with water. They predicted an enormous flood. (consequently) (13) The flood never took place; in fact, the month was even drier than usual. (14) In spite of these criticisms, astrology spread to North America, where many people still find it interesting and enjoyable.

P R A C T I C E   2 8 C

Showing Cause and Effect

DIRECTIONS: Read the following paragraph. Most of the numbered items have sentences paired together. Copy the paragraph, combining each pair of sentences. Use each of the following words at least once: <u>because</u>, <u>for</u>, <u>since</u>, <u>therefore</u>, <u>thus</u>, <u>consequently</u>, <u>as a result</u>, and <u>for this reason</u>. Check your work carefully.

The French Connection

(1) English has been influenced by many languages, especially French. (2) After England was defeated by William the Conqueror in 1066, the French controlled England for 200 years. French became the official language of England. (3) Everyone in power spoke French. Many French words eventually became part of English. (4) In addition, the French took over the government. They also had control of the courts. (5) The justice system was controlled by the French. Lawyers and judges used French for many legal terms. (6) For example, French words such as *attorney, judge, defendant, prison, sue,* and *pardon* are part of English today. They were taken from French and eventually used in English courts. (7) In addition, the people who spoke French were mainly from the upper class. They thought French was much more elegant than English, which was spoken by the lower class. (8) The people in the upper class wanted to separate themselves from the people of the lower classes. (9) In addition, the upper class had the time and the money for gourmet cooking, decorating, fashion, and etiquette. Many words used in these areas were taken from French. (10) For example, people from the upper class thought that English words such as *chicken, cow,* and *pig* were not elegant enough to describe food. These people used French and substituted *poultry* for *chicken, pork* for *pig,* and *beef* for *cow.* (11) Furthermore, French words such as *fashion, gown, robe, pleat, collar,* and *button* were used by the upper class. They thought these words sounded elegant. (12) French continued to influence English for as long as the French ruled England. Many of the words in English today can be traced to the French used over 700 years ago.

ON YOUR OWN

Ideas for Guided and Open Writing

GUIDED WRITING EXERCISE: Recently the United States government passed a law that nineteen-year-old men must register for the draft. Many people have argued whether or not there should be a draft, but one of the biggest questions is who should be drafted. Historically, only men have been drafted. Some people believe that men and women both have the responsibility to defend their country during a war. Who do you think should be drafted? In a 100–150 word paragraph, attack or support the idea of drafting women. If you wish, begin your paragraph with the following: "Women should (or should not) be drafted to fight in wars." Should all women be drafted, whether or not they are married or whether or not they have children? Should age or occupation affect whether or not a woman is drafted? In your discussion try to give clear reasons for your ideas.

OPEN WRITING IDEAS: The following topics are suggestions for open writing exercises to help you practice the structures presented in this chapter. Develop these ideas into paragraphs of 100–150 words. Focus your attention on giving reasons to support your arguments.

1. Sororities, fraternities, and other social groups to bring people together are becoming popular on university and college campuses once again. Briefly discuss three reasons that this trend is happening.

2. Many local and national radio stations are broadcasting nightly talk shows in which their listeners can ask questions of well-known guest speakers. What kind of people listen to these shows? Explain your beliefs.

CHAPTER 29

Expressing Conditions

In some situations a writer needs to tell what will follow if a certain action occurs. For example, here are two points that a writer wants to make:

The temperature exceeds 100°. The medicine will spoil.

The writer means that if one event happens, the other will too. The clearest way to show this relationship is to combine the two sentences with *if*.

If the temperature exceeds 100°, the medicine will spoil.

Notice that the condition is the *if* clause. A writer can write the *if* clause either at the beginning or at the end of the sentence, as in the following:

The medicine will spoil *if the temperature exceeds 100°*.

When the *if* clause comes at the beginning of the sentence, it is followed by a comma. The following are other examples of sentences showing condition with *if*:

TWO SENTENCES	There is a war. The economy always improves.
COMBINED	If there is a war, the economy always improves.

TWO SENTENCES	People are unhappy. They make others unhappy too.
COMBINED	If people are unhappy, they make others unhappy too.
TWO SENTENCES	A person eats 100 extra calories a day. He or she can gain a pound in ten days.
COMBINED	If a person eats 100 extra calories a day, he or she can gain a pound in ten days.

Sometimes a writer wishes to indicate that if one action does not occur, another will. He or she can show this by using a comma and *or*.

TWO SENTENCES	Drivers must carry their driver's licenses. They will be fined.
COMBINED	Drivers must carry their driver's licenses, or they will be fined.
TWO SENTENCES	All nineteen-year-old men must register for the draft. They will be arrested.
COMBINED	All nineteen-year-old men must register for the draft, or they will be arrested.

Another way of showing what will happen if the first action does not occur is to use *unless*. Notice that the form of the verb in the first sentence can change when you use this word.

TWO SENTENCES	In some cities a dog must be kept on its leash. It will be taken to the dog pound.
COMBINED	In some cities *unless* a dog is kept on its leash, it will be taken to the dog pound.
TWO SENTENCES	A car should have regular tune-ups. The engine will begin to knock.
COMBINED	*Unless* a car has regular tune-ups, the engine will begin to knock.

When the *unless* clause comes at the beginning of the sentence, it is followed by a comma. The following practices will provide an opportunity to combine sentences that express conditions.

P R A C T I C E   2 9 A

Showing Conditional Relationships

DIRECTIONS: Read the following paragraph. Most of the numbered items have sentences paired together. In most instances, the sentences will not make sense until they are combined. Copy the paragraph, combining the paired sentences with the words in parentheses at the end of each pair. Check your work carefully.

Bicarbonate of Soda: Its Many Uses

(1) Bicarbonate of soda, commonly known as baking soda, is a natural product used for over 130 years for hundreds of purposes. (2) For example, a person has acid indigestion, or heartburn, from eating too much or eating too fast. He or she can drink a glass of water with one-half teaspoon of baking soda dissolved in it in order to relieve the pain. (if) (3) However, since baking soda contains salt sodium, a person on a salt-free diet should not take this solution. He or she does it under a doctor's care. (unless) (4) Moreover, this baking soda remedy should not be used for more than two weeks. A person can feel worse. (or) (5) A person wants a relaxing, refreshing bath at the end of a tiring day. He or she can also dissolve one-half cup or more of baking soda into a tub of warm water. (if) (6) A person has insect bites, sunburn, poison ivy, and other rashes. He or she can apply a paste made from three parts baking soda to one part water for soothing relief. (if) (7) A person lightly sprinkles baking soda over the entire carpet and then vacuums it. The soda will absorb carpet odors caused by pets, food, and smoke. (if) (8) This can be used for all carpets. The colors in the carpet fade. (unless) (9) The carpet must also be dry. The baking soda will cake. (or) (10) Moreover, an open box of baking soda left in the refrigerator will absorb food odors very well. The baking soda is fresh. (if) (11) In addition, a person should soak combs and brushes in a basin containing four tablespoons of baking soda and warm water. He or she wants to remove oil and dirt from them without leaving a soapy film. (if) (12) In addition, a person can sometimes use baking soda as a toothpaste to remove stains on teeth. His or her dentist warns against doing so. (unless) (13) These are only some of the many uses for baking soda, which is an economical and handy product.

P R A C T I C E   2 9 B

Showing Conditional Relationships

DIRECTIONS: Read the following paragraph. Most of the numbered items contain sentences paired together. In most instances, the sentences will not make sense until they are combined. Copy the paragraph, combining the paired sentences with the word in parentheses at the end of each pair. Check your work carefully.

Some Useful Household Tips

(1) Many people remember their mothers giving them advice about cleaning furniture, jewelry, carpets, windows, and other household items. (2) People can still receive advice as well as share their own helpful household hints. They read "Hints from Heloise," the popular newspaper column. (if) (3) They read the column. They can learn about surprising remedies that she has tested herself. (if) (4) Most people, for example, would not usually know how to remove ballpoint ink stains from clothing. They had tried many remedies themselves. (unless) (5) They take Heloise's advice. They will find that using hairspray will remove the stain. (if) (6) In addition, they should not use soap and water. They will make the ink stay on the fabric permanently. (or) (7) Also, most people probably would never imagine that one of the best ways to clean windows is with newspapers moistened with ammonia and water. They read it in her column or someone told them. (unless) (8) Moreover, people asked the manager of a record store. They would probably not know that putting a warped record between two sheets of glass and placing them in the sun will straighten the record. (unless) (9) People wanted to know how to make their razor blades last. They could read Heloise to learn that soaking them in alcohol or in mineral oil after using them works. (if) (10) All of these practical tips make "Hints from Heloise" a useful newspaper column for many people.

P R A C T I C E   2 9 C

Showing Conditional Relationships

DIRECTIONS: Read the following paragraph. Most of the numbered items contain sentences paired together. In most instances, the sentences will not make sense until they are combined. Copy the paragraph, combining the paired sentences with <u>unless</u>, <u>if</u>, or <u>or</u>. Check your work carefully.

A Need for Immigrant Workers

(1) Unlike most Americans, Malcolm Lovell, Jr. and Kenneth McLennan, economists who worked for Presidents Nixon and Ford, believe that the United States needs to encourage immigration. (2) They predict that the United States will not have enough workers by the year 2000. The government gradually allows more immigrants to work in this country. (3) America, they point out, must have enough workers. Everyone in the country, especially the elderly, will be affected. (4) Lovell and McLennan explain that there are not enough salaries because of a lack of workers. There will not be enough money from taxes. (5) There is enough money from taxes. There will not be enough money for Social Security, which the elderly depend on. (6) Some people believe that unskilled workers in the United States will lose their jobs to large numbers of immigrants who are willing to work for low salaries. (7) Lovell and McLennan disagree, saying that the undesirable jobs such as picking vegetables, cleaning houses, and washing dishes in restaurants will not be filled. These immigrants do not come. (8) In addition, these economists state that the first people the government should allow to immigrate into America should be young, skilled workers. The economy will suffer. (9) Therefore, Lovell and McLennan believe that the economy of the United States will improve. The government encourages more young, skilled workers to immigrate to America.

ON YOUR OWN

Ideas for Guided and Open Writing

GUIDED WRITING EXERCISE: Suing people is becoming a common practice in the United States. People call their lawyers over what seem like simple problems with landlords, mechanics, department stores, police, and so on. Lawsuits are so common, in fact, that almost everyone in our society is affected by them directly or indirectly. For example, many doctors do not give emergency aid to accident victims because they are afraid of being sued later on. Teachers are also worried about lawsuits filed by parents who are disappointed with their children's education. In fact, some teachers have been sued for passing students who cannot read or write, whereas others have been sued for holding students back. Even parents have been sued by their children who claim that their parents were either too easy or too strict in disciplining them. What do you think about this common practice of suing people? In a well-developed paragraph of approximately 100–150 words, discuss whether you believe the increased number of lawsuits is positive or negative for our society. You might begin your paragraph with one of the following: "The threat of lawsuits keeps people in our society honest." or "The trend of filing lawsuits shows that people in our society are selfish and greedy." How do you think people are affected when they know that filing lawsuits is easy? In your paragraph, give personal examples or examples you have read about to support your statements. Include conditional statements in your work.

OPEN WRITING IDEAS: The following topics are suggestions for open writing exercises to help you practice the structures presented in this chapter. Develop these ideas into paragraphs of 100–150 words. Focus your attention on expressing conditions.

1. Think about an event in your past when you learned something important about yourself or about someone else. If you could relive that experience, what would you do differently? If you knew then what you know today, would you have acted the same way?

2. Think of an outdoor activity that you are familiar with, such as riding a horse, camping, flying an airplane, or riding a canoe. Remember the first time you did it and problems you might have had. Offer advice to a friend about to try that activity for the first time. Tell him or her about some of the problems that could happen and suggest ways to solve them.

CHAPTER 30

Showing Contradictions

Sometimes situations arise in which a writer presents ideas that seem to contradict each other. He gives one piece of information and then immediately follows it with more information that seems to be the opposite of what he has just said:

> Air travel is quite expensive. It is the quickest most efficient way of long distance travel.

Because these sentences are not connected, they fail to make the writer's point clearly. How can they be improved to show the contradiction he wants to emphasize? One way is to combine them with *but* or *yet*.

> Air travel is quite expensive, *yet it is the quickest most efficient* way of long distance travel.

Notice that the two sentences are combined with the word *yet* preceded by a comma. Sentences expressing contradiction can also be joined with *but*.

TWO SENTENCES	Japanese cars are expensive to purchase. Their gas economy makes them the most popular small cars in America.
COMBINED	Japanese cars are expensive to purchase, *but* their gas economy makes them the most popular small cars in America.

Connectors such as *nevertheless* and *however* also indicate that the second part of a statement contradicts or raises questions about the first part. When used to connect sentences, these words are preceded by semicolons and followed by commas.

TWO SENTENCES	*Superman II* was trite and predictable. It was a box-office success.
COMBINED	*Superman II* was trite and predictable; *nevertheless*, it was a box-office success.
TWO SENTENCES	The illness caused her great pain. She continued her work until the day she collapsed and was taken to the hospital.
COMBINED	The illness caused her great pain; *however*, she continued her work until the day she collapsed and was taken to the hospital.

Contradictions can also be shown by writing with *though, although,* and *even though*. These words can be placed in front of either the first or the second clause, depending on the meaning intended. Consider the following two sentences:

Paper diapers are quite expensive. The majority of mothers in the United States use them for their infants.

These sentences can be combined with *though*. Notice that the *though* can be placed before either one of the clauses, depending on what the writer wishes to emphasize.

COMBINED	*Though* paper diapers are quite expensive, the majority of mothers in the United States use them for their infants.
COMBINED	*Though* the majority of mothers in the United States use paper diapers for their infants, paper diapers are quite expensive.

The following sentences can be combined with *although* or *even though*:

TWO SENTENCES	Working in the copper mines is a popular occupation in Arizona. It is extremely dangerous work.
COMBINED	*Although* working in the copper mines is a popular occupation in Arizona, it is extremely dangerous work.

TWO SENTENCES	Horace could not stand the sight of blood. He became a surgeon.
COMBINED	*Even though* Horace could not stand the sight of blood, he became a surgeon.

In spite of and *despite* are very emphatic ways of showing contradiction. For example, in a composition a writer states the following sentences:

She was offered a large salary at a prominent law firm. She continued to be a rural legal aid attorney.

The idea the writer wishes to emphasize is the contradiction. *In spite of*, *in spite of the fact that*, and *despite* can help the writer emphasize the relationship.

In spite of the large salary she was offered at a prominent law firm, she continued to be a rural legal aid attorney.

In spite of the fact that she was offered a large salary at a prominent law firm, she continued to be a rural legal aid attorney.

Despite the large salary she was offered at a prominent law firm, she continued to be a rural legal aid attorney.

Notice that when using *in spite of*, *in spite of the fact that*, and *despite*, the wording of the entire sentence must be changed.

In the following paragraphs you will have the opportunity to practice combining sentences to emphasize contradictions. Look for sentences in your own compositions that can be combined in this way.

P R A C T I C E   3 0 A

Expressing Opposite Ideas

DIRECTIONS: Read the following paragraph. Most of the numbered items have sentences paired together. Copy the paragraph, combining the paired sentences with the connector that is in parentheses at the end of each pair. Check your work carefully.

Lead Poisoning

(1) Lead poisoning, which causes serious health problems and sometimes death, has existed for centuries. (2) People are becoming more and more aware of the dangers of lead. Lead poisoning is still a great threat to the health of people in modern societies. (nevertheless) (3) For example, our atmosphere contains a large amount of lead pollution. The American government has established strict antipollution controls. (even though) (4) In fact, over 98 percent of all atmospheric lead pollution in the United States comes from using leaded gasoline. Efforts have been made to encourage using unleaded gasoline. (in spite of the fact) (5) Many states require automobile emissions testing. Many cars continue to pollute the air. (although) (6) The attempts have been partly successful. People breathe in small amounts of lead that has been added to gasoline to reduce engine knocking. (neverthless) (7) Many people think that using pesticides is the only problem with crops. The lead in the air that settles on these crops is also a serious problem. (although) (8) People can wash the vegetables they eat. They cannot wash the grains that farm animals eat. (however) (9) People are careful to wash their food. They still eat a certain amount of food containing lead. (even though) (10) In addition, paint containing lead, which is used on household items such as dishes and toys, is still a health problem. Manufacturers are now trying to control the amount of lead in these products. (but) (11) Efforts have been made to educate the general public about the effects of lead-based products. Each year about 200 children die from lead poisoning, and thousands of others suffer its effects in the form of brain damage and hyperactivity. (in spite of the fact that) (12) People have become more educated about lead poisoning. Its tragic effects will continue until lead is no longer used. (yet)

P R A C T I C E   3 0 B :

Expressing Opposite Ideas

DIRECTIONS: Read the following paragraph. It is part of a letter to the editor written by someone who believes that modern medicine is not the best way to cure diseases. Most of the numbered items in the paragraph contain sentences paired together. Copy the letter, combining the paired sentences with the words that are in parentheses at the end of each pair. Check your work carefully.

Problems of Modern Medicine

(1) For thousands of years people involved in healing the sick have argued over the best ways of curing illnesses. (2) Medical science has had much success in helping cure major diseases. The arguments continue. (even though) (3) Scientific, or modern, medicine is the most popular medical theory today. It still has many problems. (although) (4) Modern medicine claims to take care of the entire body. Doctors who follow its theories think of the body as a number of separate and isolated parts, such that each organ or part works independently of the others. (however) (5) The organs of the body actually work together as a whole unit. Patients are sent to specialists who treat specific organs. (despite the fact that) (6) For example, a patient may have heart problems that have weakened other parts of the body. When the patient visits a heart specialist he or she is given medicine only for the heart. (nevertheless) (7) This medicine may help the heart. It does not help the other organs that have become weak because of the heart problems. (but) (8) The medicine is supposed to make the patient feel better. According to statistics, it often hurts other organs in the body and causes more problems. (in spite of the fact that) (9) Moreover, modern medical doctors claim to have the most complete knowledge about health. They have only recently recognized the importance of nutrition and diet in healing the body. (despite) (10) In addition, stress from a person's job, family, and money matters often causes a person many health problems. Doctors try to stop the problems without considering what caused these problems. (yet) (11) For example, drugs given for minor headaches may stop the headaches for a short period of time. The medicine does not cure the cause of the headaches and they often continue. (but) (12) Many problems exist in the medical field today. Doctors are becoming aware of these problems and are trying to make improvements in modern medicine. (though)

PRACTICE 30C:

Expressing Opposite Ideas

DIRECTIONS: Read the following paragraph. Most of the numbered items have sentences paired together. Copy the paragraph, using each of the following words at least once: <u>however</u>, <u>yet</u>, <u>but</u>, <u>nevertheless</u>, <u>although</u>, <u>even though</u>, <u>despite</u>, <u>in spite of the fact that</u>, and <u>in spite of</u>. Check your work carefully.

The Advantages of Bilingual Education

(1) Bilingual education uses two languages to teach subjects. (2) Bilingual education is common throughout much of the world. It is criticized in the United States. (3) Approximately 12 million children in the United States who do not speak English as a native language would benefit from a bilingual program. Bilingual education is still not accepted by many people. (4) Some people think that the children in bilingual education programs will learn neither language well. Statistics show that these children do as well if not better in school than students in traditional programs. (5) In addition, people argue that bilingual education is expensive as a result of having to train teachers to learn another language. Many teachers are already bilingual and teach in two languages. (6) Moreover, people unfamiliar with bilingual education argue that citizens of this country should learn English. Children in bilingual programs do learn English as well as keep their own language. (7) Another common argument is that children in the United States do not need to continue to learn their native language in school. Studies show that children who lose their native language do poorly in school. (8) Many people also believe that bilingual education helps only minority children. It gives the English-speaking student the advantage of learning another language fluently. (9) Learning a foreign language is not considered important by many people. Today, knowing a foreign language is very important in traveling, communicating, and working around the world. (10) Criticism against bilingual education continues in the United States. A growing number of teachers are starting to recognize its many benefits.

O N   Y O U R   O W N

Ideas for Guided and Open Writing

GUIDED WRITING EXERCISE: Many people are very concerned about violence as described in television, or radio, and in newspapers and the way it affects people's behavior. They talk about the assassination attempt on President Reagan's life in 1981 as an example. This violent act was supposedly copied from a movie that the assassin had seen. Another example has to do with a 1977 court case of Ronny Zemora, a teenager arrested in Miami, Florida, for murdering an eighty-five-year-old woman. Ronny's lawyer said that

Ronny should not be held responsible for the murder because the boy had been hypnotized by violence on television. As a result, the lawyer said that Ronny committed the murder under the hypnotic influence of television. The court found Ronny guilty, but many people believed that this decision was unfair. These people state that television violence does influence behavior. Do you think that the violence on television makes people act violently? In a well-developed paragraph of approximately 100–150 words, agree or disagree with the idea that watching violence on television causes people to act violently. Do you think that people see so much violence on television that they begin to imitate that violence in life? You might begin your paragraph with "Watching violence on television encourages people to act violently." In your paragraph, consider whether violence on television teaches people about violent acts such as robbery, murder, suicide, or the destruction of property. Does watching violence on television influence people to treat others violently? For example, does constantly seeing television violence, such as a man shooting his wife, cause people to accept that violent behavior as normal? Or can something mechanical such as television really be blamed for people acting violently? In your paragraph, pay attention to writing sentences that emphasize contradictions clearly.

OPEN WRITING IDEAS: The following topics are suggestions for open writing exercises to help you practice the structures presented in this chapter. Develop these ideas into paragraphs of 100–150 words. Focus your attention on showing contradictions.

1. Each year many people go to national parks, canyons, rivers, lakes, and oceans in order to go cliff diving, tubing down the rapids, or hang gliding. Because many people have died doing these things, government officials have tried to ban these activities in certain areas. Do you think that the government has the right to protect people by banning these activities in some recreational areas? Or do you believe that people should be allowed to go cliff diving, tubing, or hang gliding anywhere at their own risk?

2. Laetrile, a controversial drug many people have used for cancer, has been banned by the Federal Drug Administration (FDA). The FDA has not been able to prove that laetrile is completely safe or effective for humans. Nevertheless, many patients who have been told that they cannot be cured go to clinics outside the United States where they are given laetrile or other drugs banned by the FDA. Do you think that cancer patients have the right to look for a cure, whether that cure is proven safe or not?

UNIT E
REVIEW

Combining Sentences
for Special Purposes

DIRECTIONS: Read the following paragraph. All of the numbered items have sentences grouped together. Copy the paragraph, combining each group of sentences in the most appropriate way. Check your work carefully.

The Newspaper:
A Resource
for Advice

(1) The daily newspaper provides readers with current news. It also offers them useful advice. This useful advice concerns a wide range of topics. (2) For example, people have questions about a variety of household problems such as removing stubborn stains and wallpapering rooms. They can turn to columns such as "Hints from Heloise" in one of over 500 newspapers across the country to find the solutions to these and many other household problems. (3) Other people who have problems with their friends, relatives, or fellow employees could consult either Abigail Van Buren or Ann Landers. Abigail Van Buren and Ann Landers are well-known newspaper columnists offering practical advice to millions of readers. (4) In addition, many readers have been victims of false advertising claims or dishonest business dealings. These readers write to columns on consumer protection. (5) The problems of these dissatisfied people are solved quickly. Businesses in the community do not want bad publicity. (6) Moreover, persons with physical handicaps can consult newspaper columns such as "Handicapsules." This column informs disabled people of solutions to their physical, personal, and employment problems. (7) Of course, advice about tax and other financial matters is readily available through banks. People are able to find information about these subjects in newspaper columns as well. These columns

are written by money experts such as Sylvia Porter. (8) In addition, many readers want to make real estate investments. These investments should be safe and wise. These readers want to keep informed about the current real estate market. (9) They invest in a new house. They can consult a newspaper column for advice on current real estate matters. (10) Other readers want to invest their money in the stock market. These readers can consult columns containing current stock market news. (11) Another popular column is the "Readers' Doctor." It is a column offering medical advice. (12) People generally trust their personal doctors. They feel a sense of security in getting a free, second medical opinion. (13) Almost everyone reads a newspaper. It is one of the most effective ways of distributing information to the greatest number of people.

UNIT F

Handbook: Reviewing Parts of Speech

This unit briefly reviews English grammar. Part A discusses six parts of speech. Parts B and C show how the parts of speech are used to build various types of English sentences. Part D covers phrases and clauses, both of which are important elements of a sentence.

A. Parts of Speech

1.0 Nouns:

A *noun* is a word used to name a person (sister, Mr. Wood), place (Los Angeles, beach), thing (kangaroo, sun), idea (loneliness, beauty), or activity (skiing, eating). Nouns are easy to find because they often follow the articles *a, an,* or *the*. Nouns are also easily recognized by their three typical forms:

SINGULAR	telephone, mosquito, ox
PLURAL	telephones, mosquitoes, oxen
POSSESSIVE	telephone's, mosquito's, mosquitoes', ox's, oxen's

1.1 Common Nouns or Proper Nouns:

Nouns can be classified as either common nouns or proper nouns. A *proper noun* is the name of a particular person, place, thing, or idea (Justice O'Connor, Kuwait, *Jaws*, United Nations). A *common noun* is a noun used as the name of any one of a class or group of persons (judge, country, movie, organization).

1.2 Pronouns:

Pronouns are words used in place of a noun.

> Sid twisted Sid's back when Sid and Sheila accidentally fell into Sid and Sheila's pool.

The noun for which the pronoun substitutes is called the *antecedent*. Using pronouns makes it possible to refer to a noun without having to repeat it over again and again. Note the difference when the pronouns are substituted:

> Sid twisted *his* back when *he* and Sheila accidentally fell into *their* pool.

In the example, *Sid* is the antecedent of the singular pronouns *his* and *he*, and *Sid* and *Sheila* are the antecedents of the plural pronoun *their*.

1.3 Pronoun Antecedent:

Pronouns must agree in number and in gender with their antecedents. All personal pronouns have number (singular or plural), and the third person singular forms indicate gender (masculine, feminine, and neuter).

> The two-year-old boy ran toward *his* mother.
> The Princess of Wales is a favorite among *her* subjects.

1.4 Pronoun Forms:

Pronouns take different forms: subject, object, and possessive. The *subject form* is used when the pronoun replaces the subject.

> *Marcia* was a journalist in Viet Nam.
> *She* was a journalist in Viet Nam.

The object form is used when the pronoun replaces the object of a verb or preposition in a sentence.

> The waiter showed *the guests* to a table.
> The waiter showed *them* to a table. (*Them* is the object of the verb.)

The Vice President sat between *the two doctors*.
The Vice President sat between *them*. (*Them* is the object of the preposition *between*.)

SINGULAR PRONOUNS

	Subject form	Object form	Possessive form
First person:	I	me	my, mine
Second person:	you	you	your, yours
Third person:	he	him	his
	she	her	her, hers
	it	it	its

PLURAL PRONOUNS

	Subject form	Object form	Possessive form
First person:	we	us	our, our
Second person:	you	you	your, yours
Third person:	they	them	their, theirs

The possessive forms *mine, yours, hers, ours,* and *theirs* are used only when no noun follows the pronoun.

Those goggles are *mine*.   Which wet set suit is *yours*?
Those are *my* goggles.   Which is *your* wet suit?

1.5 Personal, Relative, Demonstrative, and Indefinite Pronouns:

Among the kinds of pronouns are the personal pronoun, the relative pronoun, the demonstrative pronoun, and the indefinite pronoun.

1.5a Personal Pronouns:

Personal pronouns change their form depending on their function in a sentence.

	SINGULAR		PLURAL	
	Subject form	Object form	Subject form	Object form
First person:	I	me	we	us
Second person:	you	you	you	you
Third person:	he, she, it	him, her, it	they, it	them

He promised to return soon.

We visited a banana plantation in Puerto Rico.

The director will give *us* the application forms.

1.5b Relative Pronouns:

A *relative pronoun* is used to introduce a dependent clause, a clause that does not make sense by itself, and to *relate* that clause to another word in the sentence. Relative pronouns are *who, whom, which,* and *that*. In each of the following examples, the dependent clause is printed in italics and the relative pronoun is in the boldface. The arrow points out the word to which the pronoun relates.

The student **who** *is waiting for me* is from Lebanon.

The film star **whom** *we met in New York* was Robert Redford.

The train, **which** *was once the greatest means of cross-country transportation*, is dying as a form of passenger transportation in America.

The only sunset **that** *I have photographed* was in Florence, Italy.

1.5c Demonstrative Pronouns:

Demonstrative pronouns are used to identify or point out a particular person, place, or thing. *This* and *that* are singular; *these* and *those* are plural. When *this, that, these,* and *those* are used alone, they are pronouns. When these words are used in front of a noun, they are adjectives.

This *book* belongs to Sarah. (adjective)

This book belongs to Sarah. (pronoun)

SINGULAR	PLURAL
This is my concern.	*These* are my concerns.
That car is old.	*Those* cars are old.

1.5d Indefinite Pronouns:

Pronouns referring to one or more of a number of persons or things are called *indefinite pronouns*. These pronouns are confusing because some of the pronouns appear to be plural, but they are in fact singular. The following are the most common indefinite pronouns:

anybody   nobody

anyone   none

each   no one

either   somebody

everybody   someone

everyone   everything

Everybody at the football game is wearing the school colors.

Someone has just reported the accident.

2.0 Verbs:

Although nouns name whatever we are discussing, and pronouns avoid repeating nouns, we need *verbs* to describe an action or a state of being. There are two kinds of verbs: action verbs and linking verbs.

2.1 Action Verbs:

Action verbs such as *deliver, run, jump, read, invent, drop,* and *pick* state an action.

Thomas Jefferson *invented* the folding chair.

The newspaper carrier *was delivering* papers in the rain this morning.

2.2 Linking Verbs:

Some verbs do not express action. Verbs such as *be, seem,* and *become* express a state of being. They are called *linking verbs*.

The weather *is* cool.

The mailman *seems* nervous.

Joan *became* an expert at wallpapering.

Desert rain *smells* sweet. (Desert rain *is* sweet.)

The coyote *smelled* the dead rabbit.

He *grew* sad at the news. (He *is* sad by the news.)

He *grew* cucumbers in the garden.

The following is a list of other linking verbs:

appear	remain	stay
feel	smell	taste
grow	sound	turn
look		

Using linking verbs requires that the noun or pronoun following the verb be in the same form as the word referred to before the verb. Therefore, in the following sentences, the pronouns on the right of the verb must match the form of the subject. In other words, since the subject is on the left of the verb, the pronoun, which is on the right, must be in subject form because it refers back to the subject.

She is calling.   *He* seems to be the leader.

It is *she*.   The leader seems to be *he*.

Some linking verbs can show action as well as a state of being. All linking verbs can be substituted with the verb *to be*.

2.3 Verb Forms:

Verbs take certain forms. Verbs change in form to show a change in time or tense, as in the following examples:

The quarterback *is dropping* behind the line, *is picking* a receiver, and *is throwing* the ball.

The quarterback *has dropped* behind the line, *has picked* a receiver, and *has thrown* the ball.

Nearly all verbs change form (for example, *fix* to *fixed* or *know* to *knew*). All verbs in the progressive tense end in *-ing* (was walking).

2.4 Verb Phrases:

A verb consisting of more than one word is often called a *verb phrase*. A verb phrase is made up of two parts: auxiliary verb(s) (or helping verbs) and the main verb.

The turmoil *has begun*.

She *was traveling* to Utah.

He *should have rested*.

Common auxiliary verbs are *has, have, had, am, is, are, was, were, been, do, does, did, should, will, would, could, can, may,* and *must.* The main verb always follows the auxiliary verb(s) in a verb phrase.

3.0 *Adjectives and Adverbs:*

Adjectives and *adverbs* are words used to modify or describe other parts of speech.

Adjectives modify nouns and pronouns. An adjective tells what kind of person, place, thing, or idea is being described.

> an *energetic* athlete   a *large* sweater   his *strong* wishes

Adjectives also answer the following questions:

> Which one? (a *rainy* day, the *final* yard)
> Whose? (*my* tie, *his* vest, *our* cat)
> How many? (*some* problems, *several* dates)
> How much? (*no* time, *five* pounds)

Usually adjectives come right before the noun they modify or right after a linking verb.

> The *awkward, trembling* monkey jumped out of my lap.
> His face was *pale* and *anguished.*

Adverbs are modifiers that describe verbs, adjectives, and other adverbs. Adverbs answer the following questions:

> When?   To what degree?
> Where?   How often?
> How?

> The cheetah runs *quickly.* (how)
> That movie star is *very* talented. (to what degree)
> Police headquarters *sometimes* patrol the park. (how often)
> She arrived *late.* (when)
> The millionaire lived *here.* (where)

Many adverbs are easily identified because they end in *-ly* or *-ily,* such as *profoundly, sweetly,* or *kindly* and *gloomily,* or *carefully.*

> The minister spoke *kindly* to the boy.
> The student read her paragraph *carefully.*

4.0 Prepositions:

Prepositions show the location or space relationship between words. Study the following sentences:

> The customer stood —— the counter.
> The pitcher threw the ball —— second base.
> The clock was sitting —— the table.

These blanks can be filled by prepositions. A noun always follows a preposition. That noun is called the *object of the preposition*. The preposition, its object, and any words that modify the object make up the *prepositional phrase*. Notice that a preposition may be made up of more than one word. The following are some common prepositions:

above	away from	down	in front of	through
after	behind	for	near	toward
against	beneath	from	next to	until
around	behind	in	of	to
at	between		on	with
	by		over	

Now fill in the missing blank of the first sentence:

The customer stood
beside
at
by
in front of
near
the counter.

Note that all of the preceding choices are prepositional phrases.

5.0 Conjunctions:

The purpose of *conjunctions* is to join words or word groups in a sentence. Coordinate conjunctions, correlative conjunctions, and subordinate conjunctions are different types of conjunctions.

5.1 Coordinate Conjunctions:

To join words, phrases, or clauses in a sentence, we use *coordinate conjunctions: for, and, nor, but, or, yet, so*.

MaryCarmen *and* Ann are friends. (Joins two nouns)

She is sweet *yet* forceful. (Joins two adjectives)

He likes to swim *but* not to dive. (Joins two phrases)

We went home early, *for* we were exhausted. (Joins two clauses)

5.2 Correlative Conjunctions:

Correlative conjunctions are used in pairs. Correlative conjunctions include *either . . . or, neither . . . nor,* and *not only . . . but also.*

Neither Elva *nor* Natalie caught the bouquet. (Joins two nouns)

Marcus *not only* plays the saxophone, *but* he *also* plays the piano. (Joins two phrases)

Either we will get the contract *or* the other company will get it. (Joins two clauses)

5.3 Subordinate Conjunctions:

Subordinate conjunctions are used to link dependent clauses, sometimes called subordinate clauses, with the clauses they refer to.

Because René was very organized, the committee asked him to write the report.

The doctor arrived minutes *after the ambulance had driven in*.

The following are the most used subordinate conjunctions:

after	because	provided that	unless
although	before	since	when/whenever
as	even though	so that	until
as if	if	than	where/whereas
as long as	in order that	though	while
wherever	just as	whether	

B. Parts of a Sentence

6.1 Finding the Subject and the Predicate:

The standard English sentence has two main parts: *subject* and *predicate*. The subject is the word or group of words that the sentence is about. The predicate is the word or group of words that makes a statement about the subject.

SUBJECT	PREDICATE
Birds	sing.
President Reagan's plan	is not working.
That gentleman	will receive a prize.

The nouns *birds, President Reagan's plan,* and *that gentleman* — the words that tell *what* sings, *which* plan isn't working, and *who* will receive a prize — are the subjects.

A predicate is usually made up of a verb or verb phrase and the words following it. *Sing, is not working,* and *will receive* are all the *simple predicates* of the sentence.

6.2 Finding the Subject and the Verb:

To find the subject of a sentence, find the verb of the sentence and then ask yourself, "Who or what does this?" Look at the following sentence:

The puppy in the pet shop window has been barking all night.

To find the verb of a sentence, first look for the auxiliaries and then look for the main verb. *Has been* are the auxiliaries, and *barking* is the main verb. To find the subject, ask *what* has been barking. The answer to the question is *puppy* — the subject of the sentence. "In the pet shop window" is a prepositional phrase; the subject of the sentence is never in the prepositional phrase.

6.3 Compound Subjects and Predicates:

When all the subjects in a sentence refer to one verb, that sentence is said to have a *compound subject*.

Swimming and *aerobic dancing* help tone a person's muscles.
The *rich* and *poor* alike were hurt by the Depression of 1929.
Rugged mountains, abundant deserts, and *blue skies* are characteristic of the Southwest.

A *compound predicate* is two or more verbs that have the same subject.

Our organization *collects* food, *stores* it, and then *distributes* it to the needy.

C. Other Elements of a Sentence

7.1 Direct Object:

A *direct object* names the person or thing that completes the action of the verb. Ask yourself the question *what?* after the verb.

> S   V   DO
> He *built* a *cabin* last year. (*Cabin* tells what he built. *Cabin* is the direct object.)
>
> Last winter brought many *hardships* in the East. (The winter brought what? Hardships. *Hardships* is the direct object.)
>
> She married *Ricardo* last May. (Whom did she marry? Ricardo. *Ricardo* is the direct object.)

7.2 Indirect Objects:

Some verbs (such as *give, offer, bring, take, lend, send, buy,* and *sell*) may have both a direct object and an indirect object. An *indirect object* tells to whom or for whom something is done.

> Elizabeth offered *me* a piece of pie. (The indirect object *me* tells whom the piece of pie is for.)
>
> Terry sold *Diana* the stereo. (The stereo was sold *to Diana*.)

7.3 Subject Complement:

Sentences with linking verbs (*appear, be, become, feel, look, taste,* and so on) have three main parts: subject, linking verb, and subject complement. A *subject complement* is a noun, pronoun, or adjective that renames the subject or describes the subject. These complements complete the meaning of a sentence.

NOUN	Anne is going to be a *principal* soon.
PRONOUN	The idea is *theirs*.
ADJECTIVE	The park seems *pleasant*.

Note that if the subject complement is a pronoun, then the pronoun must be in its subject form.

> It appeared to be *he*.
> The winner is *she*.

D. Kinds of Phrases and Clauses

8.0 Phrases:

A *phrase* is a group of related words without a subject and verb. This group of words functions as a grammatical unit. Study the following sentences:

> She always walks home *after her yoga class*.
> The owner *of the restaurant* never ate the cook's food.

The italicized word groups are prepositional phrases. In addition to prepositional phrases, which you have already studied in this review, four other kinds of phrases will be discussed: appositive, participial, gerund, and infinitive.

8.1 Appositives:

An *appositive* is a noun placed beside another noun or pronoun in order to identify or describe it more fully. Most appositives follow the words they explain; they are usually set off by commas.

> *The Rocky Horror Picture Show*, a *satire*, is considered a cult classic.
> An herb used generally in Mexican and Chinese cooking, *coriander*, is difficult to find.

8.2 Appositive Phrase:

An *appositive phrase* is made up of an appositive and its modifiers.

> That university, *a great Southern institution of learning*, is approximately 250 years old.
> The eel, *a deadly snakelike fish*, has smooth, slimy skin.
> Coral, *a skeletal deposit produced by polyps*, is considered a semiprecious stone.

8.3 Participles:

A *participle* is a verb form used as an adjective. Participles may be -*ing* words or past participles such as *exciting, closed,* and *torn*. The participles in the following sentences are in boldfaced type. The words that each of the participles modifies are in italics.

The movie was an **overwhelming** *success.*
Writing is an **exciting** *activity.*
That was a **trying** *situation.*
This is a **closed** *case.*
Please change my **torn** *sheet.*
The doctor set Julius's **broken** *arm* in a cast.

8.4 Participial Phrases:

A participial phrase consists of a participle plus modifiers.

Having studied, Pete was prepared for his exam.
Having studied biology all night, Pete was prepared for his exam.

In both of the preceding sentences, *having studied* is a participle modifying *Pete*. In the second sentence, *having studied* is only a part of a participial phrase. The phrase is completed with "biology all night."

The following are examples of sentences with participial phrases. Remember that the entire participial phrase acts as a unit. The participial phrases are in italics, and the words they modify follow.

Remembering her previous experience with the doctor, Katherine quickly recovered her good health.
Dialing the telephone quickly, DeWayne called the paramedics.
Disgusted by his behavior, Gilda soon stopped seeing her friend.

8.5 Absolute Phrases:

An *absolute phrase* consists of a noun plus an incomplete verb. An absolute phrase explains or gives more information about the action in the sentence.

The ceiling having been painted, I soon left. (*The ceiling having been painted* tells why I soon left.)

The absolute phrase can appear at the end of a sentence as well as at the beginning.

She walked on the stage confidently, *her spirits lifting when she saw her parents*. (*Her spirits lifting when she saw her parents* explains why she walked on the stage confidently.)

8.6 Gerunds:

A *gerund* is an *-ing* word that is formed from a verb and functions as a noun. A gerund can be used anywhere in a sentence that a noun can be used.

> *Jogging* has become a popular sport for senior citizens. (Subject)
> Gloria considers *roller skating* dull. (Direct object)
> Water can be purified by *boiling*. (Object of a preposition)
> The best part of the evening was *eating*. (Subject complement)

8.7 Gerund Phrases:

A *gerund phrase* consists of a gerund with its modifiers. The gerund phrase functions as one unit.

> *Buying a Mustang* was Sonny's dream. (Subject)
> Her duties include *telling the children a story* and *serving their snacks*. (Direct object)
> The boss praised Jefferson for *arriving on time*. (Object of a preposition)
> Their specialty is *catering weddings*. (Subject complement)

8.8 Infinitives:

An *infinitive* is a form consisting of *to* + a verb. An infinitive can function as both a noun or a modifier.

> *To communicate* was Helen Keller's goal. (Subject)
> She likes *to scuba dive*. (Direct object)
> Our only hope is *to improve*. (Subject complement)

8.9 Infinitive Phrases:

An *infinitive phrase* consists of an infinitive with its modifiers. The entire phrase functions as either a noun or a modifier.

> Mary Ann didn't want *to fail*. (Infinitive)
> Mary Ann didn't want *to fail her chemistry course*. (Infinitive phrase)

In the first sentence, *to fail* is the infinitive. In the second sentence, that infinitive has a direct object, *chemistry course*. Here are some other examples of infinitive phrases used as nouns and modifiers:

Lisa is trying *to do her best*. (Direct object)

To spend money wisely is difficult. (Subject)

President Nixon's greatest wish was *to be reelected*. (Subject complement)

Antonio searched for a place *to think about his problems*. (Adjective phrase describing *place*. The phrase tells what kind of place.)

Ted bought the old book *to study early types of printing*. (*To study early types of printing* functions as an adverb phrase, modifying *bought*. The phrase answers the question *why*; it provides the reason.)

9.0 Clauses:

A *clause* is a group of related words that contains a subject and a verb. There are two kinds of clauses: independent and dependent.

9.1 Independent Clauses:

A clause that is part of a sentence but can make sense by itself is called an *independent clause*, or a *main clause*. If an independent clause appears alone, it is called a *sentence*.

This university offers 2,135 classes each semester.

9.2 Dependent Clauses:

A *dependent clause*, sometimes called a *subordinate clause*, has a subject and a verb but does not make sense by itself. The following sentence has one independent clause (main clause) and one dependent clause (subordinate clause).

Because adobes require special care, many builders do not recommend adobe construction.

The sentence contains two clauses: The first clause, "because adobes require special care," is dependent. It is a group of words that has a subject and a verb, but the clause does not make sense by itself and cannot stand alone as a sentence. The dependent clause depends on the second clause, which is the independent clause. There are three kinds of dependent clauses: adjective, adverb, and noun.

9.3 Adjective Clauses:

An *adjective clause* functions like an adjective. It modifies nouns or pronouns. Like an adjective, an adjective clause answers the questions: *which one?* or *whose?*

> The girl *who lives next door* is my student. (The adjective clause tells *which* girl — "who lives next door.")
>
> The lawyer *whose client received the death penalty* will ask for another trial. ("Whose client received the death penalty" tells which lawyer.)

Adjective clauses are usually introduced by one of the *relative pronouns (who, whose, whom, which,* or *that).* That relative pronoun has two functions. First, it relates the clause to the word it modifies. Second, the relative pronoun has a grammatical function in the adjective clause. For example, the relative pronoun can be a subject, a direct object, or a possessive pronoun. In the following sentences, the adjective clause is in italics, and the word in the independent clause that the adjective clause modifies is boldfaced.

> The **man** *who usually trims my hedges* is on vacation. (*Who* is the subject of the adjective clause. The entire clause tells which man.)
>
> The **teacher** *whom the children like the most* is retiring. (*Whom* is the direct object of *like. Children* is the subject of the clause. The entire clause modifies *teacher*.)
>
> They are the **neighbors** *whose house was featured in the magazine, House Beautiful.* (*Whose* is a possessive pronoun. It tells who owns the house. The entire clause modifies *neighbors*.)
>
> The **poetry** *that Sylvia Plath wrote* reflected her life. (*That* is the direct object of the verb *wrote*. The entire clause tells which poetry.)

9.4 Adverb Clauses:

An *adverb clause* is a dependent clause that functions as an adverb. Like an adverb, it modifies verbs, adjectives, or other adverbs. Adverb clauses answer the following questions:

When?	To what degree?
Where?	How often?
How?	Why?

The following examples show adverb clauses functioning as simple adverbs:

Becky smiled *nervously*. (Adverb telling *how*.)
Becky smiled *as if she were nervous*. (Adverb clause telling *how*.)
Finally, we left the party. (Adverb telling *when*.)
After the last drop of champagne was gone, we left the party. (Adverb clause telling *when*.)

Subordinate conjunctions usually introduce adverb clauses. Some common subordinate conjunctions are the following:

after	if	though
although	in order that	unless
as	just as	until
as if	provided that	when, whenever
as long as	since	where, wherever
because	so that	whereas
before	than	whether
even though	while	

Some of these words such as *after, before, since, until* can also function as prepositions. Notice the difference in the following two sentences:

Open the box *before* you leave.
Open the box *before* noon.

In the first sentence, *before* is a conjunction introducing the adverb clause "before you leave." In the second sentence, *before* is a preposition.

The various subordinate conjunctions show the meaning of the adverbial clauses. In the following examples, the subordinate conjunction is in boldfaced type, and the entire adverb clause is in italics.

TIME	(after, as, before, just as, since, until, when, whenever, while) The traveler kissed the ground **after** *he descended from the boat*.
PLACE	(where, wherever) She always buys clothes at the store **where** *her mother works*.
REASON	(because, in order that, since) **Because** *the university lost five games in a row*, the game became boring.
CONDITION	(as long as, if, provided that, unless) **If** *the weather continues*, the roads will have to be closed.
CONTRAST	(although, even though, though, whereas, while) Modern family life is mobile **whereas** *traditional family life was stable*.
COMPARISON	(as, as if, just as, than) **Just** *as humans hold and caress their infants*, mother apes carry their young for almost the entire first year of the young apes' lives.
CONTRADICTIONS	(although, even though, though, whereas) **Although** *foreign cars are expensive to buy*, they are inexpensive to operate.

9.5 Noun Clauses:

Noun clauses are dependent clauses that function as a noun. In other words, a noun clause can be a subject, direct object, indirect object, object of a preposition, and subject complement. Noun clauses may be introduced by the following words:

how	when	who
if	where	whoever
that	whether	whom
what	which	whomever

Whoever volunteers for duty will be given two days to leave. (Subject of sentence)

That Mary is sick is sad news. (Subject of sentence)

He asked *whether or not she could go*. (Direct object)

The organization will give *whoever needs assistance* a loan of $100. (Indirect object)

She is the girl about *whom we were speaking*. (Object of preposition)

The reason for cancelling the course is *that only five students signed up for the class*. (Subject complement)

UNIT F REVIEW

Reviewing Parts of Speech

DIRECTIONS: Read the following paragraph. Then on a separate piece of paper answer the questions at the end of the paragraph.

Soap Operas: A New Campus Craze

(1) Once considered the answer to the housewife's doldrums, the soap opera is finding a strong audience on American college campuses. (2) From student center restaurants to fraternity and sorority living rooms, from dormitory lounges to student government offices, hundreds of students crowd around television sets daily to watch such programs as *General Hospital, Ryan's Hope*, and *Guiding Light*. (3) Not only are these students involved with their soaps outside the classroom, but they are also discussing the themes and effects of daytime dramas in some of their sociology, anthropology, and literature courses. (4) No longer needing the excuse of being home sick in bed to watch a soap opera, many collegians now anxiously await the next episode of their favorite soap and eagerly talk about the program to their friends. (5) What is the sudden appeal of these long-established television programs? (6) Many students say that watching soap operas provides a welcome break from the routine of going to classes. (7) Moreover, these soap operas offer a necessary escape from the students' world. (8) According to Lupe Cajero, a student at State University of New York, "I'm glad it's the characters, not I, who have to face all the predicaments in life. (9) Knowing that someone else is experiencing worse problems than you are is a real relief, especially when all you have to worry about is tomorrow's algebra exam." (10) Besides escape, the soap operas seem to offer students role models, or at least characters with whom the students can identify.

(11) For example, two popular characters in *General Hospital* have been Laura, a tempestuous yet innocent twenty-two-year-old, and her level-headed, understanding boyfriend, Luke. (12) *General Hospital* fans have watched the pair go off on adventures, encounter life threats, and still successfully resolve dilemmas. (13) Because of their energy and stamina, and because of their foolhardiness and tempers, Laura and Luke are not mere characters; they are real people to many students. (14) Indeed, many students consider soap opera characters their friends. (15) "I feel as if I know so much about these characters; I can't help caring for them" notes Tom McGreevy at the University of Utah. (16) Momentarily leaving the dreary concerns of college life and establishing a kind of relationship with the fascinating characters on soap operas are only two reasons that these daytime dramas have gained popularity on American universities. (17) Of course, everyone who regularly follows the soaps has his or her own reasons for watching the shows. (18) In fact, the current status of these programs as college fads will certainly ensure the continued success of these television serials.

1. What is the main clause in sentence 2? Underline the subject.
2. What is the subordinate clause in sentence 17? Underline the pronoun in the subjective case.
3. What is the prepositional phrase in sentence 10? Underline the pronoun in the objective case.
4. What is the adjective clause in sentence 8? Underline the relative pronoun in that clause.
5. What is the adverb clause in sentence 9? Underline the subordinate conjunction in that clause.
6. What is the subordinate clause in sentence 16? Underline the demonstrative pronoun in that clause.
7. What is the main clause in sentence 17? Underline the indefinite pronoun.
8. What is one independent clause in sentence 13? Underline the linking verb in that clause. Circle the subjective complement.
9. What is the prepositional phrase in sentence 5? Underline the preposition.
10. What is the coordinate conjunction in sentence 11? Write the two phrases joined by that conjunction.
11. What is the correlative conjunction in sentence 3?
12. What is the main clause with a compound subject in sentence 13? Underline the subject.

13. What is the compound predicate in sentence 12?

14. What is the participial phrase in sentence 4?

15. What is the participial phrase in sentence 1?

INDEX